TONY HALL

FALCONRY
BASICS

Falconry titles also available from Swan Hill Press:

The Encyclopaedia of Falconry	Adrian Walker
Falconry for Beginners: An Introduction to the Sport	Lee William Harris
The Harris Hawk: Management, Training and Hunting	Lee William Harris
The Modern Falconer: Training, Hawking and Breeding	Diana Durman-Walters

TONY HALL

FALCONRY BASICS

A Handbook for Beginners

SWAN·HILL
PRESS

Copyright © 2003 Tony Hall

First published in the UK in 2003 by Swan Hill Press,
an imprint of Quiller Publishing Ltd.

British Library Cataloguing-in-Publication Data
A catalogue record for this book
is available from the British Library

ISBN 1 904057 28 4

Printed in Singapore by Stamford Press Pte. Ltd.

Swan Hill Press
an imprint of Quiller Publishing Ltd.
Wykey House, Wykey, Shrewsbury, SY4 1JA, England
Tel: 01939 261616 Fax: 01939 261606
E-mail: info@quillerbooks.com
Website: www.swanhillbooks.com

Contents

Common (or European) buzzard (*Buteo buteo*)

Language Conventions

Throughout this book the term *hawk* is used for all falconry birds. This usage complies with falconry tradition, but not with dictionary-making which restricts the word to a group of birds known as 'accipiters' (such as Sparrowhawks and Goshawks). Similarly, the term *falconry* means the training and flying of all kinds, not just falcons such as the Peregrine.

In the sport's very long history many names have been used to distinguish one kind of falconer from another. For example, *austringer* for a person who trained and flew Goshawks; *sparviter* for one who flew Sparrowhawks; *hawker* for one who flew any kind of accipiter; and *falconer* for one who specialised in flying falcons (meaning the female Peregrine). These days, even falconers don't often use such distinctions, partly because most own and fly several different kinds of hawk, and partly because no-one outside the sport would have the faintest idea what an austringer or a sparviter was and wouldn't be enlightened by consulting any standard dictionary.

Another long-standing protocol is that all falconry birds – whatever their sex – are referred to as *she* or *her* when speaking in general terms. Female hawks are usually larger and more powerful than males. Centuries ago this probably made them more desirable, and therefore more prominent. But falconers learned long ago that males and females are just different, and each sex has its own special attributes. But the protocol is well-established, and in this book I have respected it. Similarly, when I write 'he' – meaning the falconer or his dog – no sexism is intended. It simply makes things clearer, especially when 'she' is the hawk.

On a more general level, all known forms of life have a scientific as well as a common name. Each scientific name is unique and recognised world wide. Scientific names are given firstly to describe each organism's relationship (taxonomy) with other life forms, and secondly to avoid confusion. For example, taxonomically, all falcons have something in common with each other, as do all hawks and all buzzards. Also, Britain, North America, and Australasia all have hovering falcons called *Kestrels*, but each bird is a different species. Having a scientific name for each makes it clear which one is being talked about.

There are several levels of taxonomic classification (Orders, Sub-orders, Families, and so on) but the two lowest levels, the *genus* and *species* – which provide the most precise description – are the ones we are interested in. The generic and specific names are usually all that is necessary to identify each life form uniquely, and it is customary to begin with a capital letter and to write the name in italics, as in *Homo sapiens* (human beings). The specific name often refers to some characteristic of the species – *sapiens*, for example, means 'wise' – and occasionally a second specific name is added to identify a recognisable sub-species or race. One of the many examples of this in the bird world is *Falco peregrinus anatum*, a race of Peregrine falcons originating in Canada and North America. Another useful convention when quoting a sub-species is to write only the initial letters of the nominate species, provided it is clear which you are referring to – for example: *F.p. anatum*.

Scientific terminology has also been used, where appropriate, throughout this book.

About This Book

Iacquired my first bird of prey in 1958 when I was fourteen years old. She was a young Tawny Owl, and I blundered across her at the foot of a tree. She was only half-fledged, and had somehow tumbled out of her nest. Knowing no better, I picked her up and took her home.

After a bitter battle with my parents (who were fed up with me bringing wild animals into the house), I kept her in my bedroom and sustained her with rats, mice or voles which our two cats brought in. If supplies from this quarter failed, I went out and caught my own. If I failed too, I thieved scraps of meat from the larder. One way or another, I kept her alive until she was fully-fledged. Then I took her out into a field bordering the woods where I'd found her, threw her up into the air, and let her fly. Released from my grasp, she glided gracefully into the woods and I saw her for the very last time.

I sincerely believed I'd saved her life. I know now that I probably condemned her to a slow death through starvation, and this probability has haunted me for many years. Although I didn't know any better at the time, that doesn't provide much comfort and I doubt that I will ever really forgive myself.

At the foot of a tree she was vulnerable, but her parents were probably nearby and still actively feeding her. Exposed as she was, close cover was all around and she was perfectly capable of reaching it. Had she done so, it would have provided some protection from foxes and other predators (including me). Once fully-fledged and able to fly, her parents were programmed to teach her how and what to hunt, and perhaps even assist in this process until she developed the skills and experience to do it alone. My intervention, however well-meaning, had deprived her of this vital life-saving education.

But, provoked by the sense of virtue this incident gave me and now completely hooked on birds of prey, I went on to interfere in more of their lives. I must admit, I was also inspired by a word I'd picked up from somewhere – *Falconry*. Kestrels, Sparrowhawks, and more Tawny Owls suffered my adolescent attentions. Some of these were also collected off the ground, but most were taken as fledglings from their nests.

Whilst they were in my care, I can honestly say I never killed any of them – but that was simply down to the fact that I fed them as much as they wanted because I knew nothing about the first principal of falconry – weight control. Indeed, I knew nothing about falconry. I'd heard of it, but I knew no-one who did it. One or two books had been published, but it was such a rare and specialised activity that even the best of libraries didn't stock them as a matter of course. To obtain one you needed to know the author, book title, publisher and preferably the ISBN or similar reference. All of this was way beyond my nous, as well as my available travel and communication facilities.

So these birds and I had a bad start and believe me, I grieved over every one of them. They all seized the first opportunity presented to them to claim their independence, and rightly so – even though I hadn't given them the wherewithal to survive as wild predators.

After adolescence, I wasn't able to maintain contact with birds of prey at any significant level for several years. The need to earn a living took me to the big city, and marriage, a family, and a large mortgage kept me there until I had the opportunity to take early retirement in my mid-forties. By then, the whole scene had changed dramatically – falconry centres were springing up all over the place; equipment-makers were selling their wares at country shows and by mail order; how-to-do-it books were becoming freely-available; and many people were offering comprehensive training courses. Even dedicated clubs had proliferated, and were offering memberships to 'supporters' and 'novices' as well as practising falconers. But the biggest change – and most significant for me and the sport – was that all native birds of prey had become protected by law and the vast majority of those used in falconry were bred in captivity.

Since I retired I've trained several birds of prey, all of which have flown free and hunted successfully. I've read every book on falconry I could find, and I've even been on courses. In a way, I was fortunate to have a twenty-five-year break from flying birds because, in effect, I became a committed 'townie' and saw things through a townie's eyes. Using these eyes, I found most of the books I read unhelpful in many respects. Even those written for beginners assumed a certain level of knowledge – about the countryside; it's still-abundant wildlife; and the meaning and significance of phrases like *downwind, upwind, crosswind* and *quartering*. More fundamentally, many appeared to take a basic knowledge of animal psychology and management for granted, and failed to explain the logistics of acquiring captive-bred birds, food, and other vital supplies.

One reason was that many of their authors had been born and brought up in the countryside and involved with training various kinds of hawk, as well as working dogs and ferrets, since they were small children. As such they were as remote from the problems facing townies like me as I was from a full appreciation of their knowledge and skill.

So I wrote this book in an effort to bridge the gap between those people starting from a base of complete ignorance, and those who are already half way up the ladder because of their familiarity with the countryside and its various alternative hunting pursuits. I have assumed no relevant knowledge on your part. The book is designed to satisfy any curiosity you might have about falconry – what it is and what level of skill and commitment it requires – but its primary aim is to lead you from a state of ignorance to the point of catching quarry with a bird of prey you've trained yourself.

Many practising falconers might complain that I haven't mentioned this or that; or discussed such-and-such new development; or I haven't acknowledged that there are other ways of training a bird of prey. And they would be right. But there is no-one on Earth who could write a book about all there is to know about falconry, and every publication is itself a compromise. And it is immeasurably more difficult to decide what to leave out rather than what to include.

All I've attempted to do is to get to the heart of the matter and write only about those elements which proved fundamental to me. Once the basics have been learned, training, handling, hunting, and hawk-management can all be tweaked to suit yourself – as long as you don't lose sight of the fundamentals.

But in addition to these technical issues, I have a deeper reason for writing a book of this kind. When I was a city-dweller, occasionally going back to the countryside was, for me, a therapeutic experience. It blew away the pressures of urban life – however temporarily – and provided a basis for relaxation and reflection. Resting on a rock on top of a hill taking in the whole vista on a clear sunny day did wonders for my blood pressure. And if I happened to see a deer or a fox crossing a field unaware of my presence, or even a humble rabbit scooting into cover at my approach, I treated them as a bonus.

After retirement, walking through the countryside with a working dog, whose nose was bred and trained to recognise different animal scents, was an immeasurably more enhanced experience. I began to realise how much I had previously missed, and how *alive* the countryside actually is. It shifted me from a two-dimensional world into a three-dimensional one.

Flying my first properly-trained hawk, however, took me even further. Quite apart from her use of air, wind and thermals to transport her from place to place (a 3D picture worth viewing in its own right), she saw its wildlife with eyes several times better than my own, and she reacted with it as if her ultimate survival depended on her performance. Through her, I became *a part of the landscape* – an active participant in its everlasting drama. I shared her successes; I shared her failures; and I shared her learning.

In short, the experience put me back in touch with nature – my own, as well as the complex checks and balances that control wildlife and eventually determine its future. Such contact makes any working partnership with a hawk totally unique. Nothing in our modern world can replicate the experience, neither computer-generated 'virtual reality', nor the latest technological advances in film presentation.

The writing of this book was, therefore, motivated also by a strong desire to share this discovery, and to make the same quality of life accessible to people as deprived as I used to be.

Introduction

The Nature of Falconry

One of the benefits of falconry's long evolution is that it has acquired a versatility probably unmatched by any other sport. It is possible to fly one kind of hawk or another anywhere there is suitable wildlife, which excludes very few places on Earth. Falconers everywhere have developed ways of dealing with differences in climate, habitats, and potential quarry, and they have established the training techniques and hawks most fitting for those conditions. Even on a small island like ours, there are indigenous hawks suitable for all kinds of terrain. In some cases there are several.

Despite this, some of our falconry literature will attempt to persuade you that *real* falconry is about flying a Peregrine against red or black grouse over the wild and windy moors of Britain. The falcon takes the grouse in mid-air after a fast and dramatic stoop from, perhaps, several hundred feet up. Her speed and style are what the falconer wants to see, and getting her to this pitch of perfection is, in their view, an *art* and not one that can be acquired by just anybody. The existence of other versions of the sport might be acknowledged, but they are regarded as 'humbler' and lacking the same level of artistry.

This view, to say the least, verges on snobbery. The vast majority of falconers in Britain just do not have access to open grouse moors – either because they live nowhere near them, or they can't afford to purchase hunting rights. For them, flying Peregrines at grouse is not, therefore, a viable option and the fact that they don't do it has nothing to do with their capabilities. It doesn't either make their kind of falconry any less valid. Indeed, it is possible to achieve high standards of performance in *every* branch of the sport.

Other books are more generous. They argue that falconry is really about using any trained bird of prey to hunt and catch furred or feathered game in its natural state and habitat. The title of 'falconer', therefore, is merited by a person who has trained a hawk which catches natural quarry on a regular basis.

Training any bird of prey to use its inherited expertise for the benefit of a falconer is not an art by any standards – there is simply no creativity involved. But it *is* skilful, and the process itself requires many different kinds and levels of skill, as well as a great deal of specialised knowledge.

Even a top-notch peregrine falconer could not claim that he teaches his game hawks to catch grouse for in this respect, he cannot teach them anything. If they achieve it at all, it is through their physical condition, natural aptitudes, and instincts. Of course, he has a direct influence over their condition, but his training of them will be limited to maintaining discipline in the field and persuading them to gain height for their characteristic hunting style – the stoop. Other than that, all he can do is present them with hunting opportunities, by finding and flushing game in their vicinity. What happens next is up to each individual hawk, and the falconer merely assumes the rôle of spectator.

It may already be apparent from this that there are some basic differences between falconry birds and other captive birds of prey. For example:

1. Falconry birds *fly free*
2. They are trained *to return to their handler*
3. *They catch wild quarry* – mostly for the benefit of their falconer.

Even achieving free-flight with a hawk, and getting her to return to you, require a thorough understanding of falconry techniques. But switching her on to hunting, training her to do it where, when and in the way you want her to, persuading her to relinquish her catch then carry on hunting without loss of motivation, and maintaining discipline throughout, are all additional skills immeasurably more difficult to acquire.

Some falconers limit hawks to flying free and catching a piece of artificial prey called a *lure* – for example, those employed to clear airfields of seagulls, pigeons and other nuisance birds. Similarly, others flying hawks in public demonstrations might deliberately encourage them not to hunt so that they can exert more control over their hawks within a tight time-frame and minimise any risk of upsetting their audience. Nevertheless, hunting wild quarry is of primary importance to falconry. It is, after all, the reason that birds of prey were trained in the first place, and it is the only activity which enables captive hawks to realise their full potential. As with working dogs, it gives them a purpose in life and, through that, a high quality of life.

The Nature of Falconry Birds

Hawks are not yet domesticated, and they cannot be treated like pets. They are essentially still wild, and in general display the same lack of trust and fear of human beings common to all other wild animals. Unlike cats and dogs, they will never give you loyalty or affection, and you can't alleviate their wildness just through kindness or sympathy. They can't be cuddled, stroked, played with or taken to bed like a cat or a dog. Indeed, if you let your hawk loose in the house you might find one day that she has attacked, killed, and eaten your favourite cat and left its remains all over the carpet.

Not only are hawks undomesticated, they are not naturally social animals (apart from very rare exceptions). When they are not getting together to breed, the vast majority live their lives alone. They appear to have no social conscience, morals, or codes of behaviour even towards their own kind. Any hawk straying into another's territory might find herself aggressively repulsed rather than welcomed, and this aggression could result in the death of either one of them. All hawks take their independence very seriously because it is ultimately the means of their own survival.

As a result, training and handling a hawk is very different to training and handling a dog. Dogs are pack animals. It is easy to encourage in them a 'social conscience' (however primitive) because, like their wolf ancestors and all wild dogs, they naturally define their lives in accordance with group discipline. In other words, you can give them a set of rules with which they must comply. You can reward them for doing the right thing, and you can punish them for breaking a rule they have already learned. But you can *never* punish a hawk because she doesn't bond with you in any social way. She will only consider doing what you are asking her to do if, first and foremost, she's learned to trust you. Even then she will only do it if she *wants* to, and because she's gained the *confidence* to do it, and because she's learned how to do it. If you attempt to punish her for any 'misdemeanour', you will destroy whatever trust you might already have earned. Her training will cease abruptly, and she will seize the first opportunity to desert.

Training itself is achieved by carefully regulating the hawk's food intake to keep her weight at an optimum level. This level (which falconers call *flying weight*) is the point at which she gives you her best response. Lessons proceed by rewarding her with small pieces of food when she responds in a satisfactory way until she has used up all her rations; which in turn are calculated to keep her weight stable, or reduce it or increase it by measured amounts. A similar state of affairs is perpetuated in the field, even when she is fully trained.

It is this regime of reward linked with weight control which motivates a hawk firstly to become amenable to training, then to act in accordance with it. The difficulty is that you can't reward her until she's actually done the right thing, which means that, to some extent at least, she's in control. It is by no means unusual for a hawk to educate her falconer to meet her requirements rather than comply with his. But, if training goes to plan, she will eventually become habitually responsive, at least in the essential things such as returning to you.

Once she is flying free and has caught her first head of game, control problems really begin. Confidence in her own ability will increase dramatically, and you will then have to find ways of convincing her that she is better off staying with you rather than going her own way. Usually this means flushing game regularly enough for her to regard you as a valued working partner. If you fail consistently, she will most likely find it herself and view you as an unnecessary encumbrance. That will encourage her to claim her independence permanently.

Whatever relationship you succeed in forging with your hawk will, inevitably, be extremely tenuous and can never be regarded as permanent. Her 'obedience' might last only as long as a day's food ration and could easily end with the last piece of food she takes from your hand. The next she might find for herself. By acquiring any kind of hawk you are taking responsibility for a raw piece of nature designed for hunting and freedom in the wind, certainly not life in a cage. You must be prepared to accept that you might one day lose her, but with sound training and good falconry practice, this risk is at least minimised.

The Nature of the Sport

For many practitioners falconry has ephemeral, almost poetic, qualities. It provides real contact with nature; with the wind; with the ways of wild animals and their wild habitats; with the raw beauty and power of birds of prey in flight; with the privilege of watching them do what they do naturally; with being accepted as an ally in their endeavours; and with the mutual respect that such a partnership can generate.

If you ask a passionate falconer what enjoyment he gets from the sport, he will probably tell you that it has something to do with watching a bird of prey that he has nurtured and trained behave as if she were truly wild. If you ask him to elaborate, he might add that what's important is the quality of her flights – which means to what extent she shows determination, commitment, courage, skill, and style in chasing her quarry. Press him even further, and he might tell you that what really matters is the *whole hunting experience*, which means not just being in a natural environment on any particular day, but also – through his hawk – an active part of it.

This is the point at which you will tap into his real passion and his addiction. Every hunting trip with a trained and experienced hawk has the potential to put her handler through the whole gamut of emotions from despair to ecstasy, and play havoc with his adrenaline levels. In addition, it gives him a meaningful relationship with a natural environment. As an activity, it is not only physically and emotionally demanding, but also intellectually challenging. For some, it is even spiritually fulfilling.

What he will never tell you – because it isn't even a consideration – is that he is out to kill as much game as possible. If this were his purpose, he would use a gun. Even with a top-quality bird which is well-trained, experienced, and fully fit, a fair proportion of her flights will be abortive in the sense that her intended quarry will escape. This is entirely consistent with any prey/predator relationship in the wild. In other words, all her quarry has a sporting chance to live another day, depending on the strength of its own inherited qualities – and its ration of luck.

If a falconer released an experienced hawk to fend for herself, her behaviour wouldn't be very different. Falconry training and work in the field gives her no special advantage. On the contrary, with a limited time frame – at best, two or three hours – she is at a disadvantage compared to her wilder cousins who can choose their own ground and take as much time as they want. But, unlike them, she does get regular meals whether she catches anything or not. She should also acquire at least decent housing and good medical care, although she is unlikely to recognise either as a bonus.

For me personally the sport also has an important historical perspective. Even recorded falconry extends back at least four thousand years. At that time it was already a well-established activity with a cultural as well as a practical dimension. Since then, falconers have learned to solve the problems of training, controlling and maintaining free-flying hawks in a different way, but the activity itself is essentially the same. In this respect it provides links – emotional, spiritual, and empirical – with our remote ancestors. Through these links, it has the potential to put any modern human being back in touch with his natural roots. In fact developing an understanding of wild animals – their habitat requirements and behaviour – is essential for success.

Consequently, the vast majority of falconers are committed conservationists, and it is easy to see why. The destruction of any piece of woodland, moorland, heathland, hedgerow, meadow, marshland, downland or other natural environment, is a threat to their activity because it not only destroys the habitats needed to fly hawks, but also the wildlife depending on them.

Yet the sport itself has little or no impact on wildlife populations. In Britain, hawks are no longer taken from the wild, and no falconer would be foolish enough to suggest that he could eradicate, for example, a plague of rabbits on a farmer's land in exchange for permission to fly his bird there. Even if the hawk was hunting every day and working to her full potential, in six months the landowner would probably notice little difference in numbers.

This isn't just because rabbits breed like rabbits. It's because one bird of prey, wild or otherwise, isn't capable of making that kind of impact. A wild hawk might take one rabbit, from which she will feed for several days. In contrast, a good hawk/falconer partnership might take three or four in a single day. But if they attempted to repeat this performance every day over the same ground, they would surely fail. Over-hunted game is quickly spooked, and will dive for cover before a predator is anywhere near striking range. The falconer could try persuading the landowner he has done his job, but when the hawk isn't around, the rabbits are as numerous as ever. More importantly for the falconer, the lack of flights would seriously worry him because his hawk will soon become bored. If this happens, she's much more likely to dissolve the partnership and go her own way.

Consequently serious falconers try to obtain permission from several landowners to fly their hawks over a number of locations, each covering many acres, so that they can vary the hawk's flights and maximise her chances of success. But obtaining permission to hunt over other people's land is, these days, probably the most difficult aspect of the sport. This is partly because most of the best hunting grounds have been taken up by people who use guns, and partly because of the contemporary issue of 'animal rights' and how local landowners feel about its impact on their own social standing.

Nevertheless, you would have every right to persist. People have been practising falconry since the beginning of recorded time and across almost every continent. It is one of very few activities which can claim to be part of mankind's general cultural inheritance – in the same way as working a dog or riding a horse.

Harris' hawk (*Parabuteo unicinctus*)

PART 1

Getting Started

Before You Start

A bove everything else, falconry *demands* a serious commitment. Falconry birds generally live a long time – fifteen to twenty years if they are well-managed and given appropriate medical treatment when needed. Even if you only own a single hawk, your responsibility for her general well-being and quality of life is, therefore, a long term one. Consequently, you must have a degree of passion for birds of prey before you consider taking up the sport. It is *not* an activity suitable for people who just want to dabble to see how they get on.

Even if you possess enough passion, you will probably have to indulge it on your own. Your hawk might be an object of curiosity and admiration for other people – at least at first – but you can't expect much more than that. Husbands, wives, other family members, friends, acquaintances and neighbours generally won't share your passion, and they won't want to participate. The sport has been known to become obsessive and you will be very lucky to have a partner willing to put up with your frequent absences, especially at weekends. On top of all this, you will need satisfactory answers to the following questions.

Will my work and social life allow me to spend enough time with my hawk on a daily basis?
Although you might have your hawk trained and flying free by the late summer, the flying season extends through autumn and winter. Throughout this period, she will need time and attention *every day* during daylight hours. In addition her quarters, food and equipment have to be organised and maintained properly. Many people find this difficult to achieve because there are too few hours of daylight in their 'free' time. Friends, and other members of the family might be prepared to help with peripheral chores when you're not available, but will they maintain their willingness over the next ten or even twenty years?

Can I arrange for the bird to be looked after properly when I'm away on business or on holiday?
This is a problem we all have to face at one time or another. There are very few commercial facilities for looking after falconry birds equivalent to kennels or catteries – perhaps only one or two in the whole of Britain. All hawks need a minimum amount of experience in handling just to feed and maintain them. It is neither feasible nor advisable to expect a next-door neighbour to do it on the spur of the moment while you spend a fortnight in Malaga. The best answer is another local falconer, if you can find one. But he will, understandably, expect you to return the favour, which means you will both have to co-ordinate your away-days well in advance.

Can I provide suitable housing for the bird?
Hawk accommodation is large and relatively expensive to build. You can't buy a ready-made product like a rabbit hutch or a chicken coop. Neither can you keep a bird of prey in an attic, a spare bedroom, the lounge, or anywhere else in the house on a long-term basis.

Hawks need outside quarters built specifically to meet their requirements, and sited where they can get the benefit of fresh air but providing shelter from hot sun, wind, rain, and frost. They also need protection from other animals such as foxes, cats, dogs, mink, other birds of prey, and thieves.

Do I have a ready supply of suitable food?

All birds of prey eat other animals. They can't survive on artificial diets like cat food, dog food, table scraps, 'bird' food, or any other kind of prepared food. They thrive only on whole animals – flesh, bones, fur or feathers, and internal organs. In the wild, when they catch prey, they eat all of it (given the chance), including seemingly unpalatable items like teeth and claws.

Although there are people who market such foods – primarily for institutions like zoos – they are not easy to find and usually sell it frozen down in bulk. You might have to travel many miles to collect a consignment, and you will, therefore, need a reliable means of transport as well as separate freezer capacity for at least several weeks' supply.

Do I have access to a vet prepared to treat my bird if she falls ill or suffers injury?

Where birds of prey are concerned, illness often causes death. Hawks differ in their constitutions, but all are vulnerable to infection and physical trauma, for example, when they are flying into thorny cover such as gorse or bramble, or through barbed wire fences. In particular, other birds they catch can pass on their own diseases.

Very few vets have any experience with hawks and, for this reason, most are reluctant to treat them except in a dire emergency. An avian specialist, or a least a vet who has considerable experience in treating birds, must therefore be found before you acquire a hawk. You can also expect that his surgery will be many miles away. In addition, his charges will reflect the fact that he is a specialist, or dealing with an 'exotic' animal, and they are likely to be considerably more than treating a dog or a cat.

Do I have somewhere suitable to fly my hawk?

For any falconer, this is the most important question. Different species of hawk require different types of terrain over which they can be successfully flown. Many falcons need vast areas of open space such as moorland where cross-country access is unrestricted. True hawks and buzzards can be flown over more enclosed land, or in woodland.

Whichever kind of hawk you decide to get, permission must be sought from the landowner before you fly her, and you will need to establish that there is enough suitable game there to keep her occupied and interested.

Will I be able to fly her frequently enough?

Falconry birds are not designed to be kept in aviaries for long periods. Once trained and in the habit of hunting, they benefit from being flown every day (weather permitting) in their hunting season. Even more important than the experience this gives them, it develops fitness and stamina, both of which are essential for good flights at worthwhile quarry.

Falcons need less flying time than hawks and buzzards but, as Sod's law has it, they are the least suitable birds for beginners to train. The reasons will be explained later. Hawks and buzzards need a lot longer (two to three hours each session). There are one or two – such as the Harris' Hawk – which can be taken out just at weekends if you are willing and able to take special measures to maintain fitness on non-flying days, but this situation is far from ideal on a long-term basis.

Can I afford it?

The vast majority of falconry birds flown in this country are captive-bred and most are expensive. Prices vary from a few hundred to a few thousand pounds depending on which type of hawk you want to buy. Also, there are substantial costs involved in housing and equipping any kind of hawk (and yourself) properly, not to mention food, veterinary care, and insurance.

Some of these costs can be spread over a period – for example, the acquisition of equipment and building suitable housing – but once you've acquired your first bird, you will find yourself locked in to spending money on a regular basis. This, as much if not more than the question of your time, may sorely try your partner's patience and can easily become an issue you can't mutually resolve. Falconry changes people's lives. Before you take it on, make sure you can handle the consequences.

Falconry And The Law

Falconry is a highly-regulated sport, but the laws which govern it are indirect. There isn't a single piece of legislation about falconry as such, but there are several which affect its activities. In fact it is generally the victim of legislation rather than the cause of it. For example, the *Transit of Animals (Road and Rail) Order* stipulates the standards to be applied in transporting animals. Although it was designed to regulate the carriage of farm and other domestic animals, it actually covers all species (apart from humans) and is relevant to falconers wanting to import or export birds, or simply transport them from one part of the country to another.

Legislation like this, which was probably written without any knowledge of its effect on falconers, catches them in its legislative umbrella and it is a potential minefield for perfectly innocent and sincere people. Although of course, if they are in breach of the law, ignorance of it is never an acceptable defence.

It certainly isn't necessary to be conversant with every piece of legislation affecting falconry, but it pays to know how the law encroaches on the sport, and where to look if you need to know what the law specifically requires. For the most part, people rely on general information of the kind given below.

In its generality, the law covers four different aspects of falconry:
1.   The acquisition of birds
2.   Care and housing
3.   Medical treatment
4.   What and when you can hunt

The Acquisition of Birds

1. Domestic Legislation

In Britain, all wild birds of prey (known officially as *raptors*) are protected by law. This means that you can't catch them, trap them, poison them, shoot them or otherwise destroy them. Neither can you take eggs or young, nor disturb their nests in any way. Even injured raptors picked up by the roadside (or anywhere else) are fully protected, and what happens to them from that point on is decided by the Department for Environment, Food and Rural Affairs (DEFRA).

Although birds have been legally protected since the mid-1950s, current legislation is much more stringent. The law now providing protection is the *Wildlife and Countryside Act 1981* which is administered by DEFRA. For falconers its main significance is that – unlike previous generations – they can no longer catch a wild raptor or take one from a nest for use in falconry, and the penalties for breaking this law are very severe indeed. They include:
•   fines and costs totalling thousands of pounds, or imprisonment, or both
•   confiscation of the illegal bird, and any others you might have
•   a bar from owning any raptor for at least five years

In other words, ruination as a falconer or a breeder. No club, for example, will knowingly accept anyone as a member who has been convicted under this legislation and, in addition, you might find yourself the subject of regular surveillance by people like the RSPB and other authorities attempting to make sure you don't break the law again.

Native birds bred in captivity these days originated largely from wild-caught parents which were in captivity before the Act came into force although, for the first few years after the act was introduced, it was possible to obtain a licence from DEFRA (then the Department of the Environment [DOE]) to capture a wild hawk to enhance and increase captive breeding stocks. However, no such licences have been issued for several years because, in the opinion of DEFRA, the gene-pool of native birds bred in captivity is now sufficient to meet all the present and future needs of falconers.

Until 1994, *every* falconry bird bred in captivity – native or not – had to be ringed and registered with the DOE/DEFRA. However, in 1994 the three most common native raptors (Kestrels, Sparrowhawks and Buzzards), and many non-native species such as Harris' Hawks, Sakers, Lanners and Luggers, were excused registration and ringing. Birds still requiring this formality are listed in Schedule 4 of the Act (which is reproduced as Appendix 1 on page 000), but those most commonly used in falconry are:

- Peregrine Falcon (*Falco peregrinus*)
- Merlin (*Falco columbarius*)
- Gyrfalcon (*Falco rusticolus*)
- Goshawk (*Accipiter gentilis*)

There are, of course, others such as the Golden Eagle (*Aquila chrysaetos*) and the Hobby (*Falco subbuteo*), but their use in modern British falconry is marginal. If in doubt, consult Appendix 1.

Breeders are required to ring their registrable birds when they are between ten and fourteen days old. The ring is a metal band closed permanently around one of the hawk's legs. It is stamped with a unique number, supplied by DEFRA, and is accompanied by the registration document which bears the same number. This document works vaguely like a car log book. Whenever the bird changes ownership, it is re-registered by DEFRA in the new owner's name, but on payment of an administration fee of £17.00. If the bird doesn't change ownership, registration has to be renewed every three years for a similar fee.

Some hybrids are also subject to ringing and registration – namely any whose parent or ancestor is listed in Schedule 4 of the Act. For example, a *Peregrine x Saker* cross is registrable because the Peregrine is listed even though the Saker isn't. In contrast, a *Lanner x Saker* hybrid is not registrable because neither is included in Schedule 4.

Registration with DEFRA is also required for injured wild birds listed in Schedule 4 which are unable to be released back into the wild even after care and attention. These are known as 'Wild-Disabled' birds. In this case, instead of a closed ring, they are fitted with a cable-tie ring. These birds *cannot be sold under any circumstances*.

Cable-tie rings are also used on wild birds listed in Schedule 4 imported from abroad under licence. Imported birds are dealt with by different legislation which, to some degree, overlaps our own and confuses the issue immeasurably.

2. International Legislation

Due to increasing international agreement, more and more countries are closing down the export of their native plants and animals, in particular those that are in any way classified as endangered. Unfortunately for falconers, a variety of factors makes raptors more vulnerable to extinction than most other forms of life.

The organisation which attempts to control traffic in wildlife is the Convention on International Trade in Endangered Species (CITES). It does so by prohibiting the sale of all forms of life threatened with extinction, and regulates traffic in others whose survival is not yet threatened but is likely to become so unless trade is strictly controlled. This control is exercised by the issue or refusal of licences. CITES establishes the extent of threat to a particular species of plant or animal through a network of qualified field-workers worldwide, and those life forms threatened with extinction are entered in what is called the *Red Data Book*. The Convention has a Secretariat based in Switzerland, which reviews this data every two to three years.

Although CITES itself has no legislative power, over 130 countries are party to the Convention and have introduced national legislation which complies with its principles. This includes the European Union. Generally EU legislation overrides our own unless the Government takes special steps to curtail it, but in this case, quite rightly, they haven't.

On 1 June 1997 EU Regulations (*EC Regulation 338/97*) came into force which changed the law in relation to the sale, purchase, and display for commercial purposes of all captive-bred native birds of prey (including Kestrels, Buzzards and Sparrowhawks) and many non-native ones. These birds are listed in *Annex A* in the Regulations (which is reproduced as Appendix 2 at the end of this section).

Basically the Regulation prohibits the sale, purchase, or commercial display of any bird listed in Annex A *unless* an 'Article 10' Certificate has been issued by DEFRA or other EU Authority. Article 10 Certificates (or 'Sales' Certificates as they are becoming known) are only valid for one sale unless the bird originates from a 'Recognised Breeder'. In this case the Certificate is valid for all subsequent sales as long as the Certificate travels with the bird. 'Recognised Breeders' are those known to DEFRA and who have been able to satisfy certain criteria, such as the keeping of accurate records and making them available for inspection.

All captive-bred birds listed in Annex A must be closed-ringed or, if this is not possible for one reason another, it must be microchipped. Cable-tie rings are not acceptable under any circumstances. As with Registration under the Wildlife and Countryside Act, the ring or microchip number/code must be recorded on the Article 10 Certificate.

The Regulation applies to all listed birds whether they are alive or dead, including hybrids if one of the parents is listed. It also applies to any part of a listed bird, for instance, feathers or semen.

EC Regulation 338/97 *does not* supersede the Wildlife and Countryside Act. On the contrary, they both operate independently. For example, consider buying three falconry birds from a breeder, all captive-bred in this country:

1. The Goshawk is listed in Schedule 4 of the Wildlife and Countryside Act and in Annex A of the EC Regulation. To comply with national legislation, it has to be registered and ringed. The closed ring required by UK law is satisfactory to the EU and therefore complies with both laws, but in addition the breeder has to obtain an Article 10 Certificate to sell the bird.

2. The Common Buzzard is not listed in Schedule 4 of the Wildlife and Countryside Act, but it is included in Annex A of the EC Regulation. Under national law, therefore, it does not require ringing and registering. However, under EU law it requires a closed ring and an Article 10 Certificate.

3   The Harris' Hawk is listed neither in Schedule 4 nor Annex A. It does not, therefore, need to be registered or ringed, and there is no requirement for an Article 10 Certificate.

In this country DEFRA administers both laws. They issue registration documents, rings, ring numbers, Article 10 Certificates and application forms. They also give advice to bewildered falconers and breeders, hopefully before they get into trouble. There is only one centre concerned with these issues, which is based in Bristol: Global Wildlife Division, First Floor, Temple Quay House, 2 The Square, Temple Quay, Bristol BS1 6EB. The Department also has an excellent website, which incorporates legislation affecting falconers, advice on CITES licensing and registration, and facilities for e-mailing queries. At the time of publishing, the site address is: *www.defra.gov.uk/wildlife-countryside/citesbird*

Care and housing

Once you own any animal, you must take full responsibility for its life – meaning not only its health and general well-being, but also its quality of life. This is not just a moral requirement, it's also a legal one. Failure to exercise this responsibility is recognised as *cruelty* – through abandonment, neglect, ill-treatment, or lack of care in some other way – and there is a great deal of legislation which covers this issue. For legal purposes, cruelty is defined as *any action which leads to unnecessary suffering.*

The vast majority of falconers care deeply about their birds and treat them well. Indeed, it is obviously in their interests to do so, otherwise they wouldn't retain a hawk in flying condition for very long. However, although cases are rare, several prosecutions are brought before the courts each year and convictions include such things as:

- accommodation of insufficient size to allow the bird to stretch her wings fully in every direction
- unacceptably dirty and unhygienic housing conditions, including old and rotting food
- unsuitable perches and tethering equipment
- inappropriate and badly maintained leg equipment likely to cause discomfort or injury
- untreated wounds
- other untreated conditions, such as prolonged infestation by parasites
- keeping birds at near-starvation levels.

These convictions seem fairly clear-cut, but the law is not. For example, if a hawk isn't properly tethered to a perch and manages to escape carrying all her equipment and then starves to death because she becomes entangled, you could be liable to prosecution. Similarly, if you lose a bird which has not yet learned to catch game and which subsequently starves to death, you could be guilty of a similar offence.

Cruelty legislation does not just cover the treatment of your hawks. It also deals with the way that any quarry you catch is despatched. The law requires this to be done as quickly and humanely as possible in the circumstances. If a falconer is seen to delay, or fails to promptly and efficiently despatch the quarry, he could be liable to prosecution.

All law is subject to interpretation, and these days interpretations where 'animal rights' and similar social pressures are concerned are like shifting desert sands. For instance, however good your equipment might be, tethering a bird for long periods could be construed as 'cruel' under current legislation by an 'enlightened' magistrate and, from a legal standpoint, it doesn't matter whether he or she misunderstands the reasons for it. So in many ways it pays to keep a low profile, for example by not unnecessarily displaying a tethered bird in your front garden, and avoiding flights at quarry in full view of someone else's garden even if the action is taking place on one of the bird's legitimate hunting grounds.

Aviaries, and the birds themselves, can also involve you in legal action. In the UK no-one is allowed to build just what they like on their own land. For some structures, planning permission from the local authority (LA), and sometimes Building Regulations approval, are required. It is unlikely that you will need either for a straightforward aviary unless it is likely to cause a 'nuisance' to your neighbours – for example because it is overlooking their property or restricting their view. Before you construct anything, therefore, it would be wise to consult your LA and your neighbours. If you don't, you might find yourself having to pull the whole thing down because a neighbour has successfully complained.

Even when you have the LA's and neighbours' blessings, the birds themselves can subsequently cause a nuisance. Usually this is through noise – in particular from 'screaming' – but also from smell if you progress to breeding birds. If any of your birds are judged to be causing a nuisance for whatever reason, you will most likely have to get rid of them.

The Acts of Parliament legislating on these issues are many and complex, but the main ones are listed in Appendix 3 on page 32.

Medical treatment

There is a limit to what you can legally do to assist one of your ill or injured hawks without qualified supervision. In effect, anything beyond first aid is the province of the veterinary profession and they are given this prerogative by the *Veterinary Surgeons Act 1966*. Other legislation already mentioned (such as cruelty cases) requires the involvement of a vet. In particular it is illegal:
- to dispense or administer any oral drug without the direction and sanction of a qualified vet
- to perform so-called 'invasive' techniques such as injections (except under the direction of a vet), catheters, drips or any form of surgery.

The vast majority of ill-health conditions require a qualified medical diagnosis before any appropriate treatment can be determined, and in practice this legislation incorporates a large measure of common sense.

However, in terms of first aid, there is a lot you can do, especially with injuries sustained in the field, for example, by providing initial treatment for shock and open wounds caused by game animals, tree branches, barbed wire, or whatever. You can also use proprietary remedies to control internal and external parasites, prophylactics during times of stress to avoid infections arising, and administer electrolyte by means of a crop tube to combat dehydration and low condition. These are explained further in the section headed *Illness and Injury* on page184.

What and when you can hunt

What constitutes game was defined originally in the *Game Act 1831* which gave legal protection to certain species during their breeding seasons. It also gave protection to many 'non-game' species, and classified 'vermin' which were afforded no protection at all. Although it doesn't appear that this law has been repealed, most of the provisions relevant to falconers have been superseded by the ubiquitous Wildlife and Countryside Act 1981.

The WCA allows the killing of 'game' species, but only at certain times of the year which exclude their normal breeding seasons (plus a generous margin on either side). The months of exclusion are known as **Close** seasons, and those when killing them is permitted are known as **Open** seasons. The following table lists the species currently defined as game which are protected under the Act, but which can be hunted in their open season.

GAME SPECIES	HUNTING (OPEN) SEASONS
Pheasant	1 October to 1 February
Partridge	1 September to 1 February
Grouse and Ptarmigan	12 August to 10 December
Black Game	20 August to 10 December
Moorhen, Coot and Mallard	1 September to 31 January
Snipe	12 August to 31 January
Woodcock (England and Wales)	1 October to 31 January
Woodcock (Scotland)	1 September to 31 January
Hare	1 September to 31 March

Where hares are concerned, legal protection is only given to those found on moorland or unfenced arable land, otherwise they are not protected at all. In other words, if you come across one in a farmer's well-defined field, you can hunt it at any time of the year (with the owner's authority). It is illegal to hunt any of the other species listed on Sundays and (for any open season which includes it) on Christmas Day.

Apart from this protection, there is another piece of legislation – the *Game Licences Act 1860* – which requires you to obtain a 'Game Licence' before you can lawfully hunt them (except for Moorhen) in the open season. These licences are obtainable from the Post Office, and are renewable once a year.

'Non-game' species are protected all year round, but some can be hunted with a 'Quarry Licence', in this case obtainable from the Department for Environment, Food and Rural Affairs (DEFRA). The licence will stipulate:
1. the species you are licensed to hunt
2. the dates between which it can be hunted
3. the number of the relevant species you are licensed to catch
4. the identity of the hawk you are permitted to fly at the quarry
For falconers, the only species likely to fall into this category are skylarks (normally hunted with Merlins) and blackbirds (normally hunted with Sparrowhawks).

Warning taking any game or non-game species out of season, or without a valid licence, or without the owner's permission is poaching and the penalties can be very severe. Quite apart from any punishment a court might impose, landowners are almost certain to withdraw any hunting rights they have given you on their land, and their neighbours might also follow suit.

The Game Act categorised the following potential quarry-species for a hawk as 'vermin' – rat; rabbit; grey squirrel; house sparrow; starling; wood pigeon; feral pigeon; collared dove; rook; crow; magpie; jackdaw; jay; herring gull; great black-backed gull; lesser black-backed gull. As vermin they could be hunted at any time (including Sundays and Christmas Day) in any numbers and no kind of licence was required. All that was needed was the authority of the landowner.

However, in respect of the birds listed here, the Wildlife and Countryside Act contains provisions which supersede this Statute. In effect, *all birds* found in EEC countries are protected under European Law and the WCA has had to be brought into line. In addition, the term 'vermin' has been substituted by 'pest'. For falconers, and every other hunter of previously-classified 'vermin' birds, this is a significant (and potentially disastrous) development. Its significance is that such birds can only be killed *where it can be shown* that they are pests. Otherwise they have the full protection of the law.

With the introduction of this protection throughout the EEC, the Government, on behalf of the people of the UK, issued itself with a General Licence to kill birds which domestic legislation previously recognised as vermin – a legal device which got round the contradictions in the two pieces of legislation and avoided setting up a whole new beaurocracy to issue individual licences to people killing them for 'legitimate' reasons. There are several of these – for example public health and safety, the safety of air traffic, the conservation of other wild birds – but the only one likely to affect the vast majority of falconers going about their normal business is the control of agricultural pests.

If that's what you're doing, then in theory you have the protection of the General Licence. However, if you're challenged and brought before a magistrate, *you will have to prove* that you were doing it as part of an agreed policy of pest control on that land. If you can't get the landowner to support you in this assertion, even if he's given you permission to fly your bird, you will lose your case. You would be wise, therefore, to obtain his confirmation that he is allowing you to hawk on his land in an effort to control pest species before you start – and preferably in writing.

If the landowner can't be bothered with this but is still willing to allow you to hunt these birds, you can apply to DEFRA for an individual licence which will be considered on its merits and issued on a similar basis as for other protected birds (see above).

APPENDIX 1

THE WILDLIFE AND COUNTRYSIDE ACT
SCHEDULE 4
(Birds requiring ringing and registration)

Common Name	Scientific Name
(European) Honey Buzzard	*Pernis apivorus*
Adalbert's Eagle	*Aquila adalberti*
Golden Eagle	*Aquila chrysaetos*
Philippine (Monkey-eating) Eagle	*Pithecophaga jefferyi*
Imperial Eagle	*Aquila heliaca*
New Guinea Eagle	*Harpyopsis novaeguineae*
White-tailed Sea Eagle (Erne)	*Haliaeetus albicilla*
Barbary Falcon	*Falco pelegrinoides*
Gyrfalcon	*Falco rusticolus*
Peregrine Falcon	*Falco peregrinus*
Madagascar Fish-Eagle	*Heliaeetus vociferoides*
Sclater's (Plumbeous) Forest Falcon	*Micrastur plumbeus*
Goshawk	*Accipiter gentilis*
Hen Harrier	*Circus cyaneus*
(Western) Marsh Harrier	*Circus aeruginosus*
Montagu's Harrier	*Circus pygarcus*
Galapagos Hawk	*Buteo galapagoensis*
Grey-backed Hawk	*Leucopternis occidentalis*
Hawaiian Hawk	*Buteo solitarius*
Ridgway's Hawk	*Buteo ridgwayi*
White-necked Hawk	*Leucopternis lacernulata*
Wallace's Hawk-Eagle	*Spizaetus nanus*
Hobby	*Falco subbuteo*
Black Honey Buzzard	*Henicpernis infuscata*
Lesser Kestrel	*Falco naumanni*
Mauritius Kestrel	*Falco punctatus*
Red Kite	*Milvus milvus*
Merlin	*Falco columbarius*
Osprey	*Pandion haliaetus*
Pallas' Sea Eagle	*Haliaeetus leucoryphus*
Steller's Sea Eagle	*Halieetus pelagicus*
Andaman Serpent Eagle	*Spilornis elgini*
Madagascar Serpent Eagle	*Eutriorchis astur*
Mountain Serpent Eagle	*Spilornis kinabaluensis*
New Britain Sparrowhawk	*Accipiter brachyurus*
Gundlach's Sparrowhawk	*Accipiter gundlachi*
Imitator Sparrowhawk	*Accipiter imitator*
(Celebes) Small or Little Sparrowhawk	*Accipiter nanus*

APPENDIX 2

THE CONTROL OF TRADE IN ENDANGERED SPECIES
(ENFORCEMENT) REGULATIONS 1997

ANNEX A

(Birds requiring ringing and an Article 10 Certificate)

FALCONIFORMES

Vultures

Andean Condor	*Vultur gryphus*
Californian Condor	*Gymnogyps californianus*
Osprey	*Pandion haliaetus*
Cinereous Vulture	*Aegypius monarchus*
Egyptian Vulture	*Neophron percnopterus*
Eurasian Griffon or Griffon-vulture	*Gyps fulvus*
Lammergeier	*Gypaetus barbatus*

Eagles

Adalbert's Eagle	*Aquila adalberti*
Bonelli's Eagle	*Hieraaetus faciatus*
Booted Eagle	*Hieraaetus pennatus*
Golden Eagle	*Aquila chrysaetos*
Greater Spotted Eagle	*Aquila clanga*
Harpy Eagle	*Harpia harpyja*
Imperial Eagle	*Aquila heliaca*
Lesser Spotted Eagle	*Aquila pomarina*
Madagascar Serpent Eagle	*Eutriorchis astur*
Philippine (Monkey-eating) Eagle	*Pithecophaga jefferyi*
Sea Eagles	*Haliaeetus (all species)*
Short-toed (Snake) Eagle	*Circaetus gallicus*

Kites

Common or Black Kite	*Milvus migrans*
Black-winged or Black-shouldered Kite	*Elanus caeruleus*
(Cuban) Hook-billed Kite	*Chondrohierax uncinatus wilsonii*
Red Kite	*Milvus milvus*

Harriers

Montagu's Harrier	*Circus pygargus*
Northern (Hen) Harrier	*Circus cyaneus*
Pallid Harrier	*Circus macrourus*
(Western) Marsh Harrier	*Circus aeruginosus*

Hawks and Buzzards

Eurasian Sparrowhawk	*Accipiter nisus*
Goshawk	*Accipiter gentilis*
Grey-backed Hawk	*Leucopternis occidentalis*
Levant Sparrowhawk	*Accipiter brevipes*
Common Buzzard	*Buteo buteo*
(European) Honey Buzzard	*Pernis apivorus*
Long-legged Buzzard	*Buteo rufinus*
Rough-legged Buzzard	*Buteo lagopus*

Falcons

Barbary Falcon	*Falco pelegrinoides*
Common Kestrel	*Falco tinnunculus*
Eleanora's Falcon	*Falco eleanorae*
Eurasian Hobby	*Falco subbuteo*
Gyrfalcon	*Falco rusticolus*
Lugger Falcon	*Falco jugger*
Lanner Falcon	*Falco biarmicus*
Lesser Kestrel	*Falco naumanni*
Mauritius Kestrel	*Falco punctatus*
Merlin	*Falco columbarius*
Newton's (Madagascar) Kestrel	*Falco newtoni*
Peregrine Falcon	*Falco peregrinus*
Red-footed Falcon	*Falco vespertinus*
Saker Falcon	*Falco cherrug*
Seychelles Kestrel	*Falco araea*

STRIGIFORMES

Barn Owl	*Tyto alba*
Boreal Owl	*Aegolius funereus*
Christmas Hawk Owl	*Ninox squamipila natalis*
Eurasian Eagle Owl	*Bubo bubo*
Eurasian Pygmy Owl	*Glaucidium passerinum*
Eurasian Scops Owl	*Otus scops*
Forest Owlet	*Athene blewitti*
Great Grey Owl	*Strix nebulosa*
Lesser Eagle Owl	*Mimizuku gurneyi*
Little Owl	*Athene noctua*
Long-eared Owl	*Asio otus*
Norfolk Boobook	*Ninox novaeseelandiae undulata*
Northern Hawk Owl	*Surnia ulula*
Short-eared Owl	*Asio flammeus*
Snowy Owl	*Nyctea scandiaca*
Sokoke Scops Owl	*Otus ireneae*
Soumagne's Owl	*Tyto soumagnei*
Tawny Owl	*Strix aluco*
Ural Owl	*Strix uralensis*

APPENDIX 3

PRIMARY LEGISLATION AFFECTING FALCONRY

The aquisition of birds

The Wildlife and Countryside Act 1981-1983
*The Control of Trade in Endangered Species (Enforcement) Regulations
1997 [EC Regulation 338/97]*

Care and housing

The Protection of Animals Act 1911
The Abandonment of Animals Act 1960
The Animal Health Act 1981
The Welfare of Animals During Transport Order 1992
The Town and Country Planning (General Development Order) 1988

Medical treatment

The Veterinary Surgeons Act 1966
The Medicines Act 1968
The Protection of Animals (Anaesthetics) Act 1954

What and when you can hunt

The Game Act 1831
The Game Licences Act 1860

All these can be purchased from The Stationery Office (previously HMSO) or
their agents, usually book shops. Alternatively, they should be available in
your local library, but normally only for reference purposes.

Hawks And Falconry

All birds of prey have found their own niche in life. Some are desert birds, some are arctic birds; some hunt in wide open prairies, moors or tundra; others in deep woods and forests. A few have adapted to and exploited human environments, but most never will. Species vary in their habits and physical appearance according to where they live and what they hunt. In all categories there are exceptions to their 'normal' pattern, but some general statements can be made:

1. Most falcons inhabit wide open spaces relying on long-distance speed and power to overtake and kill their prey
2. Most hawks (accipiters) are forest or woodland birds which hunt with stealth, surprise and quick sprints
3. Most buzzards and eagles are high-flyers soaring on updrafts and thermals to range over a large area.

The training and flying of each kind in falconry reflect these differences, and falconers distinguish between them by describing their wing *configurations*.

Falcons are known as 'longwings'. Long, pointed wings and relatively short tails are designed for cutting through air and wind at speed

Hawks (accipiters) are know as 'shortwings'. Shorter, more rounded wings and relatively long tails are designed for manoeuvring through dense vegetation

Buzzards are known as 'broadwings'. Large, plank-like wings and relatively short, wedge-shaped tails are designed for soaring and gliding flight

These classifications describe the birds' arrangements of primary feathers (those at the tip of each wing) rather than the wing as a whole. None of them can claim to be scientifically accurate, nor even literally descriptive, but they are immensely important to falconry because they identify a bird's propensities and lifestyle. This means falconers know how each kind should be trained and flown, what they are likely to recognise as quarry, and in which type of terrain they are most comfortable. In turn, this also means that the falconer can make choices about which type(s) he can fly – given his experience, the land and landscape he has available, and the quarry-base he will be hunting.

Compared to the numbers and variety of birds of prey in the wild, only a tiny minority are used in falconry. This is because their size, diet, habitat, hunting behaviour – or some other quality – make most of them unsuitable. Of those that are used, different species are flown against the type of quarry they are familiar with which, understandably, tends to be the kind of game humans also like to eat. For example, you can't persuade a 5oz Merlin to catch a 2lb pheasant, but it will catch larks, which were once a delicacy here. In the long development of the sport, exploiting a bird's inherited skills and propensities maximised a falconer's chances of catching something for the pot, as well as providing natural and exciting flights.

Both elements (food and flights) still drive the sport, but the emphasis in recent centuries has been centred on the bird's quality of flight rather than the gastronomic content of her catch. Since accurate guns came onto the scene, falconry birds have lost much of their value as food-providers. Nevertheless, Merlins are still used to hunt larks, and Sparrowhawks blackbirds, simply because both kinds of flight provide superb visual spectacle.

One other relevant factor is that female raptors are usually larger (up to 33 per cent) than their male counterparts – a feature known as *dimorphism*, which means 'two forms'. For both wild and falconry birds, this has consequences:

1. Females can hold onto larger prey than males, but they tend to be more ponderous in flight
2. Males are quicker and more agile, but are usually limited to smaller (though generally faster-moving) prey.

Naturalists believe that this difference in size enables breeding pairs to catch a much wider range of prey than either could individually, which ensures the best possible chance of survival for their hungry offspring, especially in times of shortage. It might also be that, where males and females tend to hunt alone outside their breeding season, they don't end up competing with each other even if their territories overlap.

Because of this dimorphism, many males and females are flown in falconry almost as if they were different species. Where this is the case, each sex has traditionally been given a different name (although this applies only to long-established species). What follows is a short summary of the birds most regularly flown in Britain, and the kind of quarry they are usually set against. Latin (or scientific) names are given in brackets.

LONGWINGS

With one or two exceptions, falcons are flown exclusively against feathered game. The classical model is for the falcon to take station (wait on) high above the falconer, then dive (stoop) at quarry flushed beneath her and catch it in mid-air. In modern falconry, especially where newer birds have come onto the scene, there are several variations on this theme. If a comparison can be made with other field sports, falcons are equivalent to game-shooting, or fly-fishing.

Peregrine Falcon (*Falco peregrinus*)
Used primarily for 'game hawking'. The female – called the 'falcon' – against grouse, duck or pheasant; and the male – called the 'tiercel' – against partridge. A falcon which doesn't make the grade as a gamehawk might be used against rooks or gulls, but a tiercel not coming up to scratch has little or no sporting future.

Saker Falcon (*Falco cherrug*)
Males are known as 'sakrets'. This species originates in Central Europe, but migrates to parts of the Middle East and North Africa. In Britain they are used as alternatives to Peregrines and are flown at similar quarry. In addition, the females can be used to catch hares. Being primarily desert or steppe birds, they do not handle wind and rain nearly as well as the Peregrine.

Prairie Falcon (*Falco mexicanus*)
These are North American longwings fairly new to the sport. They are another alternative to the Peregrine, but they are neither as fast nor as stylish, and their behaviour in the field can be unreliable. Even so, good Prairies tend to show more persistence than the average Peregrine by chasing quarry in and out of cover, which makes the species potentially useful in more enclosed country. Some falconers are still experimenting with them, but neither sex has yet established a recognisable niche here.

Gyrfalcon (*Falco rusticolus*)
The male is known as the 'gyrkin' (or 'jerkin'). Gyrs are mainly arctic birds and are the largest and most powerful of all longwings. In this country they are flown against the same quarry as Peregrines, but it is difficult to train them to wait on. They prefer using their superior speed and power to fly game down over a long distance. Consequently they are easily lost. The only quarry really worthy of their potential in this country are red grouse, migrating geese, or the extremely rare (and protected) ptarmigan.

Lanner Falcon (*Falco biarmicus*)
The male is known as the 'lanneret'. They are native to Africa where they hunt over semi-desert and savannah. They are used mainly for lure-flying, for example at exhibitions or airfields, and lannerets in particular for so-called 'hedge-hunting' against quarry such as magpies.

Lugger Falcon (*Falco jugger*)
These birds originate in the Indian sub-continent and they are used as alternatives to Lanners, but they lack the same persistence, agility and style.

Merlin (*Falco columbarius*)
The male is known as the 'jack'. Both sexes are used against first-year skylarks. A young lark flushed off the ground will 'ring up' to get above the falcon and the falcon will spiral up in pursuit. If she succeeds in gaining height on the lark, she will put in several short stoops to drive it back to earth, then catch it on the ground.

Kestrel (*Falco tinnunculus*)
Although very fine birds, kestrels are generally considered of little use for hunting unless you want to catch frogs, beetles or voles. Their primary value to falconry is that they can be used to

teach apprentices how to train other longwings without the risk of ruining a potentially first class gamehawk. Having said that, they are interesting and exciting birds to fly to a lure as long as you don't expect any more from them.

SHORTWINGS

Accipiters are primarily woodland birds and they are employed as generalist hunters in enclosed, mixed, or wooded terrain. They take feathered or furred game, usually catching it on, or close to, the ground. Some work best from trees, following the falconer from tree to tree (the follow-on method), others work best 'off the fist'. In this category, there is less distinction between males and females. Again as a comparison, they are the falconry equivalent of rough-shooting or coarse-fishing.

Goshawk (*Accipiter gentilis*)
The Goshawk is the archetypal shortwing in the same way as the Peregrine is the classical longwing. The male is often referred to (mistakenly) as the 'tiercel' or 'tiercel gos', perhaps in recognition of this status. They are generally acknowledged as one of the best of all hawks because they provide good quality flights against a large variety of quarry in virtually any weather. Basically, a good bird will chase almost anything that moves with the guts and courage for which soldiers are awarded the Victoria Cross. They work from trees or off the fist, and they are lethal against pheasants, rabbits and hares, but anything found in or around local farmland is likely to be considered fair game by one of these hawks – including the landowner's cats, lambs and chickens if she is not kept under proper control.

Sparrowhawk (*Accipiter nisus*)
The female is known as the 'spar', and the male the 'musket'. Although a miniature version of the Goshawk, the Sparrowhawk has the same gutsy and ferocious qualities. They are specialist bird-catchers, and the classical quarry for the spar is the blackbird which provides stunning, swift-moving, determined and evenly-matched flights, but both spar and musket can be used against any small birds (sparrows, starlings, etc) found in local farmland. They are, perhaps, best flown off the fist, and some falconers literally throw them to give them extra impetus, or use a sling-like device known as a *halsband* (see the section headed *Falconry Terminology* page 231).

Cooper's Hawk (Accipiter cooperii)
A North American species similar in shape and colour to the Gos and Spar but midway in size. In the USA, where wild ones can still be legally caught and trained, they have proved to be interesting and versatile. In Britain, where they are captive-bred, they have a reputation for unpredictable and aggressive behaviour towards their falconers (actually there is some evidence that they show similar aggression towards their own parents in the wild). They are flown in the same way as a Goshawk or Spar, mainly against young rabbits, partridge, moorhens, and occasionally grouse.

Black Sparrowhawk (*Accipiter melanoleucus*)
These hawks originate in the tropical forests of West Africa, and they are still fairly rare here. They are also intermediate in size, but they are predominantly black with white underparts, and have incredibly long tails which help them to manoeuvre in dense forest. They are flown the same way as Spars and, like them, specialise in feathered quarry.

BROADWINGS

Buzzards are trained much the same way as shortwings to follow-on or fly off the fist, but in addition they can be encouraged to soar (using updrafts and thermals to gain height) and stoop at quarry flushed beneath them. They are neither as specialised as falcons, nor as energetic as accipiters, and they provide a more relaxed style of hawking which is also comparable to rough-shooting or coarse-fishing. In this category, there is no working distinction between males and females, differences in performance depending entirely on individual birds.

Common (or European) Buzzard (*Buteo buteo*)
These are one of the toughest and hardiest of all hawks. Their performance is opportunistic rather than energetic, but their soaring flight in particular is stunning to watch. They are used primarily against young rabbits, squirrels, rats and moorhens.

Red-tailed Buzzard (*Buteo jamaicensis*)
This is another North American species, similar to the common buzzard but larger and more powerful. They are also more aggressive and energetic hunters, and their hunting style is closer to that of the Goshawk's. They also have some of the Goshawk's versatility, taking a range of furred and feathered quarry such as rabbits, hares, squirrels, pheasants, moorhens, rooks and crows.

Harris' Hawk (*Parabuteo unicinctus*)
These birds originate in South and Central America, the southernmost states of the USA representing the extreme northern extent of their range. They are neither accipiters nor buzzards, but a natural cross between the two. Highly sociable, they are relatively easy to train, and they take to the follow-on method of hunting much more readily than shortwings or other broadwings. Many falconers fly them as a substitute for the Goshawk, and they will take the same range of quarry. What they lack in speed and single-minded aggression, they tend to make up for with brains and guile.

Ferruginous Buzzard (*Buteo regalis*)
Another bird from North America and one of the largest of all broadwings. In the wild they roost and nest mostly on the ground or rocky outcrops, and perching in trees or other vegetation is somewhat alien to them (although in prairie lands, where they have no alternative, they will nest in trees). Persuading them to perch on the fist or work from trees can, therefore, be very difficult. They can be fast fliers, but only where they have room to build up speed. In enclosed areas they are relatively clumsy and ill-at-ease. In this country they haven't had much success with feathered quarry, and quarry-species tend to be limited to hares or rabbits.

Hybrids

Falconers are always looking for new species to fly in an effort to extend the boundaries of their sport but, because of increasing international agreement on the control of traffic in wildlife, it is unlikely that any new kinds of wild hawk will find their way into falconry. Consequently, many falconers are already experimenting with cross-breeding, which has been made possible by the success of recent captive-breeding programmes through a greater understanding of imprinting and artificial insemination (AI). Current examples of hybrids are *Gyr x Peregrine*, *Gyr x Saker*, and *Peregrine x Merlin*. Ultimately cross-breeding might lead to the full domestication of falconry birds, which will be bred – like working dogs – to suppress or enhance particular qualities. But as yet, no specific 'breeds', or reliable bloodlines, appear to have been established.

At this stage, hybridisation is controversial in the falconry world. Some see it as ethically wrong, others as a natural progression; but this is not the place to rehearse the arguments. For the moment, no kind of hybrid has usurped a raptor with wild origins from its established place in the sport. In the final analysis, there are two questions confronting every kind of falconer:

1. what sort of terrain (moorland, farmland, prairie, woods, mountains) do I have available on a day-by-day basis to fly my bird over?
2. what potential quarry does it support?

Ultimately the real art of falconry is about using a suitable hawk to catch appropriate quarry in your own landscape, and there are already enough varieties of natural species to achieve that anywhere in the world. Indeed, many overlap and, as captive-bred birds, are available here which means you might be spoilt for choice.

But, undoubtedly, well-bred hybrids will eventually extend this choice. They may even be bred to specialise in particular types of quarry which would then become easier to catch. They may also be bred to deal with certain weather conditions (such as wind and rain), or to make them easier to handle and train, or more resistant to raptor diseases, or more productive in breeding terms, or just to look prettier. Where hybridisation goes will depend on what future falconers, who will create the demand, want from their birds.

First Birds

As a beginner, you must accept that you will make many mistakes, and that failure to develop a hawk's full potential is normal with a first bird. This doesn't mean that you will be unable to train and fly a first bird successfully, but it does mean that your mistakes will be an integral part of the bird's early experience and they might limit her potential in the field – at least initially. Many early mistakes are redeemable, and as your experience grows you will know better how to correct them. To put them right, you might have to show endless patience and persistence by constantly analysing what is happening between the pair of you.

This makes it imperative that you acquire the right kind of bird to start with. All the birds described in the last chapter are well able to provide brilliant sport, but some are best avoided until you have gained experience – either because they are expensive, or because their temperament makes them intolerant of mistakes or, much more importantly, because they are easily lost, permanently ruined, or killed through innocent mismanagement.

Longwings

However much you might admire them, you should never attempt to train a longwing on your own as a beginner. Unlike computers, falcons do not have a delete button and they tend to be totally unforgiving, especially if you clout them accidentally with a lure because you are not yet fully-practised in its use. If you do attempt to train one, the most likely outcome is that you will ruin her forever and have little or no success in the field.

If you are determined to fly longwings, you should consider a kestrel as a first bird – *but only if you have access to a longwing falconer*. One or two clubs are offering 'apprenticeships' to beginners, so this is sometimes possible. Otherwise you will need to find a longwinger close by who is willing and able to help. The problem is that Kestrels are small birds which are easily killed, and you will need frequent access to a mentor to avoid this outcome. He will also be able to tutor you in the use of a lure before you use it on the bird, and in other skills such as hooding. If you manage to train one with his help, you can then move on to other species.

Shortwings

These birds are also problematical. By human standards, accipiters are hyper-active and inherently neurotic. Such qualities make their temperaments difficult to cope with to say the least, and they are all stressful to train and maintain. Accipiters reared naturally by their parents do not take to captivity easily, and getting them to tolerate human beings and their environment (a technique called 'manning') can be a long and tedious process. Even then, most will revert to a wild state at the first opportunity, and out in the field they are very easily lost.

They can be imprinted, which eliminates their wildness and fear, but this takes additional knowledge, skill and experience. Then, lack of fear can be replaced by blatant aggression towards their handler, especially when you start to reduce weight. Medium-sized and large accipiters which have been imprinted are, therefore, potentially dangerous and need careful and experienced handling.

With all accipiters, weight-control needs to be very finely-judged to get them responding adequately, but with smaller species weight easily becomes a matter of life or death. Male Sparrowhawks in particular are tiny by falconry standards, and the loss of a few grams in weight can result in a hypoglycaemic (low blood-sugar) fit or a dead hawk. Males and females alike have a very high metabolic rate, which means that they burn energy rapidly. In relation to their size they need much more food than longwings or broadwings, and much more stringent monitoring of weight. All these factors point to a need for experience in handling less frenetic birds first.

Broadwings

This group provides a selection of appropriate birds for a beginner, and the qualities that make them suitable are:
1. Their temperaments: they are laid-back and easy-going, and will allow you to get away with a few mistakes
2. Mistakes are easier to rectify at a later date
3. Their size and constitutions: they are big and robust with large weight margins, which means that they will give you plenty of warning before their condition becomes critical and you will have time to remedy the fault
4. They require less skill and experience to train.

But there is one available broadwing which should be avoided at all costs, namely the Ferruginous Buzzard which is comparable to an eagle in size, power and temperament. Any beginner taking one on is asking for trouble. You will either sustain a serious injury or lose a valuable bird. The remaining options are: the Common Buzzard, the Red-tailed Buzzard, and the Harris' Hawk.

Broadwings

It would be wholly inappropriate to view any of the birds described in this section just as 'beginners' birds', which implies that they are somehow discardable once the ropes have been learned. It is a bad label which does no justice to the birds, or to the dedication of hundreds of experienced falconers using one or other of them as mainstream hawks. Each species will give a lifetime of service if they are trained well and flown regularly, and they are all well-able to provide exciting falconry. Indeed, the older and wiser they are, the better they tend to perform.

The purpose of this section is simply to give you a comparative analysis to help you make an informed decision about which broadwing suits your circumstances best. For example, you might want to fly a native hawk, or you might be severely limited by price, or you might prefer the appearance of one more than the others. But they are all suitable, even though each has advantages and disadvantages.

The details which follow include a map of their distribution in the wild, an ornithological description, natural prey species, and an assessment of their value as falconry birds – in particular for beginners.

Common (or European) Buzzard *(Buteo buteo)*

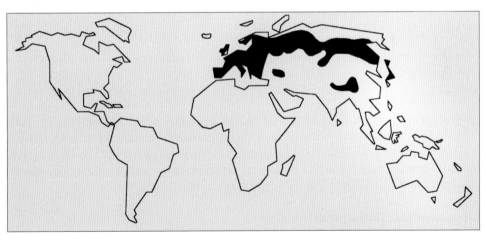

The bird we know as the Common Buzzard is not just a native one. In fact Britain is really an outpost. It is much more abundant in the rest of Europe, Russia, Siberia, China and Japan. In Britain its main stronghold is the West and Southwest, and it is almost totally absent in the Southeast (although gradually extending its range in that direction).

Common Buzzards are generally large birds, and on the whole there is less difference in size between sexes compared to other birds of prey. A large male can be bigger than a small female, and this kind of overlap is unusual in raptor populations. The significance of this to falconers is that it makes the sexing of young Common Buzzards extremely difficult. If you specifically want to buy a male, all a breeder can do is show you his smaller birds and hope for the best.

Wild buzzards thrive in semi-wooded country, farmland, cliffs, hills or open moorlands and it is their ability to exploit this range of habitats which is partly responsible for their breeding success. They are neither fast nor energetic flyers, but they can soar effortlessly for long periods – especially on warm or windy days – and this is their characteristic hunting style. In bad weather, such as fog, mist or heavy rain, they will use trees, telegraph poles or similar open vantage points to hunt for food. Their natural prey are rabbits (usually not fully-grown, or old or sick), voles, mice and rats, but if times are really hard they will eat almost anything – lizards, worms, caterpillars, large insects and spiders, carrion, and even berries from the hedgerows. Constitutionally they are incredibly tough and resilient hawks capable of withstanding chronic deprivations that would kill most other birds of prey, but their relatively small foot size makes them less capable of holding on to bigger quarry species.

Trying to describe the plumage of Common Buzzards is a nightmare. There is no specific feature, not even a generalised pattern, which can be applied to all. They are basically a blotchy brown, darker on top than underneath, but on some individuals underside plumage is a speckled cream or anything up to snow white. Upper plumage can range from mid- to sooty-brown, but often it has a ginger tinge, especially on the tail, which is heavily-barred. Most have a pale, vaguely diamond-shaped marking on the back of their head and neck, but even this isn't guaranteed.

In falconry terms, they are the ideal first bird in several respects. First of all, they are native and relatively inexpensive, but in addition:
- they are big, robust, tough, laid-back and forgiving
- they have large weight margins (ie the difference between fat weight and starvation), which means that they are difficult to kill through innocent mismanagement
- you can make many mistakes with them, yet still get them responding
- their 'laid-backness' verges on 'lazy', which means you have to operate with very fine weight control to produce an acceptable response
- to get them hunting consistently, you will need to put in some fieldcraft and a lot of confidence-building groundwork.

In other words, they develop all the basic skills required to train, manage, and hunt with a bird of prey.

However, if your main objective is to hunt, the quarry range for Common Buzzards is limited – probably restricted to rats, half-grown rabbits, and moorhens (discounting shrews, voles, beetles etc). It is unlikely that you will get a Buzzard to take a pheasant, a hare, or even a full-grown healthy rabbit. But if you just want to fly a bird, Buzzards love soaring. If you can get one to do that, and still keep it under control in field conditions, it is a real joy to see.

Red-tailed Buzzard *(Buteo jamaicensis)*

Red-tailed Buzzards mainly inhabit the USA (where they are known simply as Redtails, or Red-tailed Hawks), but also southern Canada, Mexico, other parts of central America, and the West Indies. They are similar to Common Buzzards (which don't exist there) and they may even be distantly-related but they are much larger.

Because of the spread of these birds over a huge area individuals vary greatly in size and colour, but they are generally mid-brown on top with creamy or pale orange underparts streaked vertically with dark brown blotches. They may also have a ginger tinge to their head and neck plumage, but the real distinguishing feature is their tail, which is pale chestnut or Indian red with a single black bar near the tip.

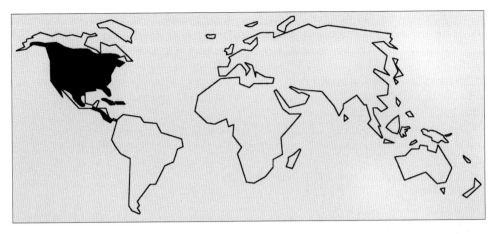

Basically a soaring bird, the Redtail has a wide ecological tolerance but prefers mixed country of open pastures or fields varied with groves, bluffs and streamside trees or, in drier climates, deserts where there is some tree-like growth. As with most *Buteos*, they are opportunistic hunters and their prey species vary from grasshoppers to jack rabbits (American hares). They also take ground squirrels, rabbits, pheasants and other gamebirds. Snakes, too, are often on the menu, including such venomous species as rattlesnakes, and they have often been observed patrolling the entrances to bat-infested caves just before dusk waiting for flocks to emerge, then picking them off one-by-one in mid-air.

Redtails are a fairly recent addition to British falconry (rarely imported before the 1960s), but they have since acquired many devotees. In the USA, where falconers have to serve an apprenticeship, they are compulsory first birds in many States. They are faster and more aggressive than our native species, and have a proportionately bigger foot size, which means that they are capable of holding onto larger species of quarry such as hares. Like the Common Buzzard, they help beginners acquire all the basic skills necessary for falconry, except that their natural aggression makes them much easier to initiate into serious hunting which is a plus in many respects, but a minus in developing fieldcraft if you lack this skill because a Redtail (if allowed) will often find its own quarry.

They are flown in similar terrain to the Common Buzzard – farmland or other open country with a few trees to work from – and they are best flown from trees with a bit of height against quarry flushed beneath them. They can be flown 'off the fist', but they really need height and distance to build up the speed required to catch up with and secure their quarry. Off-the-fist flights are usually reserved for ferreting, especially when the Redtail is prone to catch the ferret, but this technique (off-the-fist) is frowned upon by purists for anything other than accipters for whom it was developed, and in which they excel. Redtails can also be trained to 'follow-on', but their ability to get their heads around this technique is limited. It usually only works if you can flush quarry consistently for them as you move on, or if you have a well-controlled working dog which can be relied on to do the same thing.

A word of warning. Some captive-bred females are very large (the average Common Buzzard is almost a dwarf in comparison) and a few demonstrate what the Americans call 'attitude'. This means that they can become very aggressive towards you, or other people, or both. Their size and power alone make this a potentially serious problem, and often this kind of explosive aggression doesn't reveal itself until the bird is two or three years old. Males are not only smaller, but temperamentally steadier and easier to handle. They are also quicker and more agile in flight, yet still capable of catching the range of quarry you are likely to have available (including hares, although they might need your assistance to subdue them). As a first bird, the male is the better option.

Harris' Hawk *(Parabuteo unicinctus)*

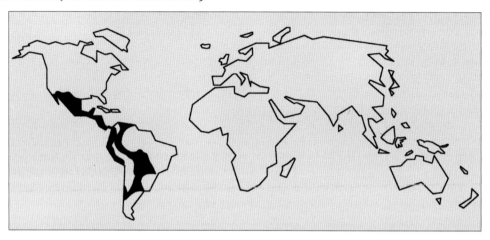

The prefix *Para* in the Harris' Hawk's Latin name is derived from *par-* meaning 'same as', which is apt because this bird is not a true buzzard (*Buteo*). In fact it is a natural cross between an accipiter and a buzzard, having some of the qualities and characteristics of each. The bird was 'discovered' by the famous American ornithologist and artist Audubon, who named it after Colonel Harris, a friend of his. An alternative name, used mainly in the USA, is the Bay-winged Hawk. Harris' Hawks are essentially South American birds, but in recent centuries they have extended their range northwards through central America, Mexico, and into the extreme southwestern parts of the USA.

The plumage of Harris' Hawks is basically sooty-brown, except for chestnut flashes on the shoulders and chestnut thighs. Their tails are black with a broad white tip and a white base (rump). As with accipiters, there is a large difference in size between sexes, and they have the same general build – long tail, long legs, large and heavily-armed feet, sturdy beak and a compact muscular body. Unlike accipiters (but characteristic of *Buteos*), their eyes are dark brown, and their head is a miniature replica of the Golden Eagle's.

For reasons not yet fully-understood, Harris' Hawks are social rather than solitary hunters contrary to the general raptor pattern. Like wolves, they hunt in packs, usually comprising four to six individuals, each playing an appropriate role in the flush, the chase, and the kill. Natural prey is widely varied depending on availability, but includes waterfowl, gamebirds and other birds; mammals such as gophers, tree-squirrels, rabbits and hares; and reptiles such as snakes and lizards. Once a kill is made, it is shared by other pack members. Naturalists believe that this enables the species to catch larger prey than they could otherwise because they can rely on group assistance when necessary. This gives each member of the group more food than it could obtain as a solitary hunter, more regularly, and more reliably. Their breeding patterns are also social, limited to one dominant pair who are supported in hunting and feeding young by other group members. Pack members are usually the siblings of, and/or the offspring of, dominant pairs.

Harris' Hawks were first imported into the UK in the 1970s, but they are already the most popular bird of prey flown in Britain. There are good reasons for this. Their group behaviour – which incorporates not only co-operation but also levels of dominance – makes them naturally predisposed to domestication and co-operative hunting with a human partner in exactly the same way as dogs. Like accipiters, Harris' Hawks can generate rapid acceleration over short distances, and they have the same willingness to pursue quarry through woodland and thick cover. For this reason, they were originally flown here as Goshawk substitutes. However, Goshawks are capable of swifter and more enduring pursuits than Harris' Hawks, which will give up within two or three hundred yards, especially flying into the wind. But their lack of equality with Goshawks in straight pursuit is more than compensated for by the intelligent way they learn to work with their co-hunters – not just the falconer, but also his dog.

If co-hunting is extended to a pair (or more) of Harris' Hawks, together with falconers and dogs, they introduce a whole new dimension to the sport and few quarry escape. Other species, such as Buzzards and Redtails, can be flown together in the sense that they refrain from killing each other, but in the artificial set-up of falconry they compete rather than co-operate. Harris' Hawks naturally work together and seldom show aggression or jealousy towards their own kind. On the contrary, they quickly learn to work together in the most efficient way – perhaps one going into a hedgerow to flush quarry relying on the other to chase and secure it; then, if necessary, coming to their aid if they're having trouble holding on.

The co-operative hunting style of Harris' Hawks has not yet been fully-exploited in this country much beyond the traditional bird/man/dog team effort, but this alone makes them outstanding falconry birds.

Harris' Hawks have one vice and that is that they are prone to screaming. Birds taken for training when they are just fully-fledged will scream incessantly from dawn to dusk. You might be able to put up with this, but your neighbours probably won't, and if they complain, you might have to get rid of the bird or face court action. Generally speaking, breeders try to minimise this by holding on to the birds for a few weeks after fledging. However, some breeders keep them too long, or rear them away from their parents, which eradicates their screaming but, in the process, destroys some of their sociability. A small minority of such birds go further and revert to accipiter-like behaviour – fearful, and difficult to train and control.

Ideally Harris' Hawks should be raised by their parents then, once fully-fledged, kept with them for a few weeks – even helping them out with raising the next batch of youngsters if the female lays a second clutch. This mimics their natural behaviour in the wild. The final stage is to put them in a separate aviary with their siblings for a few more weeks to gain a measure of independence from their parents. The whole process usually takes sixteen to eighteen weeks from hatching, after which they are ready for training. Crèche-reared birds – those fed as a brood after hatching by the falconer rather than by their natural parents – are at greater risk of losing sociability.

In terms of your longer-term development as a falconer, there is another big downside to taking on a Harris' Hawk as a first bird. Although, like the Common Buzzard and the Redtail, they will teach you the basics of managing, training and hunting with a bird of prey, the ease with which you can achieve this with a well-bred Harris' Hawk does not compare with any other hawk of whatever kind. Not only do these birds give you a false sense of security, they also give you a completely unrealistic view of how difficult falconry actually is. Once you've trained a Harris' Hawk and want to move on to something else, you will find yourself going back to the drawing board time and time again or, alternatively, failing dramatically.

Kestrels

As I have already pointed out (in the section headed *First Birds*), longwings are generally unsuitable as starter birds. The kestrel is the exception, and it has long been used to train apprentices in the skills required for longwing falconry. The keywords here are 'apprentices' and 'skills'. Kestrels are small birds which require skill to maintain without endangering their life and, as with all longwings, they require skill to fly them to a lure.

Of course it is possible to acquire both skills through trial and error on your own but, given the facilities available these days, I believe this to be an irresponsible approach especially if it results in the death or ruination of a bird. Books like this certainly help, but lure-swinging skills in particular are difficult to acquire unless you can be tutored by someone who knows what they're doing, and without a bird involved. If you are desperate to take up longwing falconry and you are lucky enough to have access to a mentor, either through an apprenticeship scheme or because you live close to a longwing falconer willing to help, by all means consider a kestrel as a first bird. Otherwise, please leave them well alone.

Common Kestrel *(Falco tinnunculus)*

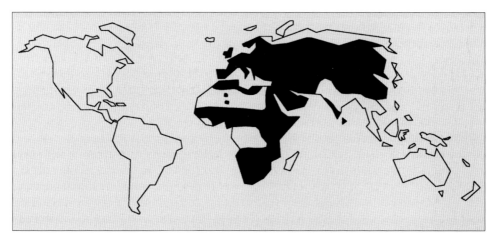

Kestrels are true falcons, commonly seen in this country hovering by the roadside. They are also indigenous to Europe, Africa and Asia, but not the Americas or Australasia. North Americans have their own species (*Falco sparverius*) which is slightly smaller, but otherwise virtually identical. Confusingly, it is commonly-known there as the 'sparrowhawk'. *Falco sparverius* is also available here as a captive-bred species. Although there are other species of kestrel in different areas of the world (including Australasia), none of these is available as a falconry bird.

Where Common and American Kestrels are concerned, the males have a grey head, rump and tail, and a chestnut-coloured back speckled with black dots. Females, which are slightly larger, are duller in plumage, mainly brown all over.

By and large, Kestrels have adapted superbly to human encroachment on the landscape, and their habitat varies from wide open country to inner-city skyscrapers. Their natural diet is equally wide-ranging, comprising mice, voles, young rats, frogs, earthworms, insects (grasshoppers and beetles as opposed to flies), sparrows and other small birds. Their characteristic hunting technique is to hover with rapidly-fanning wings and a spread tail, 30 to 50 feet above ground, searching for any prey passing underneath. They are able to maintain their position in anything from a dead calm to a raging gale, but in strong winds they scarcely fan their wings at all, maintaining suspension by changing the wings' 'angle of attack'. Although other raptors occasionally hover for short periods, none does it for as long or as efficiently as the Kestrel for whom it can be regarded as a trade mark.

It could be said that Kestrels are not true falconry birds in the sense that they don't catch the kind of quarry that falconers are generally interested in, or in the style that they want from longwings. Once trained, they no longer hover, and they are very difficult to train to 'wait on'. Occasionally they will do it, but usually only if they have help from the updraft off a hill or a close-by thermal. Otherwise, seeing them drop from 40 feet onto a beetle or a grasshopper can hardly be called classical falconry. However, as first birds, if you have access to good and consistent advice they:

1. Provide a valuable introduction to the maintenance of other small longwings such as Merlins, and ultimately to the maintenance and flying of all longwings
2. Provide a good introduction to the skill of lure-swinging because, compared to other longwings, they are fairly slow in flight and often take short rests between 'passes' giving a novice falconer time to recover his position
3. Are highly entertaining (sometimes spectacular) fliers to a swing lure.

As an introduction to training longwings, therefore, Kestrels still have a positive role to play. You can make many mistakes and, within certain limits, correct them without risking the loss or ruination of a more valuable falcon. But the big problem with using a Kestrel as a first bird is deciding what to do with it once you've learned the ropes. You might want to fly it to a lure for the rest of its life if you can fit it in with your other, newly-developed, falconry pursuits. But if you can't, you have only two acceptable options:

1 Pass it onto someone else who can fly it and care for it properly
2 Release it (hack it back) to the wild.

Provided it is a native Kestrel, hacking it back is fine as long as you can be sure it will survive. If it has never caught anything (beetles, voles, or whatever) this ceases to be a viable option. If your Kestrel isn't a native species (eg *Falco sparverius*), releasing it would be illegal anyway even if you were 100 per cent sure it would survive. Passing it on to another novice is also fine, except that they would not get the benefit of training the bird themselves, and they will have to make up for that in some other way. Keeping a Kestrel (or any other Bird of Prey for that matter) idle in captivity for the rest of its life is not an acceptable solution, and you will need to find an answer to this problem before you decide to take one on.

Peregrine falcon (*Falco peregrinus*)

PART 2

Nuts and Bolts

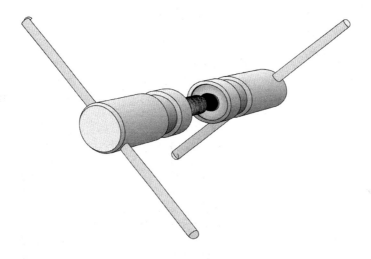

Hawk Quarters

Appropriate housing for a hawk is of paramount importance, not only to comply with the law but also for her general health and well-being. The accommodation described in this section satisfies basic law requirements as well as security, but there are other issues involved such as siting, construction, and cost.

Falconry birds are essentially wild animals and on the whole they live outdoors. They benefit a great deal from fresh air and should spend time outside whenever possible as long as the weather is not too extreme. Any place where they are put for this purpose is known as a *weathering ground*. Many falconers tether their hawks on a perch on a lawn during the day if they can be adequately supervised. Otherwise they are kept in an open air enclosure which also incorporates sheltered overnight quarters. Even if you can weather your hawk outside every day, somewhere safe and suitable to house her overnight is absolutely essential. As a *bare minimum* she will need shelter and protection from:

- high winds, heavy rain, and hot sunshine – in the wild, a hawk will find shelter for herself but a tethered one has to stay where she is put
- other wildlife – mainly foxes, badgers, rats, weasels, stoats, and even mink these days
- domestic animals and malicious persons — in particular cats, dogs, thieves and 'animal rights' extremists

The simplest and cheapest type of secure weathering is a three-sided shelter with a sloping roof and a wire mesh front.

The three sides can be made with many types of weather-resistant sheet material – for example, exterior plywood, blockboard, planking designed for sheds (which will have to be weather-proofed), or larch-lap fencing panels – depending on budget. The roof is best constructed of corrugated plastic sheeting (opaque to provide shade), or exterior plywood covered with roofing felt. The supporting posts need to be anchored securely in the ground for stability, and this is most-easily achieved by using 'Metposts' – metal sockets with spikes that can be driven into the ground providing metal 'shoes' for the posts.

The front should be covered with a strong wire-netting (but *not* chicken wire) using a mesh small enough to prevent the hawk poking her head through (a rectangular 3in x 1in mesh is ideal). Galvanised or plastic-coated netting, though more expensive to buy, is cheaper in the long-run because it doesn't rust. Obviously for access to the bird – and security – you will need to construct a meshed door fixed either by hinges, or on runners so that it can slide to one side. A stout padlock fixed to a Brent bolt will at least deter unauthorised entry. A further precautionary measure is to place a groundsheet of coarser wire netting (such as chicken wire) over the floor area before covering it. This will prevent wildlife gaining access by tunnelling underneath.

Floor-covering is also of some importance. Depending on how much your bird moves around, the whole area is likely to become fouled with faeces very quickly which can harbour potentially harmful bacteria. The floor area should be covered with a material which can be disinfected and hosed down (or at worst replaced) easily. Falconers have tried almost every substance – sand, straw, peat, sawdust, concrete, the earth itself – but uncrushed pea gravel is, in the opinion of many, the best option if you can find it. It is more or less permanent, easy to clean and rake over,

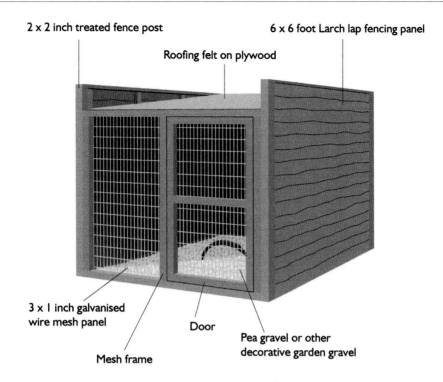

2 x 2 inch treated fence post

6 x 6 foot Larch lap fencing panel

Roofing felt on plywood

3 x 1 inch galvanised
wire mesh panel

Door

Pea gravel or other
decorative garden gravel

Mesh frame

and it isn't harmful to the bird's feet or digestive system. If you can't get pea gravel, any cleaned and washed decorative garden gravel (up to 20mm gauge) can be used as a substitute. Either should be spread over the floor to a depth of two to three inches so that it can be raked over effectively.

Several kinds of non-native hawk suffer from extremes of cold (meaning minus 10° C downwards), and a few are even susceptible to frostbite, which invariably leaves them permanently disabled. It would be wise to consider some form of heating in the event that such temperatures occur. Unfortunately oil heaters emit fumes, and gas heaters fuelled by containers can cause, or aggravate, condensation. Both are unhealthy for a hawk, and neither is practical for accommodation of this size.

Expensive though it might be, the only satisfactory form of heating is electricity. Fortunately, relatively low amounts are needed to keep the air above freezing. Pig lamps (heat-lamps used in pig sties) suspended above the bird's perch are perfectly adequate. An alternative is tubular heaters of the kind used in greenhouses which can be 'banked' (grouped in two, three or four tubes) to provide the amount of background heat required. To keep the warmth in and minimise wastage, a blind made out of a length of opaque PVC sheeting can be rolled down from the roof to cover the open-mesh frontage. It will need to be held down, with stones or some other device, to stop it flapping about in the wind and upsetting the hawk.

The need for heating, albeit infrequent, might be decisive in choosing a suitable site – in other words, near an electrical supply. Otherwise the weathering can be built anywhere. However, it is probably advisable not to put it in a front garden where the bird can be ogled by every passer-by, nor facing a blank wall, which is unlikely to do much to maintain her interest in the outside world.

Hawks and buzzards have one unsociable habit – they 'shoot', rather than drop, their waste products (mutes) out of their back end. Consequently the inside walls of a weathering can easily become soiled, and some materials – in particular larch-lap fencing panels – are difficult to keep clean. To minimise this, a loose sheet of rigid plastic about 5ft x 3ft – or something similar – can be placed behind the hawk's perch to take the worst of it. The sheet can then be removed and hosed down easily.

An enclosed weathering of this kind is perfectly adequate for the vast majority of falconry birds. If it is all you can afford for the time being, you can be assured that your hawk will at least be safe and fairly well protected.

There are, of course, more sophisticated quarters you can build if you have the space, the skills (unless you know a friendly and charitable builder), the time and the budget. Adequate though it is, the accommodation described above has one or two longer-term drawbacks:

1. It doesn't provide any appreciable flying space. Once fully-trained, most hawks are much better left untethered with a variety of perches they can use. This helps to keep them fit, and relieves boredom by enabling them to change their point of view.
2. It doesn't provide an area a hawk can retreat to out of sight, or roost in overnight.

A roost is a perch on which a bird chooses to sleep. All hawks will roost on the highest perch available, and the higher the better. To get above frost level it needs to be at least three to four feet off the ground, which will further reduce the need for heating. Having indoor quarters also means she can get away from bad day-time weather, or inquisitive eyes. A simple and relatively inexpensive way of solving these problems is shown below.

Such quarters provide flying space for an untethered (free-lofted) bird, as well as an indoor compartment for her to roost or hide in once it has been rigged with a suitable perch such as a tree branch, or a piece of cylindrical wood extending from the back to the front of the shelter. If

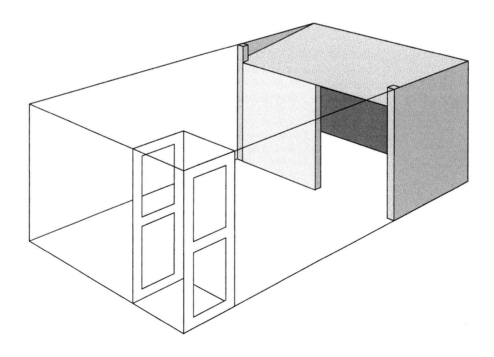

you decide to use cylindrical wood, such as 'mop-handle' banister rail (from builders' merchants), it should be covered with Astroturf or something similar, which provides a rough surface and avoids a condition known as 'bumblefoot' caused by constant and even pressure on the balls of the feet (see the section headed *Illness and Injury* Page 184).

This enclosure features a double-door entry system. With a single door, there is always a risk that the free-flying hawk will escape when you're trying to get in for whatever reason. Although some think the risk is over-estimated, it does provide a sensible safeguard, especially for beginners who, by definition, have little experience of hawk behaviour and body language. Whether you use a single or a double-door system, make sure it is large enough to get a wheelbarrow through for topping up or replacing floor covering (gravel, sand, etc) when necessary.

There are, of course, much more sophisticated quarters you can build for hawks if you have the time, money and space. Your management problems would also be greatly eased if you have a 'services' room – the more birds you have, the more important this will be. Not only will space be needed for equipment, but also the storage of food and first aid supplies. All of these can, of course, be held in the house (with the forbearance of other members of the family) but hawk food in particular is best kept separately from your own. It helps enormously to have somewhere close to the bird where food can be stored and prepared, and where ongoing equipment can be made, maintained and repaired when necessary. The diagram on page 54 illustrates a complex designed for several free-lofted hawks, together with an equipment room, and room for expansion in the event that more birds are acquired.

Here, the mews chamber is built on a concrete base which slopes from front to back (a gradient of 1 inch in 40 is sufficient) to allow the drainage of wastes when the mews is hosed down. To further assist drainage you will need to construct a gravel sump running the whole width of the chamber, which also acts as a soakaway for rainwater from the roof. A perforated drainage pipe about 4in in diameter (bearing in mind possible future expansion of the complex) should be laid in the sump and taken either to a natural drainage ditch close to the site, or to a larger soakaway. This second soakaway, which should be capable of coping with wastes and rainwater from several mews, needs to be a pit about 1 cubic metre in size filled with clean stone or clean rubble.

To minimise the build-up of condensation, the chamber should be vented close to the apex of the roof. Venting can be achieved simply by leaving a gap about 4in deep between the roof and the top of the front wall. Covering the gap with some sort of mesh will stop the bird attempting to use it as an escape route. The vent allows air to flow from the open side of the chamber over the inside of the roof and out through the other side. This will help to keep the roof area dry.

If you don't install proper drainage and ventilation you will find that the chamber is always damp – often flooded – and running with condensation on the roof and walls. These are not healthy conditions in which to keep a hawk. Such a high level of condensation will be generated by your efforts to keep the place clean – with a hosepipe, preferably incorporating a labour-saving jet-spray.

The 'feeding tube' is a plastic self-sealing WC pan-connector which can be bought at most DIY stores. It is fitted through the front wall of the chamber with the bend facing downwards, and the outside opening is covered by a hinged flap to keep out the weather. It allows you to drop food into the chamber without the need to go in, and is particularly useful during the bird's annual moult, or if at some time you decide to breed birds. The feeding table simply stops food from falling onto the floor and gives the hawk somewhere to break it up.

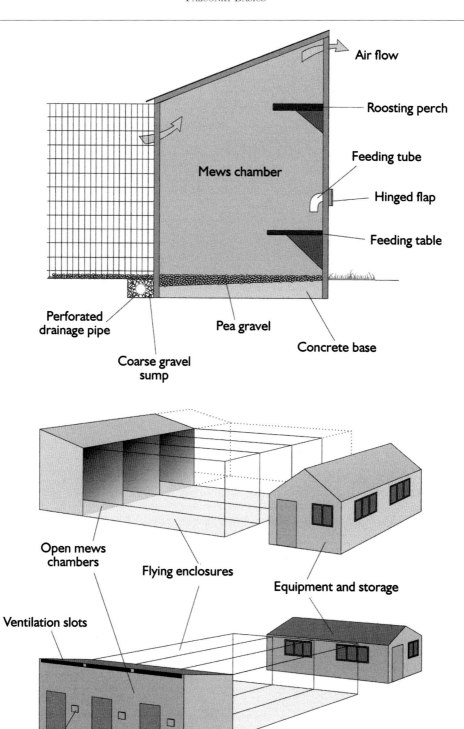

Air flow

Roosting perch

Feeding tube

Hinged flap

Mews chamber

Feeding table

Perforated
drainage pipe

Pea gravel

Concrete base

Coarse gravel
sump

Open mews
chambers

Flying enclosures

Equipment and storage

Ventilation slots

Feeding hatch

The roosting perch should be set as high as possible but leaving a generous clearance between that and the ventilation slots to avoid the possibility that she will be sitting with her head in a constant draught. The chamber can, of course, contain other perches such as logs, stones branches, etc but don't be tempted to overcrowd it. One or two are sufficient. Similarly the flying enclosure will need a number of perches, preferably at varying levels, to give the bird exercise and a change of view. Again don't be tempted to overdo it. The purpose of the enclosure is to give her *clear* flying space rather than present her with an obstacle course.

The equipment room is the area in which you can have most flexibility – it is primarily for you, and can be what you want to make it. Any reasonably-sized shed would suffice, provided it has enough room at least for a freezer and a workbench to prepare de-frosted food, weigh the bird and maintain equipment. The need for a freezer will mean an electrical supply, and building in a lighting circuit at the same time would be an advantage. Similarly, you will find some of the husbandry elements of keeping a bird much easier if the room has a sink with running water. Cupboards, drawers or both are invaluable for keeping leather, tools, spare and currently-used gear, cleaning equipment, first-aid supplies and anything else associated with the bird tidy and out of the way.

Unfortunately no-one can erect just what they want, even on their own land. Local authorities (District and County Councils) have to administer Government legislation which dictates what you can and can't build. For some new structures – or even for the 'change of use' of old ones – planning permission might be needed. Planning laws cover two separate things:

1. The site of a new building – controlled by the *Town and Country Planning (General Development Order) 1988*
2. The general standard and safety of the building – controlled by the *Building Regulations (1985)*

But, if you don't intend to erect something with a roof-ridge more than 3 metres from the ground and in a position likely to cause annoyance to your neighbours, and if you can convince the authorities that what you are constructing is, in effect, an aviary, it is unlikely that planning permission or building regulations approval will be needed.

Nevertheless, it is your responsibility to make sure that you don't breach any planning laws. Before you start work on anything major, therefore, it is advisable to consult your local authority first rather than risk having to pull the whole thing down because a neighbour has successfully complained that it doesn't comply.

If you are simply asking for advice about compliance, local planning authorities will give it to you freely. But to help them – and your own cause – it is useful to have the largest scale Ordnance Survey map you can find which shows your property and its relationship to the surrounding area. You will also need (at least) a diagram showing where on your land you want to build the complex, its main structural elements, and in particular its dimensions.

Housing Equipment

All falconry equipment – for reasons that are not very clear – is known as *furniture*, even though much of it is used on the hawk herself and has nothing to do with accommodation. As you will see in this and later sections, falconry furniture is very specialised. Each item is designed to perform a specific function, usually to do with control, training, or work in the field, and the designs themselves, in many cases, have evolved over hundreds of years.

Having built a secure home for your hawk, until she's trained sufficiently to respond to you, she will have to be tethered to something – even in her weathering. Otherwise, once you put her in there, you won't be able to get her out again with any degree of control. In addition, she will need a suitable perch to sleep on. For a falconer with a young untrained hawk, tethering her to any kind of perch presents two major problems:

1. The longer her tethering gear is, the further she will be able to fly when she attempts to get away (falconers call this *bating*). The greater the distance she is able to fly, the more speed she will generate and the greater the stress on her legs when she is pulled up short. It is common for young hawks to break their legs in this way with tethering equipment which allows them too much freedom

2. Given that a very short tether is ideal, if the hawk's perch is sited, for example, six feet off the ground she will end up dangling below it the very first time she bates. It takes several days at least for an untrained hawk to learn how to regain a perch from such a position, and, unless her owner is prepared to supervise her activity twenty-four hours a day, he will end up with a dead hawk. For her, such a death is equivalent to crucifixion.

To solve both these problems, for shortwings and broadwings falconers generally use what is known as a 'bow' perch. This device was designed to simulate the branches such birds perch on in the wild, and at one time was actually made with a tree branch bent in the shape of a bow and fitted into metal sockets. These days it is constructed entirely of metal. The perch itself is sited on the ground so that if the hawk bates, she can regain it easily simply by hopping back on. Even if she chooses not to do so, she is still safe standing on the ground and she can be left alone to work things out for herself.

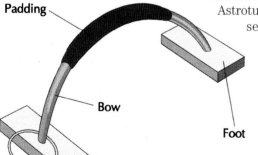

The 'bow' is padded in the centre with leather or (preferably) Astroturf, and it is encircled by a large closed ring used for securing tethering equipment. The ends of the ring should be securely welded so that there is no possibility that it will fail under stress, and it should be large enough to travel comfortably from one end of the bow to the other to allow the hawk some freedom of movement. The padded area should be just high enough off the ground to prevent the tip of her tail making contact with it when she is perching – for a broadwing this is about eight inches. This height also minimises the length of the tethering gear required, which should be just enough for her to reach the ground and regain the perch. For the largest of broadwings – such as the female Redtail – the padded apex of the perch should be at least 1½in in diameter to avoid any possibility that she will pierce her own feet with her hind talon when she grips the perch.

Specialist falconry suppliers, on the whole, are fully aware of these requirements and they make superb equipment to meet them for each category of hawk. But some don't, and it pays to be selective about where and what you buy.

The perch illustrated on page 56 is a portable one. There is a variant – the 'permanent' bow perch – with spikes instead of feet which can be driven into the ground to anchor it. Frankly, if you can only afford to buy a single perch, they are not worth considering at this stage. Your bird will only need to be tethered in the mews or weathering-shelter while she's undergoing her early training. After that, if you choose to leave her untethered, the only likely use you will have for one is to put her out on the lawn (if she hasn't got a permanent flying enclosure) or, more importantly, to carry her around in the car – to the vet, her hunting grounds or various other locations. For this you will need the flexibility a portable bow perch provides.

Another vital piece of housing equipment is a hawk bath, which is important for well-kept plumage. If you neglect to provide one you might find that, instead of hunting and chasing quarry, your hawk has flown off to find water. If you don't lose her as a result and manage to catch up with her, she will be soaking wet and interested in nothing but preening and drying herself out. Although birds of prey don't often drink, they should be given the chance to do so every day. Not surprisingly, they drink more in hot weather, but also after travelling long distances and especially when they are ill. Drinking and bathing are usually done in the same operation.

The illustration shows a custom-made polypropylene bath, but what it's made of is not that important. Circular baths are more comfortable for hawks, and for a broadwing it needs to be about 2ft to 3ft in diameter with a maximum depth of 5in. The wider the rim the better because it is easier on the bird's feet. For a tethered bird it should be placed near enough to the bow perch to allow her freedom to use it properly, then move back onto the perch to preen and dry herself out. For some reason – possibly because their plumage is not very waterproof – young hawks do not bathe very often. Indeed, you might find that you have bought one that refuses to bathe at all, at least in her first year. Even so, she should be given the opportunity to do so every day.

Ideally bathing should be done in the morning so that the hawk has time to preen and dry before you take her out into the field. Even in dull or cold weather a hawk might still bathe, and it isn't always possible to dictate when she does. The danger is that if she bathes during an evening when the temperature is likely to drop substantially below zero overnight, she could freeze to death and she will need to be dried out artificially: a standard hair-dryer is ideal for this purpose.

While we are on the subject of water, you will find a hosepipe invaluable. Not only is one essential for cleaning out the mews and enclosure, but it is the only practical way of filling a bath this size. In addition, many birds enjoy being sprayed with water once they have made the decision to bathe, and often can be encouraged to do so by giving them a gentle spray with a hose.

The final piece of housing equipment is a good set of scales, which are used to monitor the weight of a hawk as an aid to regulating her food intake. No experienced falconer relies entirely on them to assess condition, but they are an objective measure and vitally important. Ordinary spring-type kitchen scales are totally useless for this purpose – they are just not sensitive enough to register small variations in weight. Modern digital scales are viable, but can also present a risk. Because they rely on 'solid state' electronics (which means that there are no moving parts), there is no way to make adjustments and when battery power is running low they can give inconsistent readings.

For falconry the most reliable scales are old-fashioned 'balance' types which can easily be adjusted if necessary.

You can often find scales of this type languishing in junk shops. They normally come with a removable pan on one side, and a fixed platform for weights on the other. The pan should be discarded, and in its place you will need to fit a perch for the bird to stand on during weighing. How this is done will depend on the brackets holding the pan. The most common construction is two arranged cross-wise (+) and bent upwards to fit the pan base. The bracket pointing towards and away from the weight-platform should be removed by unscrewing it (if this is possible), or by sawing it off with a hacksaw. The remaining bracket should be drilled at the top ends to take fixing screws for the perch. The perch itself is best made of cylindrical wood about two inches in diameter – such as a piece of 'mop handle' banister rail, or even part of a tree branch.

Once you have modified the scales you will need to check them for balance. If they are already accurate, both ends will be suspended in a horizontal plane with neither touching any other part of the scale. If they're not, adjustment is easy. If the perch is too light, small metal washers should be placed over the fixing screws until it is brought back into balance. If the platform is light, washers, coins, lead shot, screws, nails, or any combination of these placed on top will correct it.

Balance must be checked every time you use the scales. The wooden perch will constantly absorb or lose moisture depending on atmospheric conditions and the type of wood it is made from. For example, if you hose your scales down or they are left out in the rain, the perch will become heavier. Conversely, if the scales are left out in a hot sun or a warm room, the perch will become lighter. You can minimise the absorption and loss of moisture by sealing the wood with a good external varnish, in particular at each end, which is where most moisture penetrates or escapes.

Obviously you will need a set of weights to use with the scales, and you should buy a range to give a precise measurement. The most practical combination, which will cater for any broadwing, is one each at ¼oz, ½oz, 1oz, 2oz, 4oz, 8oz, 1lb and 2lb. Where weights are concerned, consistency of use is much more important than absolute precision. So long as you use the same scales and weights all the time, it doesn't matter if they would fail an inspection by a Government official, they will still measure fluctuations in the bird's weight accurately.

If you don't want to be bothered with buying and converting your own scales, suppliers of falconry equipment sell them ready-made, together with a full set of weights. However, it has to be said that you will pay a lot higher price for them.

Hawk Furniture

Anklets and Jesses

Whether or not your bird is fully-trained, she will need to be under control at all times, and all furniture worn by her is concerned directly or indirectly with control. That is the sole purpose of its existence. For example, dogs wear collars to which a leash can be attached when needed, and the falconry equivalent is a pair of 'jesses' – simple leather straps fastened to the bird's legs. Even when your hawk is out in the fields flying free, they provide a means of bringing her under control so that she can be carried on the fist or tethered to some other perch temporarily.

Of all kinds of hawk furniture jesses are amongst the most basic, and the most important. Unfortunately they are also the most controversial. The controversy lies in the way they are fixed to the hawk's legs – whether they should be permanent (the traditional method) or inter-changeable (the Aylmer method).

The traditional jess is attached by an ingenious and a very old type of leather knot. In contrast, the Aylmeri are in two parts – the leg-fixing (called an anklet or bracelet) which itself is permanent, and the jess which is removable. The jess is threaded through the eyelet hole until it is stopped by the button-knot at its top end.

Aylmeri were invented by a modern falconer (Guy Aylmer) to avoid the possibility that the jesses would snag in tree branches, barbed wire or undergrowth. It is not the strap itself which causes entanglement, but the swivel slits which, with constant use, open up considerably and are easily caught when trailing behind a flying hawk. As I understand it, Aylmer's original idea was to remove the jesses completely when the bird was loose, but this was at the cost of full control in the field. These days slit jesses are inter-changed for plain ones which are not conducive to snagging.

Traditional jesses are still used by some falconers, but I don't recommend them for any falconry bird. If a hawk does get caught up when she is chasing quarry it will obviously spoil the flight – even if it doesn't injure the hawk – but the problem becomes much more serious if you lose her. At least in the field you are there to assist, but on her own she will have no chance and is likely to die from slow starvation, probably hanging upside down from a branch or a wire fence.

Both types of jess are easy to make if you have the right tools, and the right kind of leather. However, the next few paragraphs only describe the making and fitting of Aylmeri jesses, which must be used on shortwings and broadwings who work from trees, often crashing into undergrowth after quarry. Also, these paragraphs only describe generic types from which all other variations are derived.

If you want to make your own in preference to buying them, be advised – suitable leather is very difficult to find. All leather is prone to tear without warning, and most of what is generally available is useless, either because it tears too easily, or it's too thick and heavy, too stiff, or has too much stretch in the wrong direction. Safe leather to use is calf skin if you can get it. The best way to test potential jess leather is to take a sample about half an inch wide and three or four inches long. Cut a slit lengthways down the centre long enough to place the index finger of each hand in, then attempt to tear the leather by pulling the fingers in opposite directions. If you can

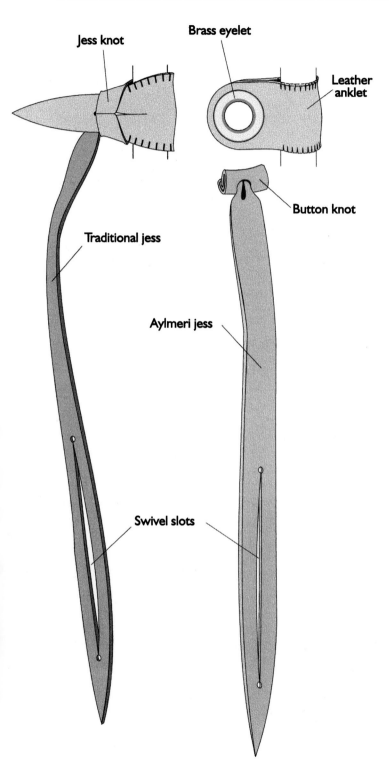

Jess knot

Brass eyelet

Leather anklet

Traditional jess

Button knot

Aylmeri jess

Swivel slots

tear it easily, reject it. One or two falconry suppliers might be prepared to sell you small amounts of jess leather (say, one square foot – enough for twelve pairs of jesses), but most won't, simply because it isn't in their interests for you to make equipment yourself.

One job you will have to master is the fitting of leather anklets, which must be attached as soon as you get your bird. These are made of broader strips of leather wrapped around the hawk's legs with holes punched through both ends big enough to take metal eyelets. You can buy them ready-made for any size of bird, but they still have to be fitted, and the means of fixing them is with eyelets.

Eyelets are made of two rings of thin malleable metal. One has a cylindrical centre-piece which is placed in the punched holes in the anklet, and the other is a washer which provides a base around which the cylinder is closed.

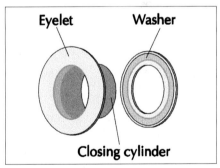

Eyelet

Washer

Closing cylinder

These are also available from falconry suppliers and come in various sizes. For a buzzard-sized anklet you will need them with a hole (meaning the internal dimension of the cylinder) at least a quarter of an inch in diameter – five-sixteenths of an inch would be ideal, and three eighths the maximum.

Eyelets need a special tool to close the cylinder around the washer under pressure. There are basically three kinds – a punch and anvil, eyelet pliers, and a screw-type closing tool. Punches and anvils are rare these days and require skill to use successfully, especially in such close proximity to a bird's leg. Pliers of the kind used in craft shops are useless for this purpose — they tend to split the eyelet cylinder. However, there are one or two marketed specifically for falconry which work very well, but they are difficult to find. In terms of availability, therefore, the best option is a screw-type closing tool.

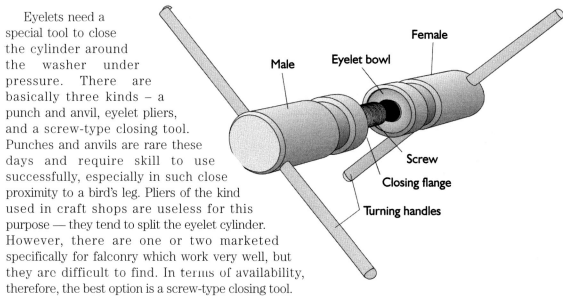

Closing tools also come in different sizes to match the eyelets you are using, and any falconry supplier will advise you about the appropriate one for the type and size of bird you plan to get. Normally, the eyelet washer fits over the screw end of the tool but, depending on supplier, designs can be very different and you will need to make sure that he provides clear instructions on how to use it properly. The illustration shows a popular and reliable type.

If you do intend to make your own anklets and jesses, you will need a few other commonly-available tools:
1. Craft knife – used for cutting cleanly through leather. The best and most economical are Plasplug or Stanley-type knives with retractable 'snap-off' replacement blades
2. Leather punch – for punching holes in various materials. You will need one with several punches of different diameters, and the most easily-obtained is the pliers-type with a rotating head
3. Rigid steel ruler – for measuring and to use as a cutting guide
4. Long-nosed pliers – these can be optional, but they make pulling pieces of leather through punched holes much easier than using bare fingers.

Making Anklets

Anklets were designed to be more or less permanent, and they should be cut from thicker leather than jesses. If they are not, they will become ragged, dishevelled, and potentially unreliable. Good quality cow-leather (rather than thinner calf-leather) is usually used – preferably taken from the belly area which is both strong and supple.

Although the eyelet takes much of the stress of a bating hawk, the anklet itself provides leg-support and acts like a shock-absorber, which is why strength and suppleness are important. Although a hawk's feet are incredibly powerful, her legs up to 'knee' joints – the area (called the tarsus) where anklets are fitted – are relatively weak. They are designed to accommodate vertical forces (for example, the shocks imposed by landing and seizing prey) rather than horizontal ones. A broad anklet spreads the stress of bating over a wider area of the tarsus and minimises it.

Some current falconry literature will advise you to make anklets *in situ*. This involves first holding the bird, then measuring, cutting and fitting each anklet from scratch to match the dimensions of the hawk's leg. This is, of course, a valid way of making them, but it is neither essential nor the only way. In fact it is unnecessary for a number of reasons:

1. There is no such thing as a 'perfect' fit for an anklet. Obviously it needs to be too small for the hawk to get her foot through, but not too tight to cause discomfort
2. The circumference of one female buzzard's tarsus is much like another's. If there is a difference, it is usually small enough to be irrelevant as far as the fitting of anklets is concerned
3. The action of the hawk bating constantly – at least in the early days of training – will stretch the anklet slightly anyway, which will nullify any 'perfect' fit you might have been aiming for.

Another reason I would not recommend tailor-making anklets – at least until you have gained considerable experience in handling birds – is that they take time and consequently prolong the stress imposed on a new hawk.

It is entirely feasible to pre-make a pair of anklets leaving only the final fixing (by means of the eyelets) when your bird arrives. Indeed, many suppliers will sell them to you ready-made to fit the kind of bird you intend to buy. They do this by categorising birds – and hence the furniture they make – as *extra-large* (for eagle-sized birds); *large* (female broadwings and Goshawks); *medium* (male broadwings and Goshawks); and *small* (birds such as the Sparrowhawk). If you intend to follow my recommendations for a bird (see the section headed *First Birds*) 'large' and 'medium' will be the only categories of interest.

Anklets are easy to make, and making them yourself will save you money if you can find good leather. In addition, because they will be made before you acquire a hawk, more time can be spent on them and their design can be improved to incorporate a central 'belly' which maximises support for the hawk's leg.

First you will need a template, which is used as a cutting guide to give you the right shape and size. This is best made out of thin sheet-metal, such as aluminium which is easy to cut and file, although if you're not confident working with metal you can substitute sheet-plastic, very thin modelling plywood (say, 1/32nd of an inch), or, as a last resort, good-quality card such as 'Bristol' board. Small amounts of sheet-plastic and plywood can be obtained from shops catering for model-makers, and board from suppliers of artists' materials. The problem with any material other than metal is that, when you are using it as a cutting guide, it is all too easy to slice bits off the edge of the template unintentionally.

The advantages of making a template are that its materials are easier to cut and refine to the right proportions (because they're rigid), and with a good template you can cut any number of anklets all the same size and shape. Whichever material you use, the template itself should be fashioned according to one or other of the following profiles:

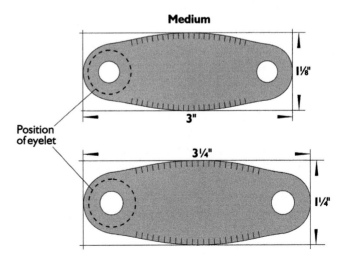

The eyelet cylinder holes at each end of the template should be made to fit comfortably the size of eyelet you intend to use. Once the template is made, place it on the leather, mark out the eyelet holes, then cut round the template using a craft knife. Punch the eyelet holes with a leather punch (which you might have to use several times to enlarge the opening) until the eyelet cylinder fits comfortably.

About ⅛in in from each eyelet hole, make slits at the top and bottom edges of the strap cutting right through the leather. These slits should be about ⅛in long and ⅛in apart, but exact measurement is not important. They simply serve to open out the edges of the anklet when it is attached to the bird's leg avoiding any possibility of abrasion.

Making Button Jesses

The reliability of any jess – particularly in the early stages of a bird's training – must be paramount. If they give way, you could lose a valuable hawk. What's worse, the bird might lose its life. Until a young hawk is properly trained and able to hunt, she won't be able to fend for herself and escape is a death sentence. As well as being a vital piece of control-equipment, therefore, good jesses are the first line of defence against such an eventuality.

To make a pair of jesses for a buzzard, or a similar-sized bird, you will need a piece of leather 1in wide, 11in to 12in long, and ½mm to1mm thick. Thickness itself is less important than pliability – if the leather is on the thin side but strong and pliable, by all means use it: if it's thick but stiff, forget it. Make sure it doesn't have excessive stretch lengthways, and if you can, choose a piece which doesn't have any obvious faults (meaning holes, scratches, tears, etc).

Don't make jesses any longer than necessary out of the misguided notion that they will give the bird more freedom. If you do, there is a good chance that she will become entangled when tethered to her bow perch, restricting her movements even more. A useful guide is that each jess, once it is threaded through the anklet, should be just long enough to hang down over the palm of the hand ending an inch or so below your little finger. The illustration opposite shows a standard jess pattern for a broadwing.

Before you start cutting, you will need to measure and mark out guidelines on your piece of leather. Turn it the 'wrong' side up and use a Biro or a fine felt-tipped pen to give you clear lines. Mark out two strips 11in to 12in long and about ½in wide. Don't worry about the curve at the bottom end of the jess for the moment, just draw them square at both ends.

Cutting leather well is not easy. In all operations the object of the exercise is to cut through it in one go to avoid furred or ragged edges, and for this you will need a very hard surface to rest it on. From experience, the best is glass. The problem is that glass blunts knife-blades very quickly (which is why you will need a craft-knife with relatively cheap and easily-replaceable blades), but this effect can be minimised by placing several sheets of newspaper between the leather and the glass. Use a steel ruler as a guide to cutting straight lines and to help you hold the leather flat and firm. Cut the two strips as cleanly as possible.

For the curved ends use a template (such as the edge of a cereal bowl or a saucer). Draw a mark at the centre of the square edge at the bottom of each strip. Place the edge of the curved template on this mark and at a tangent to the side of the strip, then cut the curve. Repeat for the other side, and the second strip. The curve itself is only a cosmetic feature, but a pointed end to the jess is important for the next part of the construction.

To make the button, fold the top end of the jess over two or three times, then punch a hole through all three layers of leather using the largest diameter punch available on your leather

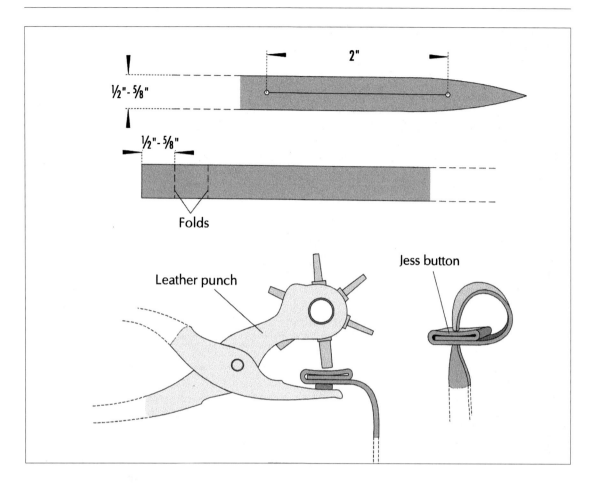

2"

½"-⅝"

½"-⅝"

Folds

Leather punch

Jess button

punch. Keeping the folds in place, put the pointed end of the jess into these holes from the top, and pull the strap right through. If you find this difficult with your fingers use long-nosed pliers, but be careful not to tear the point of the jess. Pull the knot as tight as you can.

To make the swivel-slots, mark a centre-line 2in long starting about ¾in in from the point of the jess. Punch two holes at either end of this line using the smallest diameter punch available. The action of the punch compresses the leather and makes the slit less likely to tear under stress. Cut a straight line between these two points, being careful not to nick the outer edges of the holes in the process.

Swivels

The sole purpose of a swivel is to minimise twisting of the jesses when the bird moves around her perch. The Falconry swivel is specially designed to function properly under stress and accommodate the jesses and a leash. It is usually made of stainless steel with two basic constructional elements – the first is a ring fixed to a free-turning rivet, and the second is a modified ring, or U-shaped piece, fixed to a straight bar. The best swivels are 'D'-types, so-called because of the shape of their top ring.

In these two examples the leash ring is completely closed and welded to the rivet shaft: similarly, the 'D' (jess) ring is welded to the central bar. Both of these design-features ensure that the risk of failure under pressure is minimised.

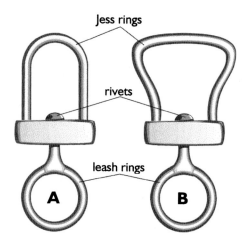

Swivel A is the generic design-type, and B is a refinement which has a flattened top on the jess ring. Both work very well, but in A the knot securing the jesses can slide down to the central bar and interfere with the action of the swivel, especially if you are using relatively thick jess-leather. The design in B holds the jess-knot in place better whatever leather you use.

Jesses are attached to the swivel using the slits at their lower ends. They are not permanently tied. On the contrary, they must be capable of quick separation and attachment. In addition, the knot has to be easy to tie with one hand (the other is used as a perch for the bird). To tie the knot, hold the swivel with the leash ring pointing to the floor. Thread the jess through the jess ring from the back of the swivel and pull it through to the top end of the slot (1). Push the leash ring and central bar through the slot (2), then pull the knot tight (3). Repeat the procedure with the second jess.

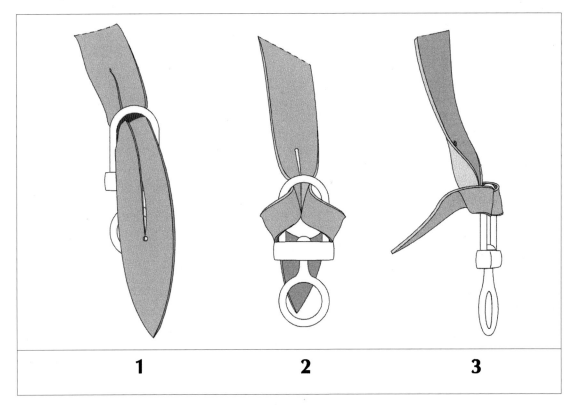

This is the traditional way to attach jesses to a swivel, but there is a much quicker method which is no less reliable. The knot is exactly the same, but it involves tying both jesses together. To accomplish this, align the swivel slots on each jess then follow steps 1, 2 and 3 treating the pair as one. Yet another variation is to tie each jess separately, but thread one through the back of the swivel and one through the front so that the two ends finish up pointing in opposite directions. Some falconers consider this to be neater, and the jesses sit easier on the swivel compared to the traditional method. In the end, it's all a matter of taste and preference.

Leashes

The leash was designed specifically for tethering a hawk to her perch, but it is also used to assist with control when carrying her around on the fist and (to a very limited extent) during her initial period of training. Because of the long-term unreliability of leather, leashes these days are made of strong braided nylon – either round in section (cord) or flat, like their traditional leather equivalents.

For a broadwing the finished leash should be about 3ft long. If you are using cord nylon it needs to be about ¼in in diameter and pliable. The kind rock climbers use, which is easily-obtained from shops catering for them, is perfectly adequate. Some DIY stores also sell suitable cord these days, but be careful to distinguish this from simulated rope which is generally much too stiff to knot with one hand. If you can find strap nylon, it should be about ½in wide. Strap leashes are made in the same way as Aylmeri button jesses except that they don't have swivel slits. For additional peace of mind, you can make the button larger by incorporating an extra fold or two in the top end.

Bear in mind that any braided nylon which is cut has to be heat-sealed to stop it from fraying. With a strap-leash this means the holes punched for the button knot, as well as the edges cut to a point at its bottom end. Heat-sealing is easy to do with a lighted taper, a match, or a cigarette lighter. The object of the exercise is simply to melt the nylon sufficiently to 'weld' the cut fibres together. Apply the flame to the exposed fibres until they melt. With wet fingers (to avoid burning yourself), squeeze the fibres together and allow them to cool before proceeding.

Cord leashes also need to be sealed, but they don't have the same kind of stop-knot. For these leashes falconers have developed a variation of the marine 'figure-of-eight' knot, which incorporates an extra twist making it bulkier and flatter.

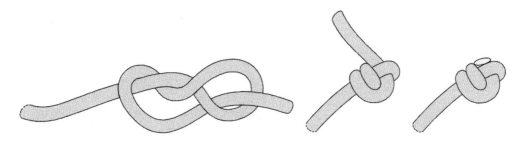

Once the knot is tied and pulled tight, the surplus cord should be cut off near to the knot and heat-sealed. It helps to make the whole thing secure if some of the melted nylon spills over onto the knot itself, which has the effect of welding the end to it. Finally, cut the cord to length and seal the other end.

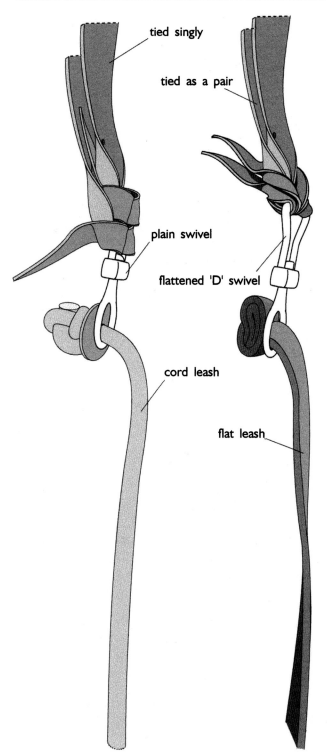

tied singly

tied as a pair

plain swivel

flattened 'D' swivel

cord leash

flat leash

The leash is not attached to the swivel as such. It is simply passed through the leash ring until the knot stops it. Cord leashes can come apart under pressure from a bating hawk but to prevent this, cut a leather disc about the size of a ten pence coin. Punch a hole in the centre just big enough to thread the leash, then pull it all the way through until the disc is tight against the knot.

The illustration left shows two variations in the jess, swivel and leash assembly, but of course, either swivel can be used with either kind of leash and, as I've said, the way the jesses are tied is entirely a matter of preference.

Tying a Falconer's Knot

The so-called 'falconer's knot' is used to secure a leash to a perch by means of the large welded metal ring attached to the perch. It is actually an enhanced version of the slip knot, and is the same whichever kind of leash (or perch) is used. Its primary virtue is that it is capable of being tied with one hand (the other is either being used as a temporary perch by the bird, or is trying to keep her under control in some other way). It is also the second line of defence against escape.

Although the knot is basically simple, circumstances can make it very difficult to use. Often it has to be tied in the freezing cold, in wind or rain, or in a restricted area, all with a powerful bird bating furiously off your fist. Obviously the more you practise the easier it becomes, and you would be wise to rehearse it until you can do it blindfolded – in any weather conditions – before you get a bird. Trying to tether your first hawk with an instruction manual on your lap is not a sensible option.

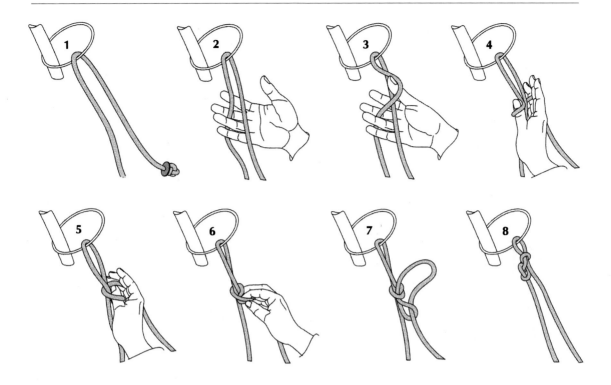

1. First, put the leash through the perch ring with the stop-knot on the right and the loose end on the left. Pull it through until there is 6in to 7in between the stop-knot and the ring.
2. Place your hand underneath the leash so that both strands run across all four fingers, then position the third and fourth fingers over the left strand.
3. Put your thumb over the right strand and under the left, then draw it outwards.
4. Keeping the loop over your thumb, and with the left strand gripped between your second and third fingers, pass your hand underneath the right strand by rotating your wrist anti-clockwise.
5. Maintaining the existing loop over your thumb, make a second loop by pushing your thumb underneath the left strand.
6. Thread the second loop through the first using your index finger, then extend it 2in to 3in.
7. Thread the loose end of the leash through this extended loop drawing it all the way. Pull the stop-knot (or button) to tighten the completed knot against the perch ring.
8. The finished knot should now look like diagram (8). To untie the knot, simply thread the end of the leash back through the second loop and pull.

Some hawks are capable of unpicking this knot, but it is unlikely that a hawk will manage two of them. Tying a second with the surplus end of the leash is, therefore, a good habit to develop.

Field Jess and Leash

Any jesses with swivel-slits are known as mews jesses and they are associated directly with tethering a bird – usually in indoor quarters (the mews), but also temporarily on the fist or weathering ground. The invention of Aylmeri equipment made the development of other kinds of jess possible because it provided potential for interchangeability. For instance, many falconers use what is known as a 'field' jess. Its size and general construction are the same as a mews jess, except that it has only a small hole at the pointed end instead of a slit. It is designed to take two different kinds of equipment – the creance (see the next section *Training Equipment*) and the 'field leash' – both of which are made of fine braided nylon cord about 2mm in diameter.

The field leash usually has a fixed loop at one end for slipping over the little finger of the glove. The free end is threaded through the hole in the jess then tied with a normal falconer's knot. When the bird is ready to fly, the knot is untied and the bird cast off with the jesses still in place.

Field jesses are certainly a viable option, and a much better one compared with keeping mews jesses on the bird. However, several falconers have experienced hawks snagging standard field jesses on barbed wire. On these occasions the bird has landed on a fence post, and the punched hole in the trailing end of the jess has caught in a barb of the wire fence. These days plain button jesses with neither holes nor swivel slits are normally used, and they work very well. Once the bird is fully trained, it is possible to dispense with a leash altogether in the field, and how to do this will be explained later.

Radio Telemetry

Out hunting a hawk will often disappear from view into woodland, under-growth, behind a hedgerow or over the brow of hill. It is essential, therefore, to have a means of tracking her movements. These days many falconers use radio telemetry for this purpose. Telemetry comprises a radio receiver with a tracking antenna, and a transmitter in the shape of a small cylinder which is attached to a leg or the tail of the bird. The transmitter gives out an intermittent signal which is picked up by the receiver, and the strength of it increases as you get closer to the bird. The best sets have a potential range of several miles over flat, featureless ground.

Telemetry is one of very few pieces of equipment – alongside such things as hoods and Aylmeri – which can legitimately claim to have revolutionised falconry. There is no doubt that it is of great benefit in tracking down missing hawks. These days it *essential* for flying longwings, which can fly long distances in pursuing quarry, and especially for locating them on their kill. It is also essential, though perhaps to a lesser extent, with the larger shortwings such as Goshawks.

Telemetry is usable on any kind of hawk. Indeed, its origins lie in the study of any moving animal from a shrew to an elephant, and was developed by naturalists for that purpose. Even though it is now widely-used by falconers it isn't, strictly, falconry equipment but some manufacturers are fine-tuning their products to fit the market. Valuable though it is in certain circumstances, it has one or two drawbacks:

- good telemetry is expensive – probably a lot more expensive than the bird you are trying to find
- it is another equipment burden to carry with you out in the field, and most of it is not designed with portability in mind
- depending on the quality of equipment, effective range is severely limited in broadwing flying country – hills, valleys, woodland, etc.

As a measure of its importance and general effectiveness in falconry, many clubs will not allow you to participate in a field meeting with your bird unless you are using telemetry. However, this is primarily because it enables 'missing' birds to be tracked down quickly and easily keeping disruption to a minimum. This does not, in itself, equate to an endorsement of telemetry as an essential tool for use in the field with broadwings.

Apart from the expense, another big problem with telemetry in falconry terms is that it gives the falconer a false sense of security – ie, that he will always be able to find his bird. Even if the equipment achieves this (which is highly unlikely), it doesn't guarantee that she'll come back to the fist or a lure; and if the telemetry fails for whatever reason – batteries run out, drop off, get wet, the bird goes out of range, or whatever – he will still end up with a lost hawk. In other words, telemetry is no substitute for good training, good falconry practice, and fieldcraft. By all means use it as an adjunct to these if you can afford it, but *never* as a substitute.

Bells and Their Fixings

For broadwings at least, bells alone are adequate to track them over the few hundred yards they are likely to stray and, if properly sited on the hawk, pinpoint *exactly* where they are – especially if they're on a kill in deep cover. Telemetry might get you within a few feet, but in thick cover that might as well be a few miles. Telemetry is useful over long distances, but at close range and for pinpoint accuracy bells are invaluable.

Falconry bells are usually sold in pairs, and they are made from thin sheets of brass, nickel, monel, silver, or alloys of any of these. To be effective they need certain qualities. Apart from durability, they should be clearly audible from a distance of a few hundred yards, and they should be small and lightweight to hinder the bird as little as possible. Also, a good pair of bells will have notes which *do not* harmonise – the difference between the two should be about a semitone. This is because a pair with mutually discordant tones are much more easily heard from a distance than a single bell or two with the same tone. Consequently two bells – one on each leg, or one on a leg and the other attached to the tail – is the most common configuration for all falconry birds.

As with all falconry equipment, they come in various shapes and sizes, but three generic types are widely available – Lahore (1), Asborno 'Acorn' (2), and Steve Little bells (3).

All of these are good bells for falconry, but they vary enormously in price. Lahore (from Pakistan) are the cheapest, Asborno (from America) the most expensive, and Little (from England) are in between. However, what's most important is not what they're made of or even their price, but how much you like their sound, and how far you think it will carry. Once they're fitted to the hawk you will hear them constantly as she moves around, and some sound sweeter than others.

A bell is fitted to a hawk's leg by a piece of equipment called a bewit – a narrow leather strap knotted in such a way that the bird can't untie it. It should be fitted above the anklet and below any leg ring the bird might be wearing. How narrow the bewit is will depend on the width of the bell-keeper (meaning the 'handle' on top), but it should be as wide as possible (a) because the wider it is the more comfortable it will be for the bird; and (b) because it will be easier for you to fit.

Jess leather should be used, and you will need a piece about six inches long cut to a point at both ends. How these points are fashioned is irrelevant – they're only used to thread each end through punched holes and will be trimmed off the finished bewit.

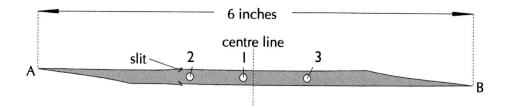

Once you have cut the strap and made the pointed ends, fitting procedure is as follows:
1. Fold the strap in half to establish its mid-point and punch the first hole **(1)** slightly to the left of centre.
2. Thread point **B** through the bell-keeper and hole **1**, then pull it tight to fix the strap to the bell.
3. Wrap the strap around the bird's leg and mark a position about half way around the leg for hole **2**. Remove the bewit and punch the hole.
4. About ⅛in beyond this hole, cut a nick in both edges of the strap angled towards point **A**.
5. Wrap the bewit around the bird's leg again, then thread point **B** through hole **2** until the strap is firm but not too tight – it should be capable of rotating around her leg, but not riding up or down it.
6. In the plain half of the bewit (without the slits) punch hole **3** as close as you can to the crossover point, then thread point **A** through this hole until the two nicks pass all the way through.
7. Trim off the excess leather.

This is the traditional way to fit a bell to a bird's leg and, fiddly though it might seem, with practice it can be tied reasonably quickly with a manned bird perching on someone else's fist. However, there is a more modern alternative, called a button bewit, which is quicker and easier to fit. Some falconry books don't recommend them because they are 'too loose-fitting' and can become snagged in a hawk's talons. But, if they're properly made, and fitted above the Aylmeri anklet, this should never happen.

The button bewit's basic construction is exactly like a miniature mews jess, but it has an extra hole for fitting the bewit to the bell-keeper.

To make a button bewit, cut a strip of jess-leather wide enough for the bell-keeper and about 4in long. Cut one end to a point. Make the button, then punch a hole ½in to ¾in from the button. Thread the point of the bewit through the bell-keeper, then through the hole pulling the strap tight to fix the bell. Test the length of the bewit by wrapping it around the bird's leg, then mark out the button slit (which should be just big enough to take the button – in other words, as tight as the button-hole on a shirt or a blouse). Cut the slit. Wrap the bewit around the leg again and push the button through the slit to secure it.

The second bell of the pair is normally attached to the hawk's tail, in a central position, and close to her rump. Tail bells are of particular value when flying accipiters and buzzards, both of which have a habit of waggling their tails when resting on a perch. Because these birds work largely from trees – often out of sight – a tail bell is an additional aid to finding them quickly. The bell's position in the centre of the tail, and as close to her body as possible, interferes least with her flight and it still enables her to fan out her tail-feathers whenever they are needed for flight-control.

The feathers constituting a hawk's tail are layered one on top of the other when they are folded in. The two uppermost feathers (called deck feathers) are positioned in the centre. Traditionally the bell is fixed, by a strip of leather, to the quill of each deck feather as close to the base as possible. A plectrum – a flat triangular piece of plastic or horn designed for plucking guitar strings – is used to stop the bell from lodging between the deck feathers. Plectrums are easily obtained for a few pence from shops selling musical instruments. In addition you will need:

- a matching bell
- a piece of paper (about A5 size)
- a large paper clip (or a small bulldog clip)
- a strip of jess leather about 6in long and ¼in wide
- a small pair of scissors
- strong glue such as 'Araldite' or general-purpose 'Superglue'
- a few cotton-wool balls and a bowl of cold water.

Some of the work can (and should) be done before you get your bird so that all that's left to do when she arrives is to assemble the various ready-made parts. The first step in this preparation is to punch three holes in the plectrum in the positions shown. They allow the leather strap to be threaded in and out of the plectrum, which itself forms a base for the whole assembly.

You will need to use the largest diameter punch available on your leather punch to give maximum leeway for threading the strap, but it has to be said that punching holes through a plectrum requires a fair amount of brute force and persistence. Another alternative is to drill the holes. If you use this option, make sure that any rough edges are smoothed out to avoid damaging the leather during fitting.

The strap itself can also be pre-made. It should be cut to a point at each end to aid threading through the plectrum and between the hawk's deck feathers. As with a bewit, these points will be cut off after final fitting so it doesn't matter how they're fashioned. Punch a hole in the centre, then fix it to the bell-handle by passing one end through the handle, then through the punched hole. Pull the knot tight. To complete the initial preparation, pass both ends of the strap through the central hole of the plectrum and pull the strap through until the bell is sitting neatly on top of the plectrum. All this preliminary work can be carried out hours, days, or even weeks before the bird arrives. But whenever you decide to do it, the assembly should be ready and waiting well before the hawk is secured to complete the fitting.

Fixing the bell to the hawk's tail is yet another task which requires her to be held for several minutes, which means that you will need an assistant. The bird should be held so that her tail is pointing towards you. The fitting procedure is as follows.

1. Be careful to identify the two deck feathers correctly, then isolate them from the rest by folding the sheet of paper over them. Hold it in place with the paper (or bulldog) clip.
2. Brush back the soft body-feathers (tail coverts) with a damp cottonwool ball to expose the deck-feather quills. With the scissors, carefully cut off the hair-like out-growths from each quill at the base of each feather until the quills are bare.
3. Thread the two ends of the leather strap between the deck-feather quills, wrap them round, then back through the remaining holes in the plectrum. What you are aiming for is the following scenario.
4. Before you pull the straps all the way, coat the undersides (meaning any area of leather likely to come into contact with the quills) liberally with glue. Then pull them tight, and give the glue a little time to set.
5. On top of the plectrum, cross the right hand end of the strap over the centre of the bell-keeper knot, mark the place, then punch a hole in the strap. Cross the left hand end over the bell handle in the same way, mark the centre, then make two nicks angled towards the end of the strap, and slightly further from the point than the centre line (this will ensure that the fixing is as tight as possible).
6. Thread the left hand end through the punched hole in the right hand end, then draw it tight until the nicks are all the way through. Cut the surplus ends off the strap. For additional security, glue the two ends down. Final assembly is shown right.

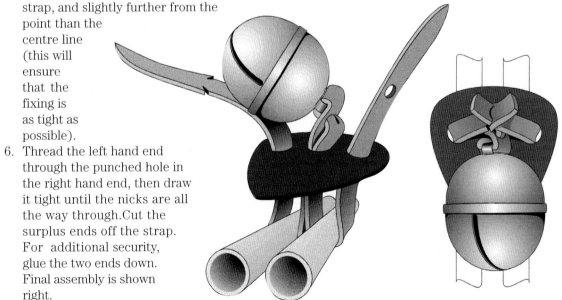

Fitting a tail bell is one of the most difficult operations routinely performed on a hawk. It is doubly so with an untrained and unmanned one – especially if you've never fitted one before. Although all hawks get used to them fairly quickly, there is no doubt that they dislike them to start with, and will pick relentlessly at the fixings in an attempt to remove them. Unfortunately they are all too often successful, which means you either have to decide to abandon the project, or go through the whole procedure again. They are, nevertheless, optional – the alternatives being to use only one bell, or fix the second to the other leg with another bewit. This combination works, but perhaps not as well. You need to balance the difficulty of fixing a tail bell against reduced tracking ability in the field. In particular, lack of a tail bell makes it more difficult to find a hawk which has gone astray (see the section headed *Missing Hawks* on page157).

Hoods

A hood is simply a blindfold. It is a piece of falconry equipment designed primarily for longwings (falcons), several of which might be taken out into the field to be flown one at a time. Placing a hood on those not yet required to fly prevents them from becoming excited at the sight of quarry. It maintains a placid state of mind until their turn arrives, and placates them again after they've flown.

Hoods work in much the same way as blacking out a canary's cage with a blanket. In the dark, any diurnal bird's physical and mental activity winds down and she may even orient herself towards sleep. Total darkness, therefore, has a calming effect, and this makes hoods potentially useful in other situations.

The general run of falconry literature suggests that there is no need to use hoods on shortwings and broadwings, which are mostly flown on their own. However, there are some good arguments for training any kind of hawk to accept a hood:

- Redtails and Harris' Hawks will bate at cats and chickens, and carrying one through a farmyard to get to a flying ground can provoke such behaviour if these animals are around
- carrying one past an area the landowner has asked you to avoid, such as pheasant pens, can have the same result
- there might be occasions when you want to join up with other falconers, such as field meetings organised by clubs. In this case your hawk will be expected to wait her turn. If she is hooded in the meantime, she will be in a much better frame of mind when she is allowed to fly
- manhandling a hawk – for example to fit essential equipment or deal with an injury – is much easier to achieve if she is hooded
- a hawk which constantly bates when riding in a car will accept it much more readily if she is hooded.

Bating provoked by restraint at the sight of 'forbidden' quarry can cause ill-temper in any hawk, which is not the best way to start, or progress, a day's flying. So, whilst a hood might not be strictly necessary for flying Redtails or Harris' Hawks, it is a useful control option to have. More importantly, it is a priceless tool for keeping hawks relatively calm during the many manhandling operations every falconer has to undertake at one time or another.

Hoods are generally made of leather. They come in various shapes, sizes and designs, but most are slitted at the back to aid fitting and removal. Opening and closing is achieved by two pairs of leather straps called braces, which are loosely-woven into the neck of the hood. Each pair has a single function – pulling on one opens the hood, pulling on the other closes it. Function is identified by the way each pair is knotted at the business end. One has a jess-like button knot, the other an ordinary 'granny' knot. Hoods also have a *top-knot*, which is simply a decorative handle for slipping the open hood over the hawk's head, or removing it when it is no longer needed.

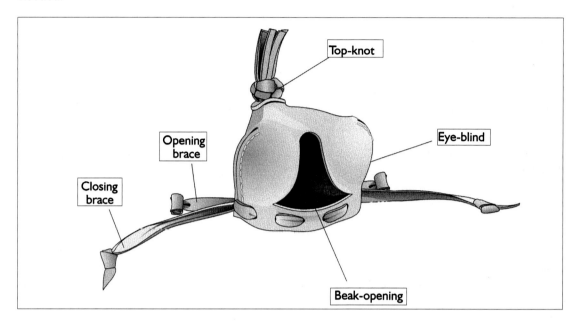

There are three basic types of hood which reflect their origins. The illustration shows an *Anglo-Indian* design, but in addition there are *Bahreini (Arab)* and *Dutch* hoods. The pinnacle of craftsmanship is undoubtedly the Dutch-style hood which is made on a wooden block carved into the shape of a falcon's head, then 'moulded' through a wetting, drying and hammering process so that it follows the contours of the head as closely as possible. This process also gives it some resilience to losing its shape in all weather and flying conditions. In contrast, the Bahreini hood is made from very soft and pliable leather which fits over a falcon's head like a tea cosy rather than a close-fitting balaclava. Some attempt is made with the Anglo-Indian design to fit the hood to the bird by measuring the widest part of the head (just behind the eyes), but the finished product doesn't look much like any hawk's head.

Because it is 'tailor-made' and more or less rigid, the Dutch hood doesn't suit broadwings whose heads and necks have different relative dimensions to those of falcons. The softness and pliability of Bahreini hoods makes them feasible for broadwings, but they look vaguely out of place and rough treatment easily takes them out of shape permanently. Anglo-Indian hoods are more 'generalist' in their design, and the fact that they can be made to fit the hawk's head-measurement rather than her 3D profile means that they can be used on longwings, shortwings or broadwings.

Of all falconry furniture, hoods tend to inspire a euphoric and often displaced sense of aestheticism. Indeed, some falconers will hood a hawk simply to 'improve' her looks without much regard to any functional value the hood might have. But don't be fooled. Whatever its artistic merit, a hood is just a hood. The only things that really matter are that it fits the hawk comfortably and it does what it was meant to do. If it happens to look good as well, treat that as a bonus. An ill-fitting hood will have one or more of the following characteristics:

1. Pinched neck feathers when the hood is closed; or, conversely, excessive movement of the hood
2. Moisture inside the eye-blinds after fitting. Alternatively, check for evidence that the hawk still has some vision: if you wave a finger in front of her head, does she react to the movement?
3. Check that the hood's beak-opening fully exposes her nostrils and 'gape' (the furthest extent of her mouth). She should be able to breath and yawn without restriction.

Faults in **3** can be corrected by enlarging the beak-opening by paring it with a sharp knife. Points **1** and **2** indicate that the hood is too small or too large and should be rejected.

Selecting the right hood from a supplier is a problem. There are only two ways to do it: (1) take the hawk to the hood-maker and fit one from his selection; (2) persuade him to send you a selection to chose from. The second is the most difficult to achieve – it depends on whether you know the hood-maker and whether he's prepared to trust you. As an alternative, he might be prepared to send you hoods one at a time on a 'sale-or-return' basis. Another option is to make your own, but you will probably end up making two or three before you get one that fits satisfactorily.

Spares

In addition to mews jesses, it is always advisable to have spare items of other essential equipment to cover loss through accident, bad luck, or any other unforeseen circumstance. For example, swivels are easily 'misplaced' when you are constantly switching from mews to field jesses, and vice versa. If you loose your only swivel, you will have no satisfactory means of tethering your hawk safely, and it might take up to twenty-eight days for a supplier to send you a replacement by mail order. My advice is, therefore, to have at least two sets of all essential control-equipment available, and carry spare tethering equipment (mews jesses, swivel and leash) with you wherever you take your hawk.

One exception is hawk bells. If you carry a spare set of these around with you, their ringing will confuse you no end when you are desperately scrambling around looking for a missing hawk. If you lose one during a flying session (a common occurrence) it is unlikely you will be able to replace it out in the field anyway, so they are best left at home.

Leather Dressing

Through constant use in all kinds of weather, any equipment made with untreated leather becomes stiff and eventually unusable. To avoid this all leather-based equipment attached to the hawk (apart from tail-bell fixings, which are protected by glue, and hoods) should be greased regularly with a suitable dressing. This will
- prolong its useful life
- retain its pliability
- make it waterproof.

Mews jesses in particular should be kept greased. They are subjected to much more stress than other pieces of equipment, and if they are allowed to stiffen and dry out they are much more likely to snap without warning. In fact it pays to have at least two pairs of mews jesses for each bird. This will enable you to replace one pair with the other each week, then examine the old pair for damage and, if they are still usable, grease them ready for replacement the following week.

Other types of jess are not subjected to anything like the same amount of stress. Consequently they will last much longer. Even so, greasing these makes it easier to interchange them out in the field because it enables them to travel through the eyelet holes in the anklet much more readily. Anklets and bewits should also be greased occasionally. If you allow either to become stiff and dry they might eventually cause discomfort for the hawk.

These days most falconers use a product called *Ko-Cho-Line* which is available from saddlers, other establishments catering for outdoor leather gear or, of course, falconry suppliers. From experience, falconers have learned that *Ko-Cho-Line* does no harm to the hawk's digestive system even if she picks at or nibbles the treated leather relentlessly. It also works very well.

Ko-Cho-Line does, however, take some time to be absorbed and tends to leave messy and sticky residues. There are other kinds of leather dressing on the market, but be careful to use only those based on animal fats – such as *Lanolin* (sheep fat) – as opposed to petroleum products.

Training Equipment

As far as broadwings are concerned, there are only two pieces of equipment which were designed for use in training and nothing else. The first is known as a creance, the second as a quarry lure. But there is another item which features heavily in training, although it is primarily used as a permanent tool in the field. This is the swing lure. The creance and quarry lure can usually be put away once your hawk is flying free and catching game, and this might sound like an unreasonable expense. But, of course, they will last a long time and they can be used to train any number of birds, or help recover one in an emergency.

The Creance

The name of this equipment is pronounced *kray-onss* and was brought to our language by the Normans. Some falconers believe its meaning has something to do with string, but it is actually an old French word which originally meant 'credit'. However, 'string' is a much better description because that is precisely what it is. In effect, it is an elongated string-like leash.

These days a creance-line is made of fine braided nylon about 2mm in diameter and 50yd long. It is used to train any falconry bird to fly increasingly longer distances to the fist, at the same time enabling control to be maintained if she decides to fly off somewhere else. The line itself is very lightweight, and hinders the hawk's flight not at all – unless it becomes snagged en route around an obstacle, or you decide to pull her up short because she is veering away from you.

To make handling easier, the line is wound around a short turned stick which has a hole drilled in its midriff so that the end of the line can be secured with a knot. Before you let her loose, your hawk will be flying the full extent of the line and a stick is much easier to control in an emergency than a rapidly-moving length of fine braided nylon. In addition, it provides a means of coiling the line away when it is no longer needed.

Traditionally the creance is wound around the stick in a 'figure-of-eight' pattern – in other words, it is looped first round one end, then the other but in the opposite direction. The reason is that this method makes it easier to reel the line in at the end of each training session using only one hand. A secondary consideration is that it is less likely to work loose compared to winding it around the stick like a fishing line on a reel. However, this technique is difficult to master and needs a lot of practice.

Firstly, it helps to create some tension on the line when you are winding it in (pulling it through gloved fingers is the usual method), otherwise it will be too loosely coiled and will come apart very easily. In this case you are likely to end up with a frustrating mess which can take hours to disentangle. Secondly, each time you wind the line in, you need to rotate the stick slightly so that the coils are evenly distributed around the circumference of the stick. If you don't do this, all the cross-over points will be in the same place which not only makes it cumbersome to handle but also difficult to unwind quickly and smoothly.

Unwinding is much simpler. The loaded stick is held loosely in the palm of one hand, and the free end of the line is pulled through the two middle fingers with the other hand. The stick should be allowed to rotate as you pull, and several feet of it can be unwound with each tug. The free end is attached to field jesses (see the previous section *Hawk Furniture*) with a falconer's knot. Unlike many other pieces of equipment, the braided nylon used is not made just for falconry and you can buy suitable line from haberdashers, curtain-makers, or even DIY stores, for a few pence a yard. If you buy it yourself, remember to heat-seal each end with a lighted taper to stop it from fraying. Similarly, if you know someone who enjoys wood-turning, they might be prepared to make a stick for you. It doesn't matter what kind of wood it's made of, as long as it is sealed and varnished to withstand wet conditions. If you can get a homemade one, it needs to be about six inches in length and one inch in diameter. Otherwise you can buy the whole thing from any falconry supplier.

The Static Creance

This device was developed by Graham Wellstead, a falconer with fifty years' experience. In other areas of this Guide, I've avoided describing every equipment variation being tried (such as braided slit leashes) which, useful though they might be, haven't yet established themselves universally. Instead I've limited description to generic items from which all others are derived. However, I've made an exception with the 'static' creance because it solves some of the major problems associated with using a creance (eg winding / unwinding; line snagging on obstacles; fouled lines, etc). It is also very simple and easy to use if set up properly, and invaluable to beginners attempting to use a creance for the first time.

The line itself is no different: it is the same length, and made from the same material, as a traditional creance. However, the stick is dispensed with, and in its place is a stiff metal rod capable of being pushed into the ground and at least four feet long – the longer and stiffer the better so that it can be well-secured in the ground. The most practical are those with an 'eye' for passing the tape or wire through.

One end of the creance line is tied to this rod with a standard falconer's knot. The other is attached in some way to the training post from which you want the hawk to work. How it's attached is not important, as long as it's secure – for the static creance to work well, the line needs to be under tension. The final piece of equipment is a metal ring large enough to run easily from one end of the line to the other. The ring doesn't have to be specially made and the kind used on purse nets (used for ferreting) are ideal, or even one designed to run along a curtain rail will do, but bear in mind that it might occasionally have to take some stress from a bating hawk or one trying to fly off elsewhere. The following diagram illustrates the arrangement.

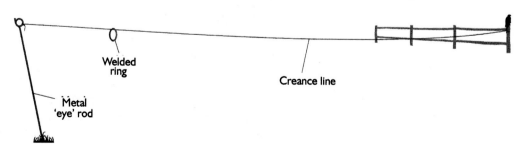

Welded ring

Creance line

Metal 'eye' rod

The hawk is tied to the ring by a short field-type leash (see the previous section *Hawk Furniture*). 'Short' means long enough only to allow her to rise up to the fist from the line, or perch on her training post, or reach the ground. This arrangement enables her to fly forwards along the line when she's called, or back to the perch ready for the next call.

Because of the tension on the line, combined with the leash and ring attachment, the hawk can only fly backwards or forwards over the length of the creance. If she attempts to fly away in any other direction, the device prevents her from succeeding. In addition, the line itself is kept snag-free because it doesn't move, and it is easy to put away after each training session – you just remove the rod from the ground, keep the line under tension, walk to the fence line with it, then push the rod back into the ground ready for collection again the following day.

Swing Lures

The swing lure was developed to encourage falcons to identify and catch specific kinds of feathered game, and as a means of recall in the field, but for the non-specialist broadwings its primary function is to recover a free-flying hawk in a difficult situation, or get her to return from a distance. It is a combination of several elements. The main bulk of it is a stuffed U-shaped leather pad which is designed to accommodate a set of cured quarry-wings. The wings themselves are taken from real birds, usually the kind the falconer wants his hawk to catch. Swinging the lure with a set of wings attached simulates the flight of the intended quarry – sufficiently at least for the hawk to be interested. The lure-pad also incorporates a means of attaching food which the hawk takes as a reward when she is allowed to secure the lure.

The two wings – a left-handed one and a right-handed one – are pushed into the pockets made for them and can be removed and replaced with a different set if required. Their 'supports' simply help to keep them in place and add body to the whole structure making it better balanced. Food is tied onto the platform with the cord ties provided, which are deliberately placed towards the front end of the lure to encourage the hawk to target the head of the quarry. The lure-pad is exactly the same on its upper and lower surfaces so that wings and a piece of meat can be secured to either or both. If both are 'garnished' (meaning tied with food), it doesn't matter which way up the lure is when the hawk catches it – she will still get her reward.

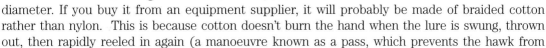

The lure is swung with the aid of a cord line about 3m in length and 4mm in diameter. If you buy it from an equipment supplier, it will probably be made of braided cotton rather than nylon. This is because cotton doesn't burn the hand when the lure is swung, thrown out, then rapidly reeled in again (a manoeuvre known as a pass, which prevents the hawk from catching the lure and helps to develop her speed and fitness). But the problem with cotton is that it rots easily when it gets consistently damp. In this respect British weather conditions don't favour it.

However, swing lures are only fully-used with falcons for whom they are a vital part of training. Where broadwings are concerned, they are basically employed as a means of retrieval and complicated passes are unnecessary. If you want to make your own lure-line, braided nylon with similar dimensions (which is cheaper and more easily-obtained) is perfectly adequate.

Whatever it's made of, the line should be attached to the lure-pad by means of the split ring (which is, in effect, a key ring). Again, if you buy the line from a supplier, it will include a small swivel intended to prevent the line from twisting when the lure is swung. If you want to make your own line, angling swivels designed for use with spinners or 'spoons' will do the job. As with the creance, the other end of the line is tied to a short stick which is, in every respect, the same as a creance stick. It also serves a similar purpose, which is to carry the line and aid in its control. The line is also wound around the stick in the same figure-of-eight fashion.

Although the swing lure was primarily developed for longwings, many falconers no longer use lure-pads for this purpose. Because of their bulk, they can cause minor injury (such as bruising) when the falcon makes contact at high speed. As an alternative, longwing falconers commonly make their own lures with just a set of cured wings tied back-to-back, and use the food offering alone to add weight.

However, for broadwings the lure pad is an acceptable – and a necessary – piece of equipment. It is used mainly as a means of retrieving the hawk, which usually catches it on the ground, and it is swung only to attract her attention. Everyone knows that a hawk's eyes are vastly superior to our own, but they are attuned in particular to movement, and a few simple swings of the lure will make it visible to her from a great distance. In addition, it is unnecessary to attach wings to the lure as any broadwing can be trained to respond to the lure-pad as it stands. Indeed, because you want her to be a generalist hunter, it is better not to encourage her to specialise by using a set of wings.

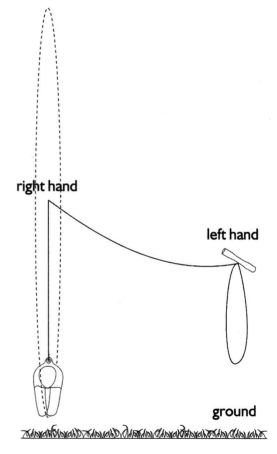

For retrieving a broadwing, swinging the lure is easy. If you are right-handed:

1. Unwind the line and grip it in your right hand between the first finger and thumb two feet or so from the lure itself.
2. Hold the stick in your left hand, and coil the remaining portion of the line loosely between the fingers to keep it clear of the swing.
3. Tuck your right elbow into your side and, keeping your forearm parallel to the ground, swing the lure in a vertical plane by rotating your hand and wrist.

If you are left-handed, the procedure is the same except that it is a mirror image. The figure right illustrates the basic technique.

The swing is usually maintained until the hawk is about fifteen or twenty yards away. Then, keeping hold of the stick, the whole line is released from both hands so that the lure lands on the ground in front of you. The momentum of the swing will carry it as far forward as the length of the line will allow. Although, from a hawk's point of view, it doesn't matter one iota which way you swing the lure, if you are right-handed you will find it much easier to cast the line with a clockwise swing simply because it will then be travelling in the right direction for release. If you are left-handed, an anti-clockwise swing will achieve the same result.

Quarry Lures

Quarry lures are used with broadwings to train them to catch ground game – for example rabbits and hares. It isn't swung, but dragged along the ground to simulate the action of the real thing. It has elements in common with a swing lure. In particular, it utilises the same kind of stick and line, which means you will only need one set of these which can be interchanged when needed.

If you buy a quarry lure from a supplier, it is usually constructed to look something like a rabbit. Indeed, it is often called a 'rabbit lure', or even a 'dummy bunny'.

The 'body' is usually a small stuffed and weighted canvas sack covered with simulated fur. The food-platform and ties, which are similar to those on the swing lure, are also located on the 'head', represented by a leather pad.

The lure illustrated doesn't have legs or ears, but it does have a white tail. This is because it is believed that the tail of a rabbit is the feature that hawks recognise most easily. This might be so, but if it is, you could expect your hawk only to chase ground game with a white tail – including roe deer – and not to attempt other species without one. Experience shows that things don't always work out like this. The tail is only fixed to the upper surface of the 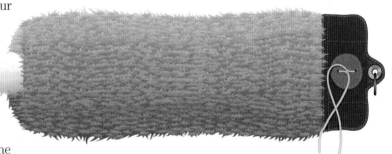 lure. Although the equipment is weighted in an attempt to keep it upright, it often lands upside down when it is thrown out to the hawk, or turns over when it is being dragged along bumpy ground. In both cases the tail is obscured, and cannot, therefore, feature heavily in the hawk's recognition.

What makes any quarry lure work is simply that it is carrying a type of food which the hawk recognises. This persuades her to view the object itself as a source of food. Then, it is the action of dragging it along the ground which switches on her instinct to chase it. Once conditioned to chasing something moving along the ground, a good broadwing in her first couple of seasons will chase almost anything, including squirrels, stoats, weasels, rats, ferrets, even small dogs and cats if you're not careful – none of which have fluffy white tails.

Even so, a quarry lure in one form or another is essential. Any kind will give the hawk practice and experience (however limited) in securing moving objects, but in addition a well-designed one will encourage her to target the head of the quarry. This is especially important with rabbits and hares, both of which have powerful hind legs capable of bucking a hawk off their body if she doesn't bind to it properly.

Personal Gear

This section concerns equipment you will need to improve your own comfort, and make things easier when training or flying hawks. Much of it is down to personal preference, and as you gain experience out in the field, you will acquire a set – or even several sets – of gear which suit you best in different flying conditions. But the emphasis is on *personal* – there is no regulation kit you have to have. Even so, there are some items you will find it difficult to do without, although there is plenty of choice in terms of design, style, cost, quality, size, type and so on.

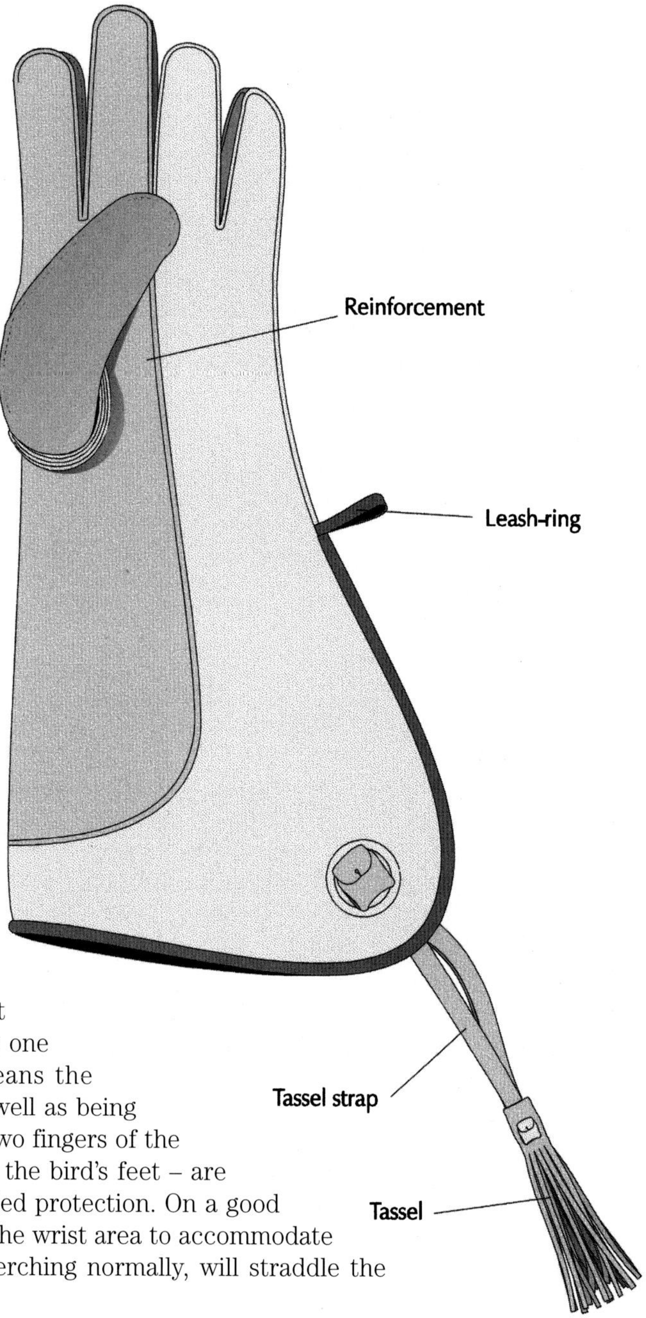

Perhaps the most important piece of personal equipment is a glove or gauntlet. It is an easily-recognisable item of falconry gear, but it certainly isn't worn for show. Any bird – particularly in training – will spend a great deal of time standing or landing on the fist. In their wild state hawks catch and often kill prey with their feet which, for animals of their light weight, are extraordinarily powerful. Their talons can be needle-sharp, and it is therefore foolish to expect to be able to handle even a trained hawk with bare hands, or a normal leather glove. A typical falconry glove, suitable for a buzzard-sized bird, is illustrated here.

Considering you only need one (and you can buy them left or right-handed), a glove is an expensive piece of equipment. A heavy-weight one is usually made from buckskin because it is one of the densest leathers obtainable (which means the hawk's talons are less likely to puncture it), as well as being durable and supple. The wrist, thumb and first two fingers of the glove – the areas which have most contact with the bird's feet – are normally re-inforced with a second layer for added protection. On a good glove, this re-inforcement will extend well onto the wrist area to accommodate large hawks whose feet, even when they are perching normally, will straddle the thumb and wrist.

Reinforcement

Leash-ring

Tassel strap

Tassel

The tassel and straps look decorative – and they are superficially – but they, too, have a definite function. The glove is not only a perch for your hawk, but also a feeding platform on which she will tear up and eat her food. Through constant use it will become saturated with meat juices, however diligent you are at keeping it clean. Consequently, other animals – mice, rats, but in particular dogs – love falconry gloves and will chew them to pieces given half a chance. The tassel straps simply enable them to be hung well clear of temptation.

Opposite the thumb, on the lower edge of the glove, is a small 'leash-ring' which is either made of strong leather or a metal loop sewn into the main body of the glove. It is used for securing the normal leash during a hawk's early training, or later as an anchor for a field leash.

Above all, the glove must be comfortable. Considering that it will become stiffer with the bird's constant feeding and your efforts to keep it clean, it is advisable to obtain one slightly larger than you would normally consider for other types of glove, otherwise you'll find that after a season's use you will have difficulty bending your fingers at all. If you ask a falconry supplier to send you one by mail order, he will probably ask you to provide him with a tracing of your hand, in which case he will take into account the fact that it needs to be slightly larger.

Although they were never specifically designed for the purpose, falconry gloves are also very good at handling barbed wire fences, as well as brambles and other thorny thickets, all of which you might have to negotiate during the course of a day's flying.

Out hunting you will need a means of carrying equipment for use in the field, such as a swivel and leash, field jesses, a swing lure, knife, or whatever else you might want to take with you. Just as importantly, you will need somewhere clean to put the hawk's food and any game she might catch. Normal clothing might be able to accommodate smaller pieces of equipment, and even one head of quarry, but two or three rabbits or pheasants can be difficult to handle. You could loop them over your belt, or even around your neck, but if they are visible to the hawk she might constantly attack them. It is safer, therefore, to carry them out of her sight and reach.

Traditionally falconers wear a specially designed bag made of heavy-duty canvas or, more expensively, fine quality leather and suede. These can usually be obtained for use with a shoulder strap, or a leather belt-loop. Falconry bags normally rest on the hip and upper thigh so that they are easily-controlled and manipulated by the free hand.

Internally falconry bags are divided into two large compartments – one for game, and the other for hawk food and equipment. The belt (or shoulder strap) attachment is centred on the top ridge of the bag and includes a swivel which enables the bag to be turned easily from back to front (for access

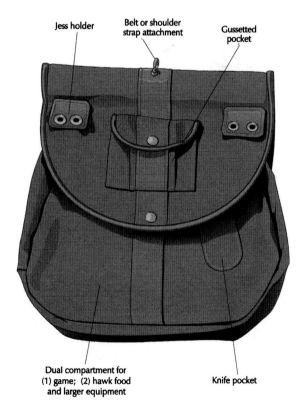

Jess holder

Belt or shoulder strap attachment

Gussetted pocket

Dual compartment for (1) game; (2) hawk food and larger equipment

Knife pocket

85

to the game pouch) or vice versa (for access to food and equipment). Both halves have an external closable lid to conceal the contents from the hawk. The front compartment should have a removable food pocket made from vinyl (or some other waterproof material), which makes it easy to clean. In addition, the outer lid usually has a means of carrying mews or field jesses, such as a leather flap with appropriately-sized eyelet holes, and it might also have a pocket or two for smaller pieces of equipment.

As a means of carrying food and essential equipment they work very well, but in the kind of field conditions met when flying broadwings they lose out on practicality because they are free-swinging – it's a bit like lugging around a large handbag. They hinder passage in wooded or enclosed country, through undergrowth, over barbed wire fences, or even field gates that won't open – especially if the bag is holding three or four rabbits. Their position on the hip and thigh, although essential for easy access to the contents, some falconers find cumbersome when the bag is not actually being used for retrieving food or equipment.

A modern alternative, developed in America, is the 'hawking vest'. These are made with artificial canvas-type materials (such as Cordura) which are tough, durable and washable. They look like a combination of a rucksack and a sleeveless bodiless jacket. Bag-like pockets are arranged on each hip, and a large game pouch covers most of the back area. One pocket has eyelets fixed into the flap for carrying jesses, the other contains a detachable food pouch. The whole thing is held together by a belt and shoulder straps which are made of fully adjustable webbing. These garments don't themselves provide any protection from the weather, but the range of adjustment available means you can wear them over anything from a T-shirt to a Parka.

Hawking vests might look vaguely ridiculous, but they are very practical for flying broadwings in rough country. Unlike bags, they don't snag on difficult vegetation or get in the way when climbing obstacles. The two pockets are large enough to hold all the field-equipment you will need (including spares), and the game pouch is enormous. In addition, it is much more comfortable to carry three or four rabbits in a rucksack-like game-pouch than it is in a free-swinging bag on one thigh.

The main problem is that good hawking vests, presumably because they are a recent innovation, are currently very expensive and only a few falconry suppliers stock them. Hopefully they will eventually become widely-available and cost much less. In the meantime, many falconers are making do with a substitute – the lightweight fly-fishing, stalking, or shooting 'waistcoat' which is obtainable from angling or other country sports suppliers. These have several flapped and gussetted pockets, as well as a large game (or spare clothing) pocket situated across the small of the back.

If you choose this option, buy a waistcoat with the largest and most accessible 'game' pocket you can find. There is nothing more frustrating than trying to place a limp, full-grown rabbit one-handed into a pocket behind you which has a top flap held firmly closed by a velcro strip. The most practical game-pockets, for falconry at least, are those giving access to the sides of the pocket – like the back-pack of the hawking vest – which can be kept permanently open and enable game to be slid in easily with your free hand.

You will also need to reserve one of the gussetted pockets for hawk food and line it with waterproof material for easy cleaning. Alternatively, make sure it is capable of carrying a removable vinyl pocket which can be taken out and washed (these can usually be obtained from suppliers of falconry equipment). Any of the pocket-flaps of the waistcoat can be adapted for use as a jess-holder by fitting eyelets in exactly the same way as for Aylmeri anklets, but again make sure that they are fixed in a position easily accessible with your free hand. Other field equipment, and such things as licences, can be distributed around the remaining pockets according to preference.

Whatever the weather, you would be well-advised to wear a pair of comfortable wellington-type boots – normal walking boots are virtually useless for falconry. Even when the day is hot and dry you will find yourself wading through bogs, streams, ponds or rivulets, particularly when your hawk has connected with game on the other side. There is nothing more guaranteed to spoil your enjoyment of a day's flying than wandering around the countryside with wet feet.

Where wellingtons are concerned, the emphasis must be on comfort – you might end up walking several miles in them. The ordinary black, hard-rubber variety are really not up to the task, but there are several types of sporting wellingtons on the market which are light, flexible and waterproof. If you can afford them, buy a pair with steel-reinforced soles which are designed for climbing over barbed wire fences or other sharp obstacles, and to improve grip on slippery surfaces.

More on the subject of clothing, wet-weather gear is also useful. Hawks certainly don't relish rain, but they will fly in it if it is reasonably light or intermittent. The trouble is that if you are only prepared to take your bird out on dry sunny days, you won't get much sport and it will be difficult to keep her fit. You will need head-wear, a waterproof jacket, and waterproof leggings. If you intend to use a waistcoat rather than a bag or hawking vest, make sure it is large enough to be worn over the jacket. Leggings are useful for two reasons:
1. Wet-weather jackets shed water straight onto the legs.
2. They will keep your legs dry when you are wading through vegetation covered in rain or snow. They also give added protection in dense undergrowth such as gorse or bramble. Again, make sure that the leggings are large enough to wear over a pair of wellington boots.

For any clothing it is best to wear colours sympathetic to the countryside, such as greens or browns. This isn't just a matter of style. If you choose to wear a luminous multi-coloured anorak, however warm and weather-proof it might be, game will see you coming for miles.

Similarly, you will find that your hawk is also sensitive to what you wear. Her recognition of you will tend to be holistic rather than specific – in other words, she will only partially recognise your face, walk, stance, voice or other attributes. If you are accustomed to handling her in a particular set of clothing, she will have difficulty recognising you if you suddenly appear in a three-piece suit. At best, unfamiliar clothing will simply confuse her; at worst, she might show aggression.

Optional Extras

There are two other items which are often useful in the field and these are a whistle and a knife. Much as you might dislike the idea, some form of limited butchery will be necessary on occasions. This will involve feeding the hawk a great deal more than her normal rations on the spot when she catches her first heads of quarry, and it is always preferable to use part of the animal she has caught.

However, it is both unnecessary and inappropriate to obtain a large 'Bowie' or 'Rambo' type knife in a smart leather sheath. These are not only cumbersome to wear, but also virtually useless in hunting conditions – their blades were not made for cutting up small animals. Many falconers use 'Opinel' knives which were designed for the job. The blade folds away into a wooden stock like a penknife, and can be carried around safely in any pocket of a bag or waistcoat. They come in different sizes, each with a number which refers to the length of the blade in centimetres;

numbers 7, 8 or 9 are the most practical. These knives are internationally known and are available from falconry suppliers, angling shops, and many other sporting establishments.

Whistles require a bit of advanced planning. Much will depend on whether you intend to use a dog (see page 160 *Hunting Aids: Dogs*). If you don't, then you can make use of any whistle on the market for retrieving a hawk. If you do intend to use a dog, it is vital that he takes precedence and is trained with one suitable for dogs. You can't use the same whistle for both hawk and dog: you will simply confuse them and encourage poor response from both.

A whistle is essential for keeping any working dog under control in the field, and there are two basic types – the so-called 'dog' whistle, which is shaped like a small cigar, and the 'shepherd's' whistle which is placed wholly inside the mouth. Both are pea-less, and produce high-pitched sounds that dogs respond to best and which they can hear from quite a distance. The shepherd's whistle can be made to produce a variety of sounds, each relating to a separate command, but it takes a great deal of practice to use properly. The dog whistle only produces one sound, and dogs are taught to respond to different sequences similar to a primitive type of Morse code.

Where broadwings are concerned, such complicated sequences are unnecessary because it is only possible to train them to respond to two 'commands':
1. To return to you
2. To follow-on.
Indeed, some hawks only get as far as learning the first. Many falconers rely on using their lips, and if you are proficient at whistling, this is perfectly adequate for the relatively short distances broadwings tend to stray. However, you will need to be proficient enough to make yourself heard in all conditions – in particular cold and wind – over several hundred yards.

If you're not especially accomplished at whistling with your mouth, it is helpful to have a 'back-up' whistle which can be used – in conjunction with the swing lure if necessary – to retrieve a hawk in an emergency. If you are out of her sight and she has flown a long way after quarry, the whistle not only attracts her attention, it also gives her an audible clue to your position. For this purpose an ordinary 'referee' whistle can be used, which produces a totally different sound to either kind of dog whistle and doesn't, therefore, confuse the dog. However, if you choose this option, buy a plastic one rather than a metal one for two reasons:
1. On a freezing mid-winter day, plastic is much more sympathetic to the lips than cold metal
2. In a metal whistle, the 'pea' rattling around inside sounds remarkably like a distant hawk bell. If you are frantically scrambling around looking for a missing hawk, it can add confusion to panic.

Handling Hawks

Introduction

A significant proportion of any hawk's management requires carrying or manhandling her. Indeed, when she isn't flying, or tethered to a perch, or confined to her quarters, you will probably be carrying her on the fist – either to tame her, move her from one perch to another, or transport her to, from and around parts of your hunting ground. Manhandling – which means holding her firmly in both hands – will be necessary to undertake such tasks as fitting equipment, trimming her beak and talons, repairing damaged feathers, and dealing with illness or injury.

Carrying a hawk on the fist is a primary method of keeping her under control when she is outside but not flying – the equivalent of walking a dog on a lead. She has to be *trained* to accept it, and in this book her instruction starts on day one. Maintaining control – particularly for a first hawk – takes practice, but there are techniques for carrying her, with the aid of full or partial tethering equipment, which make things as simple and secure as possible.

Similarly, there are safe ways of holding a hawk to immobilise her dangerous feet, pinion her wings, and keep her as still as possible without causing injury to her or to you during essential tasks like treating wounds. This kind of control is known as *casting*. The word has other meanings in falconry, but for an explanation of these, see page 227 *Falconry Terminology*.

Carrying a Hawk

Educating a hawk to accept and use the fist as a perch is one of the most important aspects of her early training. It takes time and, where most broadwings are concerned, a lot of patience. Indeed, you might spend more hours on this activity than any other. Falconers call this education *manning*, which involves exposing the hawk gradually to everything likely to be encountered in human environments – you, other people, rooms, houses, roads, vehicles, cats, dogs, horses, sheep, cattle, and so on. The long-term objective is to get her so accustomed to such sights that she no longer views them as frightening and ceases to bate at them. During this process she also learns to balance on the fist, whatever your walking pace or however rough the terrain is; and she learns to regain her stance on the fist, unaided, whenever she bates.

Even so, a trained hawk which never bates is a rarity. Bating might be provoked, for example, because the hawk is anxious to get to a familiar hunting ground and is impatient with your progress; or because she's seen potential quarry on the way; or because you're trying to carry her in the face of a strong wind which she would much rather shelter from. The difference here is that she is bating not from *fear*, but because she's been *stimulated* by something in the environment. Whatever reason a hawk finds to bate, she must be kept under full control until you decide what it is you want her to do next. For any hawk, therefore, carrying is simply a mobile means of tethering her.

Any well-trained tethered hawk will step (or hop) onto the fist from another perch whenever the fist is presented to her, and this is usually the first action in shifting control from perch to fist. Once she is settled, the jesses, swivel and leash-knot are placed behind the gloved thumb and laid over the palm. The top end of the leash is then wrapped tightly around the little finger before any attempt is made to undo the knot(s) securing her to the perch. If she gets loose with a full set of equipment attached, she is almost certain to become entangled in the first tree she lands in. If you can't locate her it means certain death. Even if you can, you will probably have horrendous problems trying to retrieve her.

Collecting an untrained and unmanned bird from a perch is, of course, much less straightforward. She certainly won't step up to the fist. On the contrary, she will bate away from you furiously. Even so, the procedure is much the same except that you will need to grab the jesses with the gloved hand, coil the leash round the little finger in the same way, then yank her clear of the floor before releasing her from the perch. The remaining portion of the leash is wrapped loosely around the third and fourth fingers, then the whole assembly gripped against the palm of the hand by closing the last three fingers into a fist.

Coiling the leash around the third and fourth fingers simply keeps the trailing end out of the way if the hawk bates. If you allow the leash to hang loose, it will become entangled around her wings and body when she does attempt to fly off or get back onto the fist. There should also be enough leeway at the top end of the jesses to give the hawk freedom *at least* to shift the position of her feet on the fist if she wants to. A bating hawk generates a considerable amount of power very quickly, and what really prevents her from getting loose is the tight coil of leash around the little finger which acts like an anchor. Gripping the equipment against the palm of the hand with all three fingers is, at best, only a secondary insurance.

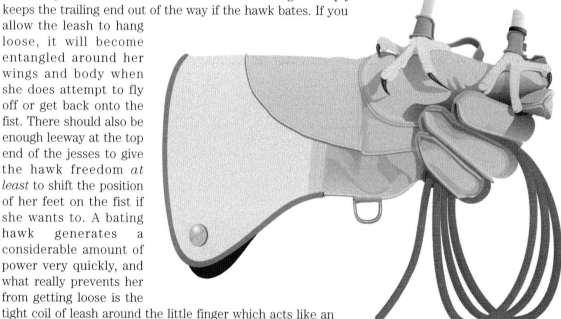

Once on the fist, the most comfortable carrying position for both hawk and human is with the forearm, wrist and thumb in a line roughly parallel to the ground, pointing forwards, and with the elbow tucked into the side of the body. For a large hawk such as a buzzard, the wrist and thumb are particularly important because her foot-span might straddle both, and they must give her a stable platform on which she can perch and maintain her balance. The thumb should, therefore, be uppermost and roughly in line with the top surface of the wrist. The first finger acts as a nominal support for the thumb, which is bearing most of the weight of the hawk.

Whenever a hawk is perching on the fist, she should be facing you – in other words, with her tail overhanging the back of the glove. This has nothing to do with style. If she's pointing the other way, she will splash your midriff with her mutes whenever she feels the need. If she is perching the wrong way, you can turn her easily by applying gentle pressure with a finger of your free hand to the base of her tail-feathers, pushing them in the direction you want her to turn.

Carrying a hawk on the fist over some distance is not easy until you get the knack but, whether she is trained or not, you should walk normally. Mincing your steps because you are afraid of provoking a bate, or holding her as far away from your body as possible, will achieve little in the long run. Similarly, if she does bate, keep your forearm and fist parallel to the ground. Don't be tempted to drop them towards the floor in an attempt to ease her discomfort. She will eventually learn to regain the fist herself, but only if you keep it roughly where it was. In the meantime, you will have to replace her manually.

There are basically two ways to do this. The first is to take hold of her body where it meets her thighs with your free hand and lift her gently onto the glove: the second is to put your hand underneath her swinging body, cradle her back, then grip between her wings and lift her so that she can replace her feet on the glove. The second method avoids any possibility that she might catch you with her beak, but if you hold her low enough on her body with the first method, her beak shouldn't be able to reach you anyway. In the end, how you replace her is a matter of personal preference.

After carrying the hawk, putting her back onto a bow-perch presents yet another problem. Her jesses will have to be secured in the fist in case she bates, but you will need the whole of her leash free to enable you to tie a pair of falconer's knots to the perch ring. Considering the speed, power and weight of a large hawk, simply holding the jesses and swivel in the palm of the hand is not a good idea – she could drag the whole lot out of your grasp before you have sufficient time to react. This is because a stiff buckskin gauntlet is not a very sensitive piece of equipment, and it is difficult to feel whether you have a good grip or not.

Falconers have devised an alternative means of securing the jesses – known as a 'glove lock' – which avoids this outcome. It involves uncoiling the leash in its entirety, then slotting the jesses between the two middle fingers of the glove. This puts the knot securing the jesses to the swivel outside the closed fist so that, if the hawk does bate, she can't free it from the fingers.

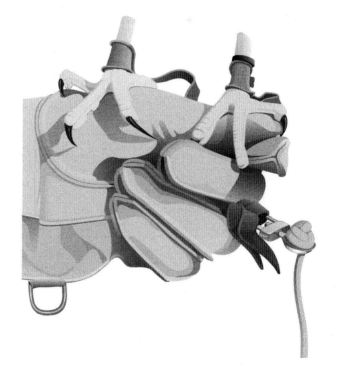

No hawk should ever be allowed to transfer from fist to bow perch until you have secured the leash to the perch ring. A trained hawk, once she is in close proximity to a familiar perch, might attempt to hop onto it before you are ready to let her go. Not only is this bad discipline, but it could give you problems securing her, particularly if she bates before you've finished.

You can prevent her from jumping onto the perch too soon simply by holding her directly above it – even to the point of resting your gloved hand on it if necessary – until you have secured the leash properly. Then, when you are ready, move your fist away from the perch and let her hop on.

An untrained hawk still standing on the fist might need some encouragement to step onto the perch. Back her up to it until it puts pressure behind her legs, then she should step backwards. For some reason, hawks find this a much more comfortable way of gaining a perch compared to stepping forwards even though, for humans, the latter might be a natural choice. If your novice hawk is dangling upside down when you have secured the leash, you will have to do the best you can, either by getting her to stand on the fist first then persuading her to back onto the perch, or trying to place her on the perch directly. If she refuses to do either, put her on the ground close by and leave her to sort herself out.

These manoeuvres – collecting your hawk from a perch, carrying her around, then replacing her on the perch – will probably be repeated dozens of times every season and they should quickly become second nature. However, the temptation to relax control through familiarity or over-confidence will also tend to dominate. But remember: whatever confidence you gain, it only takes one fundamental mistake in control to lose a bird, and if she is wearing full tethering gear, she won't have any chance of surviving if you fail to recover her.

There is an alternative method of securing the leash when carrying the hawk around – by tying it with a falconer's knot to the glove ring. In fact, with your first unmanned and untrained hawk, this method is probably advisable. To achieve it, first put the jesses in the glove-lock position, then tie the end of the leash to the glove ring with a falconer's knot. Once the knot is tied, place the jesses, swivel and leash-knot in the palm as before and coil any surplus out of the way.

The glove-lock is also useful for securing field jesses, whether or not a field leash is used. In this case, the jesses are slotted between the middle fingers in exactly the same way, but they have to rely on friction to keep them in place. Normally the method is only used during flying sessions when it is necessary to bring the hawk under manual control temporarily – for example, if you need to by-pass an area the landowner has asked you to avoid, such as pheasant pens.

If the jesses are well-greased (as they should be), this will reduce the friction and make it easier for a bating hawk to free them. However, you can increase their security by putting a twist in the exposed ends of the jesses, and slotting the points back between the third and little finger of the glove.

If you intend to make use of a field leash (see the section headed *Hawk Furniture*), you have two other options:

1. You can loop the trailing end of the leash around the little finger of the glove or
2. You can dispense with the loop and tie the free end to the glove ring.

Using a loop is more practical in field conditions because it is one less knot to tie and untie.

Casting a Hawk

The first thing to bear in mind is that *all hawks abhor being handled*. It doesn't matter how often you do it, or how dextrous and sympathetic you are, they never entirely get used to it. They will always resist, even though their determination to do so might wane as the years go by. Even then, any reduction in a hawk's determination can't be taken as approval of what you're doing, only as a measure of her sense of futility. Any lack of acceptance makes casting a stressful experience – for you certainly, but much more so for her.

A second thing to remember is that handling a hawk affects her plumage in one way or another. Degradation can range from loss of weatherproofing oils from the surface of her feathers to the fracture of those vital for efficiency in flight, depending on how heavy-handed you are. The former she can put right given time but the latter she can do nothing about. It is possible to carry out repairs (see page 191 *Maintaining Beaks and Talons*), but it is obviously much better to avoid this level of damage in the first place. Besides, repairing plumage will involve casting her yet again and introduce the risk of another accident.

Casting a hawk invariably involves two people – one to maintain control of the bird, the other to carry out the necessary action. Before you attempt it, therefore, it is essential to decide who is going to do what. It is also advisable to carry out the procedure in a closed room. There is always a possibility that the hawk will escape – especially if she is being held by someone with little or no experience – and if she is able to fly away outside, you will probably lose her forever. She might prove difficult to catch indoors, but at least she will still be captive.

Casting is normally initiated by getting the hawk to perch on the fist with any tethering equipment coiled out of the way. The sight of a second person (whose responsibility it is to cast) close behind her or coming towards her will usually provoke a bate, and she needs to be kept under full control if this happens. Obviously it is preferable to use someone she is familiar and comfortable with rather than (to her) a complete stranger, but this is not always possible as for example when you take her to see a vet.

The object of the exercise is to hold the hawk's wings against the sides of her body so that she can't flap them, and at the same time hold her thighs against her belly so that she can't lash out with her feet. This is accomplished by a special grip using both hands – the palms pinion the wings, and the fingers secure the thighs with the help of the thumbs, which lie parallel to each other along the hawk's spine.

The easiest way to achieve such a cast is to approach a perching hawk from behind. A well-manned one with a steady temperament might allow you to cast her without much fuss, apart from spreading her wings slightly as your hands draw near. She might also twitter, which is another sign of nervousness. If you are lucky enough to own such a hawk, casting is easy. Simply gather her wings in against her body, grip her thighs, then lift her off the glove. Hold her firmly, but *don't squeeze*. If you do, she will panic and try to escape.

However, no hawk is likely to be anywhere near compliant until she is fully trained, especially when you are expecting her to perch on a stranger's fist. Even then, the extent to which she will co-operate depends on her temperament, as well as her familiarity with the procedure. In such cases it is usually better to get your assistant to attract her attention – for example, by stroking her breast – then make a swift grab for the hawk before she has time to react. Make sure the cast is firmly established before she is released from the glove.

An alternative method of achieving the cast is to throw a light towel (or something similar) over the hawk's head before the cast is attempted. The theory is that this prevents her from spreading her wings and puts her in the dark so that she can't see what you're doing. In addition, use of a towel is supposed to protect her plumage from loss of weatherproofing oils.

However, in my experience, just the *sight* of a towel close by more often than not provokes the hawk to bate. If she doesn't bate at the sight of it, she will probably bate as soon as it makes contact with her body, which means that the towel will fall to the floor. Once she's learned that she can get rid of it that way, she'll bate every time you attempt to cover her head. Also, I have never seen any evidence that a towel protects plumage any better than a bare hand. Indeed, it seems more likely that it will soak up any weatherproofing oils.

If all else fails, you will have to make the cast while the hawk is dangling below the glove after she has bated – especially with a young, unmanned one. Fortunately, this is not as difficult as it might seem. While she is hanging by the jesses, she will keep her wings spread once she has stopped flapping them. Fold them in *gently* against her body with your hands taking care not to damage her flight-feathers, then hold her thighs with your fingers. When you are satisfied with the grip, lift her up and release her from the glove.

Your first bird newly-arrived from the breeder will be a difficult proposition. She will be in some sort of container, and how you bring her out of it will depend on
• whether it is a cardboard box or a commercial pet-carrier
• whether the breeder has already fitted anklets and jesses
(see page 108 *Buying a Hawk*).

If she is wearing jesses, they can be used to bring her out of either kind of carrier. Open the container just enough to get a gloved hand inside, take hold of at least one jess (preferably both), then open the container fully and pull her out. Make sure that when she bates there are no obstacles in the way. If she will stand on the fist (which is unlikely) cast her in the normal way, otherwise you will have to make the cast while she is hanging by her jesses.

If the bird hasn't been fitted with leg equipment, getting her out of a cardboard box is much easier than out of a pet-carrier. Open the lid slightly so that you can peer inside to establish her orientation. Use a torch if necessary. Once you know which way she is facing, open the lid just enough to get both hands inside the box, then cast her. The comparative darkness of the box, her restricted space, and the fact that you are approaching her from above, will all serve to minimise any action she could take to resist.

The only way I know to extricate a new hawk which is wearing no equipment out of a front-loading pet-carrier is by opening the door and putting a gloved hand inside. If she attacks the glove with her feet, draw her closer to the door and take hold of her legs with your free hand. If she doesn't grip the glove, use that to take hold of her legs. Once she is secured, pull her out and get your assistant to cast her as if she was bating.

New bird or old, before she is cast, you will have to decide how the action you want to take is going to proceed. For example, fitting leg-equipment (anklets and bewits) can be accomplished easily with your assistant holding the bird upright with her feet facing you. But this position is useless if you want to fit a tail-bell, or repair wing or tail feathers. Several operations therefore require manoeuvring the hawk into the required position *after the cast has been made*. To aid manoeuvre, a cushion placed on a table is an invaluable asset. It gives the hawk something to grip with her feet if she is laid down, or something comfortable to rest on if she has to be placed on her back for access to her underside. Another useful extra is a handkerchief, a small scarf, or a tea-towel which can be draped *lightly* over her head to block out her vision. Alternatively, if you have a well-fitting hood, that is an even better solution. Whatever, you use, the fact that she can't see what you are doing should keep her relatively calm.

Casting from behind the hawk can serve most purposes, but there is one common operation (fitting a tail bell) which requires her to be held the opposite way round – with her tail facing the person fixing the bell. The objective of this cast is the same – to pinion her wings and thighs – but in this case the hawk is grabbed *from the front*. With a compliant hawk perching on the fist, this is no more difficult than a standard cast, but with a new bird bating furiously it is almost impossible to achieve without experience.

However, you can end up with the same result by casting the hawk in the standard way, *but the person fitting the bell will have to do the initial cast*. Once the hawk is placed on the cushion (and has been blindfolded), your assistant should first establish control of her wings before you release them. Pressing her gently down on the cushion will stop her using her legs and feet in the meantime. When your assistant has her wings under control, let go of her and give him time to work his hands underneath her body to bring her thighs under control. Once she is firmly cast, proceed with the operation.

Weight And Condition

Introduction

With all predators, the instinct to hunt is greater than the instinct to feed. If this were not so, a fox in a chicken coop would kill only those chickens needed for sustenance; a domestic cat wouldn't kill small mammals and birds when all its feeding requirements were met by its owners; and birds of prey wouldn't cache food in times of plenty. However, leaving such complications aside, hunger is the primary stimulus that triggers responsive behaviour in falconry birds, which includes not only coming to the fist, but also showing the commitment required for catching quarry under field conditions. Without hunger, it wouldn't be possible to train either wild or captive-bred birds, and in this respect some general statements can be made.

The more food a hawk has in her digestive system, the less motivated she will be to hunt. Also, if she has been especially successful (meaning that she has caught enough prey to build up significant energy reserves in the form of fat), she will be less inclined to hunt. A fat hawk with no food in her digestive system might launch herself on a hunting foray on instinct alone, but her efforts will probably be half-hearted. It is just as likely that she will sit in a tree for most of the time and enjoy the benefits of not having to work for a living – at least until it becomes necessary again.

The combination of an empty gut *and* minimal fat reserves produces the strongest hunting response. In this condition, a hawk will be fully committed to catching prey and she will make use of whatever experience, aggression, and energy she has to secure it. In falconry terminology, this condition is known as *flying weight*.

Hawks have two other characteristics related to food which also make it possible to train and fly them. The first is their metabolism (the process by which food is converted into energy). Compared to mammals, all birds energise food, and burn it, rapidly. One large meal ingested by a hawk will increase weight significantly within twenty-four hours. Similarly, if she eats no food at all in the course of a day, her weight will drop noticeably. This makes it possible to regulate weight from day to day simply by giving her greater or lesser amounts of food or, put another way, to control her response to both training and hunting.

The second characteristic is that all hawks have a *crop* – a pre-digestive storage area which enables them to gulp food down quickly, then fly somewhere safe to digest it. In other words, when a hawk swallows food, it doesn't satisfy her hunger immediately. In fact she has to physically transfer food from the crop (which is situated at the base of her throat) to her main digestive system before she can begin to digest it. She does this by writhing her neck, each time passing a small portion into her stomach (falconers call this *putting over the crop*). From the falconer's point of view, this means that, out in the field, he can feed a hawk several pieces of food over a period of time and she will still be hungry and responsive. The only limiting factor is what she is capable of storing in her crop. Once that's full, she will no longer be motivated to hunt or respond. (As a matter of interest, owls do not have a crop and pass food into their digestive systems as soon as it is ingested, which is why they are not, strictly, falconry birds.)

There is no exact match between 'flying weight' in falconry birds and 'hunting weight' in wild ones. Generally speaking, wild hawks hunt at a higher weight because (with the exception of imprints) most falconry birds never entirely lose their fear of humans. As a consequence, their hunger has to be more pronounced, not only to overcome this residual fear, but also to maintain a willingness to respond and produce the commitment required for catching quarry in a limited time frame. However, all this means that falconry birds have lower energy resources 'in the bank' if things go wrong.

Flying weight is probably best described as *the weight at which each bird gives optimum response and commitment*. Without knowledge of it for your hawk, you will have no means of controlling her free-flight behaviour. It is, therefore, the key to successful falconry but establishing it, and the amount of food necessary to maintain it in varying circumstances, are two areas of falconry likely to give the beginner more problems than any other.

Weight Parameters

Where captive birds are concerned, a fat hawk is one which has been offered more food than she wants over a period of several weeks. She will show no immediate interest in any food given to her, and the next day there might still be some left over. This condition is known as *top* (or *fat*) weight.

The difference between top weight and flying weight is enormous. For example, there is a much-publicised 'guideline' of 20 per cent to 25 per cent for broadwings. Whilst it is *positively dangerous* to use a guideline like this in training a new hawk (because you can never be sure that the bird you've just acquired is at top weight), it does illustrate the point. On this basis, a broadwing with a top weight of, say, 2lb 8oz would have to lose up to 10oz to reach flying weight. This is equivalent to a fifteen stone man shedding almost four stones. Even allowing for the speed at which hawks gain and lose weight, this can *not* be achieved in a day, or even a few days.

If you feed a broadwing at top weight anything at all, albeit much less than she needs, she will lose about ¼oz of weight per day. Feed her nothing and she will lose something like ½oz per day. Both are significant amounts even for a broadwing. In which case, reducing weight by 10oz will take between forty and twenty days. However, well before she reaches flying weight, she will start responding by taking food off the fist – with a broadwing, anything from two to ten days.

Any weight above flying weight is what falconers call *high condition*. Even with fully-trained, experienced, and normally highly-responsive hawks, the closer they are to top weight the worse their response is likely to be. In fact, well before they reach top weight, it is likely to become non-existent. Although in this condition falconry birds still *remember* their training, most totally disregard it.

A trained hawk at flying weight will give you an immediate and a consistent response, which is what you're aiming for. Lack of immediacy when your bird starts feeding off the fist will cause you to reduce weight more until it is achieved. Once it is, you will move onto the next stage of training, reducing weight if necessary until you achieve an immediate result, and so on until she's flying free.

However, there is also a 'bottom' weight – called starvation. Anything less than flying weight is known in falconry terminology as *low condition*. A few percentage points below flying weight also results in lack of response, but in this case it is because the hawk doesn't have sufficient energy resources to achieve what her falconer expects.

Weight Control: Complicating Factors

In theory, weight control is about regulating a hawk's intake of food to keep weight constant, or increasing it or reducing it by measured amounts, but there are several factors which make this very difficult to achieve when training and flying a bird. As with all healthy animals, weight is directly related to energy consumption – food intake has to match energy output to keep weight stable. The harder a hawk works, the more food she will need to replace the energy she's used. This is particularly relevant during the later stages of training where she will be asked to come further and further for food and, once entered, in the field when she's using large amounts of energy to catch and secure quarry.

The quality of food she ingests also has a profound effect. Put simply, certain kinds of food increase a hawk's weight more than others, and this has nothing to do with quantity. For example, the volume of a day-old chick is greater than that of a mouse, but the mouse will increase a hawk's weight by much more. Considering the range of foods available these days (including any quarry they might eat), all of which produce a different result on weight, the potential for chaos in weight control is obvious. Unfortunately, because birds (like humans) are so individual, you can only learn the effect of different foods on your hawk's weight through trial and error.

There are more subtle difficulties. For example, if the temperature overnight falls below freezing, a hawk will burn greater amounts of energy just to maintain body temperature, even though she's fast asleep. Even less obvious, a hawk in low condition will need a lot more food to maintain her weight than one in high condition. With no energy reserves in the form of fat, the muscles of a hawk in low condition slowly waste away. In effect, her body absorbs its own muscle tissue to keep vital organs functioning, and lost muscle is much harder to replace than fat. By way of example, an inactive broadwing at top weight will probably need only a couple of day-old chicks to maintain it, but one in low condition might eat five and still lose weight.

To cap it all, flying weight itself is not a static measure. By the time your hawk is flying free, you could be excused for believing that you have established *precisely* what it is. However, as soon as she achieves hunting success, her confidence will soar dramatically and you might find that she is becoming much too independent-minded. In this case you will have to cut her weight again to maintain discipline. But, later on, when she is in the habit of working with you, it should be possible to fly her at a higher weight without jeopardising response – with the onset of habitual behaviour, response becomes semi-automatic. As the season progresses, she will also build up muscle which itself will increase weight. Sticking slavishly to a fixed idea of flying weight will not allow her to do this, and performance will be affected as a result.

Throughout her working life, it is the *quality* of response which should always determine the weight at which she is flown. But you should aim to fly her at the highest weight feasible which is still conducive to field-discipline – in other words, as close as possible to her natural 'hunting' weight.

Whatever the difficulties, flying weight is the essence of falconry. It is, nevertheless, only a *considered judgement* on your part, not a scientific fact. Occasionally you might need to review your verdict – however much you want to believe that you've got it right.

Recognising Low Condition

A hawk in low condition has already begun the long soporific slide towards death. If her condition continues to deteriorate, how long she will take to die is impossible to say. It depends on many things – her species; her size and constitution; the amount of food she's given; her metabolism; environmental factors such as temperature; whether she succumbs to infection; and so on.

The degree of difference between 'bottom weight' (starvation) and flying weight is unknown. Falconers themselves – because they don't deliberately mistreat hawks by starving them – have no measure for it. Nevertheless, from occasions when it has happened, it is clear that the difference is very small compared to a hawk's top weight/flying weight ratio. What is better known is the effect of low condition on a hawk's behaviour, and it is this which guides falconers in taking appropriate measures. But, because the margin is so small, diagnosis – and in particular remedial action – has to be swift to bring about full recovery.

Even for experienced falconers (though they might not admit it), flying weight itself is a slightly grey area. It is, perhaps, best described as a quivering needle-point somewhere on a sliding scale which encompasses a hawk's total inactivity due to a surplus of food, and her total inactivity due to death from starvation. It's a bit like tuning a radio to get the best reception – one day it will be perfect at a particular spot; the next it might need a little tweek on one side or the other. But beyond any greyness, the behaviour of a hawk in low condition will give you clues to where she is on this sliding scale.

A hawk at or near flying weight will show interest in you whenever you approach, but especially near to feeding or flying time. For example, if she's being weathered on a bow perch on the lawn and you walk around her, she will shift position so that she is facing you in the hope that you will call her off the perch for a morsel of food. If you then walk away, that will be the end of it until you come near her again.

With a hawk moving into low condition, this attentiveness will be much more exaggerated. It will become intense to the point of harassment, and she will probably bate off the perch towards you. When you feed her, her appetite will be voracious. She will gobble food down as if she's never seen it before, and if she spies another piece in your hand she might attempt to snatch it even as she's struggling to get an overload down her throat. Food – and the acquisition of it – will become the sole focus of her life.

If she's still involved in creance-training at this point, she might come to you before you've called her, and before you've walked as far away as you want to be. Out in the field flying free, her attention will stay fixed on you rather than on hunting. She might try to harass you, for example by flying close, then 'thumping' you with a clenched foot as she goes by, or constantly landing on the ground in front of you instead of flying on to another tree.

Such behaviour indicates the lowest possible weight you can work her with. In this respect knowledge of it is valuable. Its value is similar to that of top weight which, on the basis of the 20 per cent to 25 per cent rule, provides an approximate guide to her flying weight.

If the hawk's condition drops below this level, her responses will deteriorate. For example, if you call her off a perch expecting her to come the full length of a creance, she might land on the ground before she reaches you. Similarly, if she's already flying free and normally follows on well, she will lag behind and show much less enthusiasm for chasing quarry, however catchable you might think it is.

From here onwards, behaviour becomes even more abnormal and things start to happen quickly. Her weight will drop dramatically overnight – perhaps by an ounce compared to a more normal quarter ounce. Physical weakness will become apparent. For example, the hawk might have difficulty getting back onto the fist after a bate, or onto a bow-perch from the ground and bates themselves will be much less energetic.

There will also be changes in her demeanour. In particular, she will no longer be bright-eyed and bushy-tailed. Interest in her surroundings will wane, and her movements will become much more sluggish. She will rarely preen, if at all. Similarly, she will no longer adopt the normal posture of standing on one leg occasionally. Firmly rooted on her perch with both feet, she will face straight ahead possibly with her eyes half closed and plumage puffed up. She may even doze off frequently in broad daylight.

Remedial Action

A hawk on the verge of starvation is a sad sight indeed. She will show interest in nothing except, perhaps, the chance of reaching oblivion where all her problems will be solved. If she has also acquired an infection – which is common for a hawk in this condition – she probably won't even eat. If you tempt her with lots of food, she might encourage you by instinctively grabbing it and defending it by mantling. Then she will pick at it for hours without devouring anything of real substance.

It goes without saying that low condition must be arrested and reversed as soon as possible if you want to keep your hawk. If she will eat, the 'cure' is to feed her as much good-quality food as she wants, even if this means breaking it up into easily-swallowed pieces (doing that for herself will take up a lot of her remaining energy). If she won't eat, first, crop-tube the bird with glucose (see the section headed *Illness and Injury* for the method) and leave her in a dark place for half an hour. Then feed her with meat soaked in a glucose solution. If she still won't eat, you must get specialised veterinary assistance immediately. If you don't, she might only have a few more hours to live.

Avoiding Diagnostic Confusion

Unless you have actually witnessed a hawk in low condition, the early signs can be difficult to recognise. Conversely, it is easy to persuade yourself that they exist when in fact they don't – especially with a first bird whose behaviour you don't yet understand. This, coupled with your own desire not to do the wrong thing, can give you all sorts of emotional traumas, and cause chaos in weight control and training.

Ambiguity in the reason for unsatisfactory response has already been mentioned, but there are others. For example, terms like 'puffed-up appearance' and 'half-closed' or 'slitted' eyes can be very misleading. Most hawks will puff-out their plumage whilst they are being weathered on a perch outside, particularly on a sunny day. Slitted eyes can also be taken as a sign of contentment and well-being, particularly when the hawk has just been fed a substantial meal. Similarly, landing on the ground in front of you and begging for food when she is meant to be hunting can also be due to boredom, especially if she's just spent an hour following you without any sign of potential quarry; and failing to reach the fist from a perch can simply be due to lack of fitness.

An experienced falconer would recognise these subtle differences in motivation immediately, but it is difficult for a complete beginner because you won't have any frame of reference with which to make a comparison. Obviously you must try to be as objective as possible, but what should really trigger concern is that the abnormal behaviour and the changes in demeanour described occur in combination. In other words, if you're worried about your hawk's puffed-up appearance and slitted eyes, look for unambiguous and additional symptoms to confirm the diagnosis.

Having said that, you must also have the courage and humility to seek help when it is obviously needed.

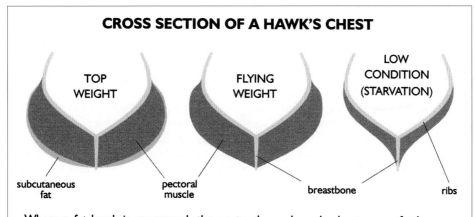

CROSS SECTION OF A HAWK'S CHEST

TOP WEIGHT

FLYING WEIGHT

LOW CONDITION (STARVATION)

subcutaneous fat

pectoral muscle

breastbone

ribs

Where a fat hawk is concerned, the pectoral muscle and subcutaneous fat have a convex profile. In low condition it is markedly concave, and at flying weight it is neither. Although assessing a hawk's condition accurately by feeling her breast takes practice, the technique does provides some guidance — especially at both extremes.

Hawk Food

The important constituents of any diet are water, protein, fat, carbohydrate, minerals, vitamins and roughage. In the wild a healthy bird of prey will obtain all of these from its kills, but to a large extent the diets of falconry birds are artificially produced. This makes it easier to regulate food intake (and therefore the hawk's weight and condition), and ensures that there is a consistent supply.

On the other hand, artificially-produced foods for captive hawks are neither as commercially-organised nor as scientifically-motivated as, say, those of poultry, beef, or other domesticated animals. There is always a risk, therefore, that birds used for falconry will suffer from an improper balance of important constituents, and any excess or deficiency in these over a period can result in illness or disease. Similarly, the lack of veterinary input and supervision in the production of hawk food can also result in ill-health, even death, through preventable infections.

This makes it *imperative* that you find a reputable supplier who produces food specifically for falconry birds. Usually these are practising (or ex-) falconers, and they are acutely aware of the importance of 'clean' food for hawks. Many other people produce potentially viable hawk food for all sorts of reasons – for example to supply zoos, which also use it for a large range of other animals. In this case, the animals concerned are not required to maintain peak fitness, and the organisation has ongoing resources to ensure that they get any necessary veterinary care if things go wrong. Failing that, they have adequate insurance to cover their loss. For them, therefore, bad or inappropriate food presents much less of a risk than it will do for you and your hawk.

Diet

Hawks eat other animals. This means not just their flesh but fur or feathers, skin, bones, beaks, teeth, feet, claws, eyes, brains and other internal organs. In short, *everything*, although indigestible material – such as teeth and fur – will be thrown up later as a pellet or 'casting'. Bearing all this in mind

- *never* attempt to feed your hawk with fruit, vegetables, bread, grain, 'bird' food, cat food, dog food, or cooked food of any kind
- except for limited periods (such as during early training or illness), don't feed her with flesh alone
- feed her only freshly-killed food (frozen animals are fine provided they were put in the freezer as soon as possible after killing and are offered shortly after de-frosting).

In falconry terms, different animals have different *food values*. This means that, ounce for ounce, one kind of animal will have a different effect on a hawk's weight compared to another. For example, although the weight and volume of four day-old chicks might be significantly greater than a small rat, the rat will increase her weight by much more.

Regulating a hawk's intake with the object of producing a fairly precise result in weight terms is not, therefore, simply a matter of giving her greater or lesser amounts of food, *unless* you feed her the same animal type over a period of time. This is precisely what most falconers do during the hawk's training, at least until flying weight has been established. Difficulties in weight control only then arise if and when she is fed game she has caught, or other kinds of food to vary her diet.

Nevertheless, it is advisable to give your hawk different types of food occasionally for three main reasons:
1. It helps to keep her diet properly balanced
2. It will give you experience of the impact different foods have on her weight
3. Feeding her animals she has caught will help develop her commitment to catching them.

As far as I know, no-one has yet produced a proper scientific analysis comparing one type of food with another and the effect each has on a hawk's weight, but most falconer's learn this, in a rough-and-ready way, through experience. I can't therefore give precise comparisons, but the following table should provide a reasonable guide to the most commonly-used food species.

Value	Food Type	Comments
Low	Day-old chicks (DOCs)	These are the staple diet of most falconry birds because (1) they are cheap and easily-obtained in bulk; (2) each can be broken up into convenient-sized pieces; and (3) their low food value means that more pieces can be fed to extend a hawk's training or flying time without compromising weight. On the downside, they tend to be low in calcium (because their bones aren't fully grown), and the quality of roughage they provide is not very good
Low	Rabbit	Although rabbit flesh is low in value, their fur provides very good roughage. Leg meat is relatively tough and hard to clean from the bone which gives hawks plenty of neck exercise. This process, and the hardness of the bones, helps to keep a hawk's beak in trim. Such assets, rather than their nutrition, are their main value to falconers
Low	Beef	Falconers normally use shin of beef or similar, but whichever cut is used, *all fat must be removed*. Beef's advantages are that it is clean to use and readily available. The meat itself is nutritious, but lacks roughage and calcium which have to be provided from other sources. Weight-for-weight it has a similar effect to day-old chicks and can be substituted for them – for instance in training or with a swing lure – without causing complications
Medium	Grown-on (or seven-day-old) chicks	Compared to DOCs, their flesh and plumage are much more fully-developed, giving additional nutrition and roughage, and their bones provide a full measure of calcium

Value	Food Type	Comments
High	Rats and Mice	Except in volume, these species are more or less identical in food value. Rats in particular tend to be smelly, and some birds find them unpalatable. But both species provide a high quality diet and they are useful especially during the moult or convalescence after illness
High	Quail	These are an excellent all-round food source. Their flesh is rich, and most hawks seem to enjoy it. Because of their cost, many falconers feed them only occasionally, but they are good for building up hawks during the moult or the breeding season, and after a period of illness

With the exception of rabbit (which, hopefully, your hawk will catch for herself) and beef (which you can get from any butcher), the rest are only available from specialist suppliers. Most sell them ready-frozen and in bulk, although items like quail you can usually buy singly. DOCs, for instance, come in lots of 200 to 250 – two to three months' supply for an average hawk. Many suppliers will deliver to your home, but generally only for large orders: if you only have a single hawk and limited freezer capacity, it is unlikely that your order will be large enough. In this case you will have to collect the food yourself.

Apart from these foods there is, of course, game itself:
- squirrel is roughly equivalent to rabbit (but tougher)
- rooks have a similar effect to grown-on chicks
- pheasant, duck, moorhen, coot and pigeon are comparable to quail (but see below).

Pigeons are notorious for carrying disease and they should never be fed unless they have been frozen first. Having said that, they are probably the best food for hawks. Like all water birds duck, coot and moorhen are fatty and should be skinned before you give them to a hawk. No such strictures apply to pheasants.

Nutritional Supplements

In certain circumstances captive hawks benefit from vitamin and mineral supplements added to their food, in particular
- during periods of stress, such as illness or convalescence
- if they are fed exclusively on one particular animal type for prolonged periods, especially day-old chicks
- during their annual moult
- when they are breeding.

Many falconers use a supplement called *SA-37*, which is sold in powder form and incorporates a wide range of essential nutrients. According to the manufacturer, a pinch of the powder sprinkled onto food once a week is sufficient to maintain the balance of these nutrients. *SA-37* is, therefore, very easy to administer, and a 200g carton will last a long time. In addition, it is very well-known and available from any vet. However, *SA-37* was formulated primarily for dogs and cats and contains elements designed to promote healthy fur and help lactating bitches produce the milk their puppies need, both of which are of little use to hawks. On the other hand, they won't do a hawk any harm. Despite such reservations, *SA-37* is certainly a useful adjunct and infinitely better than providing no supplement at all when it is most needed.

As an alternative, there is a much more expensive supplement on the market developed specially for birds of prey called *A1-Raptor*. Its makers argue that birds of prey are different to mammals in that they do not store vitamins and minerals in their bodies and therefore need a daily (rather than a weekly) intake. In addition, they claim to have formulated *separate* supplements for every falconry situation – for instance, newly-hatched chicks, growing chicks, breeding adults, moulting hawks, hunting hawks, as well as a general-purpose concoction.

A1-Raptor is complicated to use. According to its makers, the dose needed is directly related to the quantity of food the hawk eats, which involves weighing both the food and the supplement so that it is added in the correct proportions. This is a lot more fiddly and time-consuming than sprinkling a pinch on her food but its focused accuracy should increase its effectiveness.

Obviously any supplement targeted specifically at birds of prey is a better option if you can afford it. However, over-use of any supplement might cause more problems than it solves, and my recommendation is to use one only in the situations listed above. Indeed, during the moult, when weight control is no longer necessary, it is better to vary a hawk's diet by giving her a range of good whole foods (rats, quail, rabbit, or whatever else you have available) rather than rely on supplements.

Food Preparation

First and foremost, *everything* likely to come into contact with a hawk's food should be clean. This means not only your hands, but also freezers, fridges, knives, chopping boards, food-pockets in your bag, vest or waistcoat, your falconry glove, and so on. Just like wild hawks, falconry birds risk picking up all sorts of diseases and infections from their quarry or even from the hunting process itself (barbed wire fences immediately spring to mind) and it is senseless to increase this risk by feeding prepared food which is potentially unsafe. The best way to minimise risk is to treat all her bought-in food in the same way that you would treat your own.

In particular, frozen food must always be de-frosted thoroughly. The trick to killing harmful bacteria through freezing is to freeze slowly then de-freeze quickly. Length of time in the freezer is, in this respect, irrelevant. The quickest way to thaw frozen food is in a bowl of hot (but not boiling) water. Using this method, day-old chicks will thaw out in about twenty minutes. Larger animals will take longer, but in every case the essential requirement is that there is *enough* hot water to completely submerge the food. Any dead animal will float, but if the water-level is high enough to enable you to push it below the surface, that's the minimum you will need. The only disadvantage with this method is that fur and feathers get soggy and less pleasant to handle. Your hawk won't mind a bit and it is also a good way of getting additional fluid into her system but if it bothers you, dry the food out with paper towels. However desperate you are for instant hawk food, *never* attempt to de-frost it in a conventional oven or a microwave – you will cook the skin and flesh before sufficient heat reaches the internal organs even to melt the ice.

No food should be left lying around for days – the older it is, the more unsafe it will become. It is preferable to de-frost a day's supply at a time, or at most three days' rations if you can keep them in a fridge.

When weight control is not a consideration, you can throw your hawk whole lumps of food such as the hind leg or the head of a rabbit and she will break it up herself. Mice need no cutting up at all, but with rats some people snip off the tail with a pair of scissors. Rat tails don't provide much nutrition, and most hawks won't eat them unless they're desperate. Removing them saves collecting them later from her quarters.

With captive-bred mature poultry such as quail, many falconers cut off the head, remove the contents of the crop, and take out the intestines. This is a precautionary measure. Whole quail can be fed to hawks without any ill-effects, but butchering them in this way avoids the possibility that chemical additives and pesticides from grain and other foods poultry are fed might enter the hawk's digestive system. These elements tend to concentrate in the brain and intestines of poultry, and their crop often contains undigested feed. The contents of a quail's crop are irrelevant to a flesh-eating hawk's diet anyway, but the head and intestines contain essential vitamins which you will deny her by removing them. However, if you vary her diet sufficiently, she will retrieve all she needs from other kinds of food.

As you see, it is incredibly easy to become obsessive about food hygiene and dietary balance, but you must be sensible and pragmatic about it. One way is to draw a line between wild-caught quarry and artificially-produced foods allowing the hawk to feed on wild food (apart from pigeon) and let her take her chance. When you feed her bought-in food, take precautions and avoid crying all the way to the bank if you have to consult a vet.

Day-old chicks have a yolk sac inside their bodies. Whole chicks can be fed to hawks, but many falconers remove the yolks first. Although there is a lot of cholesterol in yolk, it doesn't appear to do hawks any harm even on a long-term basis. For those who do remove it, fears about the theoretical effects of cholesterol seem to be far outweighed by their dislike of the awful mess that punctured yolk sacs inevitably generate. Hawks themselves *relish* egg yolk. When they've taken in a beakful, they will stand on the fist and savour it with their tongues. The problem is that a beakful does not account for the contents of a yolk-sac. Whilst a hawk is standing on the glove enjoying the taste like an enraptured gourmet, the rest dribbles all over the working area of the glove and, if you're not careful, onto any clothing or footwear beneath it. Even worse, an over-enthusiastic hawk trying to swallow the whole sac will spray it all over the place.

Despite this, many falconers still give the yolk to their hawks, primarily because they enjoy it so much. The alternative could be considered gruesome. If you prefer to remove it, there are two methods. The first is to squeeze the belly of the chick so that the yolk is ejected out of its rear end. This takes practice, but done properly it is very effective. The second is to cut out the yolk sac with a small knife. This involves opening up the chick's belly and severing the sac's attachments. The problem with this method is that the chick's intestines are also liberated, and usually they refuse to stay in place. But, whatever you decide to do about the yolk, you need to make up your mind how you're going to deal with it before you start to train your hawk. If you feed her de-yolked chicks one day and whole ones the next, weight control will become even more difficult to achieve.

For training and work in the field, you need to decide on a staple diet for your hawk – firstly to make weight control easier; and secondly to give you plenty of food to work with. Even from the earliest stages, a hawk's rations will need to be broken up so that you can feed her small quantities at a time either to persuade her to respond, or reward her for doing the right thing. Bearing in mind that her diet should incorporate all an animal's body parts, this is difficult to achieve with some types of food. For example, even if you were prepared to separate it, the foreleg of a mouse is unlikely to tempt your hawk to do anything.

This is one of the main reasons why day-old chicks are so popular with falconers. One chick can be broken up into four substantial pieces – two legs, the head and the body. Because of their comparatively low food value, a Redtail at flying weight might eat three to four of them, which gives her handler up to sixteen tempting morsels to work with, and at the end of the session she will have eaten whole animals. In addition, the largest portion (the body) can be reserved as a bigger reward for doing something special (such as catching game) without exceeding her ration, or it can be withheld if you need to reduce weight further.

In contrast, a single rat or quail will put your hawk out of action for two or three days because either will increase her weight well beyond flying-weight limits. Of course, you can cut them up into little pieces and feed her only what she needs to keep her weight stable, but you will find that you have many fewer pieces to work with and she won't get the benefit of the 'whole animal'. How, for example, would you deal with the internal organs?

Breaking up day-old chicks is easy enough once you get the hang of it. Each leg is dislocated from its hip-socket by supporting the body either side of the joint with the finger and thumb of one hand, then pulling the leg out with the other. Chick bones still have some elasticity, and the operation requires only a small amount of force. You should end up with the whole leg from foot to hip with the meat of the thigh exposed. The head is removed simply by pinching the neck vertebrae between finger and thumb. Sever the neck as close as possible to the chick's body so that you have more to hold onto when you present the head to the hawk on the glove – if you want her to be tempted by it, she will need to be able to see the whole head.

An alternative for training and flying hawks is beef, which is also very easy to handle and provides a reasonable number of worthwhile portions in a day's ration. A strip ¼in by ¼in and about 1½in long should be sufficient to tempt a hawk back to the fist if she's familiar with this type of food. A dozen strips – or whatever constitutes her ration – are tidy and easily accessible compared to fumbling around in your pocket for a chick leg or a head.

However, there are two main problems with recommending beef as a means of controlling weight on a long-term basis:
1. Unlike day-old chicks, it doesn't come in conveniently-sized packages. If you buy a shin of beef, a day's ration for one hawk might only be 10 per cent of it. You can keep the rest refrigerated for two or three days, but after that it is too old to feed safely. If you own several hawks, it can be economical, but with only one the wastage-rate makes it expensive (unless you eat the rest yourself).
2. Beef is not a natural food for hawks. They don't normally feed on cattle, and what is available is basically doctored flesh for human consumption. For hawks it doesn't provide the range of ingredients necessary for a healthy diet. In particular it loses out on calcium (from bones), roughage (from fur or feathers), minerals and vitamins (from internal organs) – all of which have to be provided from other sources.

Even so, in the early stages of training, it can be useful to get a hawk started because a hungry hawk will always be attracted to raw flesh, whatever form it takes.

Buying A Hawk

Unfortunately, where falconry birds are concerned, there are no established pedigrees that you can depend on. This is partly because breeding hawks in captivity is a profession which has only come to the fore over the past few decades (much too short a period to develop reliable bloodlines), and partly because captive hawks are mainly reproductions of their wild counterparts. Unlike working dogs, which have been bred and cross-bred over many centuries to perform specific functions, hawks are hawks, all much the same as their wild cousins.

As in the wild, some will perform well and others won't. The difference is that a wild hawk which doesn't catch game won't survive. Indeed, it is estimated that something like 75 per cent of wild birds of prey die in their first year, although many of these deaths are caused by accidents, or bad luck, rather than starvation through inherited weaknesses.

One or two breeders are trying to address the problem by breeding only from hawks which have proved themselves in the field, but there is no guarantee that this will produce a good hawk. All wild parents 'prove' their competence by finding and catching enough prey not only to feed themselves but also to raise their young. Yet a proportion of their brood will still die when they try to go it alone. This is a basic law of nature, and if it were not so the world would be swamped by all kinds of hawk looking for food. This natural control means that any breeder's brood will probably contain a similar proportion of 'weaker' birds, whatever their parents' prowess in the field.

There is nothing you or the breeder can do about this, and it is impossible to tell, looking at a group of young hawks, which of them will become the best performers. However, if you happen to pick one which might not survive its first year as a wild hawk, with proper support and training, it can still be made into a successful – even a good – falconry bird.

Sources of Information

Breeding birds for falconry is a specialised activity for a highly specialised market. It is generally confined to practising falconers, or people who used to fly birds themselves but now make a living by breeding them. Falconers, through their own involvement with the sport, know who these people are, where to contact them, what kinds of bird they specialise in, and how good their reputations are in terms of the 'quality of their product'.

For an outsider, though, it can be very difficult to find even a starting point. You are unlikely, for example, to find hawks for sale in any of the regular national, regional or local newspapers. Neither will you see breeders advertising or even mentioned in Yellow Pages (or similar business directories), and you certainly won't find falconry birds in pet shops. However, there is a weekly publication called *Cage and Aviary Birds*, which is produced for owners of all kinds of captive-bred species from finches to vultures. Many hawks for sale are advertised in its 'classified ads'. This isn't a magazine normally available off-the-shelf in newsagents, but most will order it for you on a regular basis.

Although this is an interesting publication in its own right, you need to remember that classified ads – wherever they appear – don't give you enough information. Nevertheless, it can be a valuable starting point.

Alternatively, organisations associated with birds of prey such as The Hawk Conservancy, The Welsh Hawking Centre, or The National Birds of Prey Centre are always good sources of information. They will know of, and might be able to recommend, someone who is breeding the kind of bird you want. Indeed, they could be involved in such breeding projects themselves.

However, if you are interested in buying one of their birds, they might first want to know something about you – such as your experience, your training, why you want the particular species you're enquiring about, and whether you've got suitable housing. By doing this they are trying to ensure that all their hawks go to good homes, and will be trained and cared for by someone who knows what they're doing. They may ask similar questions before recommending other breeders. Another alternative is a falconry club. Some have breeding programmes of their own, but they are usually set up to provide birds for members only. If you're already a member (which is possible in some clubs, even if you don't possess a hawk), you should know what's available and what conditions will be imposed if you acquire one. But even if you're not a member, any club might still be prepared to give you advice on where to go.

Deciding What You Want

From all this you might have gathered that a reputable breeder will avoid selling his birds to just anybody, and you will need to prepare yourself for any questions he might ask. Honesty is by far the best policy. Where falconry is concerned, it isn't difficult to establish whether you've trained and flown a bird before. If you tell him the truth, you will find him a lot more helpful and accommodating. If you don't, he might refuse to supply you with any of his birds.

Of course, you have a right to ask questions too, but before you do, you need to sort out in your own mind exactly what you want him to supply. In particular:
- the species of bird you're looking for
- its sex
- whether you want an adult or a fledgling (eyass)
- if it's an eyass, how you want it to be reared.

Species of broadwings, and their sex, are largely matters of personal preference. Bearing in mind what has already been said in the section headed *First Hawks* (where it is suggested that the Common Buzzard is one of three species suitable) there is much less difference in size between buzzard males and females than with other broadwings.

For juvenile birds overall size (perhaps more accurately, leg size) is often the only guide to gender the breeder has. Where buzzards are concerned, therefore, no-one can guarantee to provide one sex or the other. If, for instance, you want a male, all the breeder can do is to rely on his experience and choose smaller individuals. Size difference is more pronounced in Harris' Hawks and Redtails, so you should have less difficulty. But even with these birds, sex can't be guaranteed without surgery.

Adult hawks are usually available all year round – either because a breeder has a surplus from a previous season, or because someone is advertising a bird already trained which, for some reason, they want to sell on. Another source is rescue centres where birds are handed in because they are no longer wanted. Don't consider any of these at this stage. An adult hawk which has lived in an aviary for many months is a very difficult training prospect, and may be too set in her ways to change. Similarly, a previously-trained bird – rescuee or otherwise – could have acquired bad habits which might prove very hard to eradicate. With an eyass you can start (almost) with a clean slate.

Most broadwings breed fairly easily in captivity either naturally or through artificial insemination (AI). In terms of the biological quality of the bird, it doesn't really matter which of these methods is used, but what does matter is how the bird is reared after hatching. Her early up-bringing will determine her personality – in other words, how she behaves towards her own species, and in particular how she views human beings and their environment.

Some hawks are deliberately 'imprinted'. Imprinting is the learning process in very young animals that fixes social preferences towards a parent, or a substitute for a parent – in this case, human beings. Through imprinting, hawks can be conditioned into believing that people are:

1. Their sexual partners (these are known as sex imprints, and are produced for the purpose of breeding by means of AI)
2. Their social partners (known as social imprints – a method useful for manning difficult species such as goshawks and sparrowhawks)
3. Their sole food-providers (called food imprints – see below).

The science of imprinting any animal is a highly technical subject, and in detail it is way beyond the scope of this manual. Although it has definite uses where accipiters are concerned it does, on the whole, tend to favour the breeder rather than the falconer.

For example, feeding a clutch of chicks by hand can usually result in another batch of eggs from the parents who will lay again if their first clutch is removed. Obviously this means that the parents will produce more young, and therefore more birds to sell. This is clearly important in terms of meeting the demand for certain birds, but hand-rearing the first clutch will produce food imprints – unless specific action is taken to foster them with at least one non-breeding adult of the same species.

Total food imprints (which will also be social and sex imprints) will have been fed exclusively by human beings since hatching. From a falconer's point of view, these are the very worst birds he could acquire because:

*   they're trapped for the rest of their lives in an infantile behaviour pattern, which means that every time they see (or hear) a human being they will scream for food. Even if you can put up with the noise, your neighbours probably won't
*   they have no fear at all of (or respect for) human beings and once you start reducing their weight they might become unacceptably aggressive towards you.

Frankly, if you intend to buy a broadwing, no kind of imprint will be of any benefit to you. On the contrary, the bird is likely to be a liability. You need, therefore, to make clear to the breeder that you want a hawk which has been parent-reared (foster parents are acceptable as long as fostering was initiated within a week or two of hatching).

Whatever contact a parent-reared bird has had with human beings should be minimal – confined to hand-feeding for the first few days (if necessary), and attaching closed rings (if any) to her legs. Even food should have been placed in the aviary by a hatch system enabling parents to take it to the young themselves without any obvious signs of human involvement.

To be fair, no respectable breeder these days is likely to sell you even a partially imprinted hawk unless you specifically ask for one. Not only is it a time-consuming process but it is not in their long-term interests to do so. Reputations are built on the quality of their hawks and on the willingness of past customers to come back for more. Even so, the maxim *caveat emptor* (let the buyer beware) still rules.

Choosing a Breeder

Captive hawks start breeding at roughly the same time of year as their wild cousins, usually some time in April. Normally their young will be fully-fledged and will have left the nest by mid-July. You are more likely, therefore, to find advertisements for eyasses just before the breeding season begins. However, if you want a species in great demand, such as a Harris' Hawk, the earlier you contact the breeder the better – even before the start of the breeding season if that's possible. Many deal with clients on a 'first-come-first-served-basis', so the sooner you order one, the more chance you will have of getting what you want.

This is especially relevant if you are particular about the sex you want your bird to be. No breeder has any influence over the sex of his birds' chicks, and he might not be certain of the mix until the whole brood is (more or less) fully-grown. If he has six males and seven people wanting one, the last to place an order will be disappointed.

A good breeder will place a closed ring around one leg of a new hawk even if this isn't legally required (see the section headed *Falconry and the Law*). It will be stamped with a unique set of characters which will identify him as the breeder. Documentation (such as an 'Article 10 Certificate') detailing the bird and its origins may be required by law, but even if it isn't, good breeders will provide something along these lines. Usually this includes identification details (yours, the breeder's and the hawk's) and the condition the bird is in when you collect her.

If he doesn't provide either of these as a matter of course, be careful. Should you be dissatisfied with the hawk's condition later on when you've had a better chance to assess it (perhaps even after a veterinary examination), will he willingly take her back and give you a replacement? Or is he more likely to argue that whatever's wrong happened after you took custody? The worst scenario is that he could deny having sold the bird to you at all and you will possess no evidence that he did.

Some breeders attach a second ring, stamped with a phone number, in case the bird subsequently becomes lost. If she's found, he will then be able to tell the finder who owns the bird (or at least, who bought her) through his records. Such schemes are particularly valuable for birds which no longer have to be registered with the Department for Environment, Food and Rural Affairs (DEFRA). If the breeder doesn't provide this service, there are other organisations – such as the *Independent Bird Register* – which do and which might be worth exploring at a later date.

To sum up, I would offer the following advice:
- only choose a breeder from those that falconry organisations (or falconers you know and trust) are prepared to recommend
- find as many as you can which will potentially meet all your requirements (because they breed the kind of bird you want)
- if you have a choice, select those that are as near as possible to you geographically
- contact them to compare prices and breeding methods
- make a final selection and confirm your order with a deposit (if required)
- find out how the breeder will want you to pay the balance, and ask him to estimate when you will be able to collect your bird

The breeder might offer to send the hawk to you via a specialist animal courier. This is, of course, an option, but it means that you don't get to choose the bird. However, if the breeder has only one of the kind of bird you want, and you are prepared to accept it, then sending it by courier will obviously save you a return journey. Otherwise, you should always choose your own bird, which means collecting her yourself.

Depending on how far in advance you've ordered your hawk, the breeder might not be able to give you a precise date for collection. He will want to make sure that the whole brood is at least hard-penned (fully-fledged) and that each individual has already gained some independence from its parents – in other words, that they've all properly 'left the nest'. You will need, therefore, to contact him again nearer the estimated time to make final arrangements.

When you make these, bear in mind that you have to get there, spend some time with the breeder, get back home, then fit essential equipment to keep the bird under control. Considering that you're likely to be collecting an eyass in late July or August, you should avoid driving home during the worst heat of the day (say, between 10.00 am and 2.00 pm), though this depends on how far you have to go, and what sort of weather conditions you expect. However, one or two breeders might want to retain their birds longer – perhaps until late September – in an effort to minimise 'screaming' which is more of a habit in some broadwings than others. If this is the case, weather becomes less of a problem.

What You Should Take With You

Well before you start out to keep your appointment, you will need to acquire a strong cardboard box with a floor-area about eighteen inches by two feet, and walls about two feet high. This is for transporting the bird back home. A cardboard box might sound like a crude way of carrying a valuable hawk, but in fact it's one of the best because:
1. It is sympathetic to feathers – there are no sharp corners or other hard surfaces on which a bird could damage them if she decides to thrash about inside
2. It isn't airtight, so there is never any danger of suffocation
3. It provides good insulation against draughts, heat and cold
4. It's light and relatively easy to carry
5   It's top-loading.
With a top-loading carrier like this, it is much easier to cast a bird properly before taking her out to fit anklets and jesses, and a cardboard box is both free and disposable.

Secure the base with packaging tape to make sure the flaps can't come apart, and place an old piece of carpet inside to give the bird something to grip with her feet during the journey. Make sure also that the box has flaps at the top which
can be closed securely to stop her breaking out. The recommended method of closure is as shown.
Although this method is fairly secure, panicking hawks have been known to break out of them and a wild 3lb Redtail flapping around in the car on the Motorway home does not help concentration. As additional security therefore, the flaps should be taped down
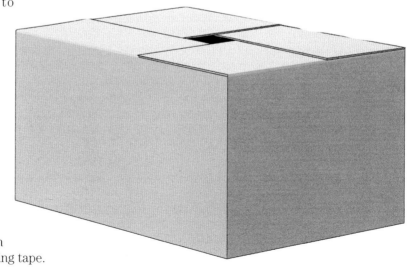
with normal plastic packaging tape.

As an alternative to a cardboard box, there are many types of plastic carriers available in pet shops (designed primarily for four-legged animals) which can also be used. If you intend to take one of these, the mesh door should be 'blacked out' – for example, with a piece of cardboard or plastic bin-liner cut to size – which will help to keep your bird calm on the journey home. Covering the door will also ensure that the hawk doesn't damage her feathers by inadvertently poking them through the mesh when she moves around. However, useful though these carriers are for transporting trained birds, you should be warned that it is difficult to extricate a wild hawk from one while still keeping her fully under control.

The problem lies in the fact that they are front-loading. You can place a cast hawk inside easily, but when you open the door to get her out again she will immediately make for daylight and attempt to fly out. Even if you can avoid this, as soon as you put your hands inside to cast her she will use her feet to defend herself. The only way to get her out is to open the door just enough to slide your gloved hand inside, grab her feet, then yank her out before she has time to damage her plumage on the carrier by flapping her wings.

Another item to consider is some kind of tape to protect the bird's tail-feathers. Whatever container you use, she will move around inside – circling, backing up, moving forwards, etc – if only to ease her tension. Consequently her tail will come into contact with the walls of her container much more than any other part of her anatomy. Wrapping tape over the full length of her tail will stiffen it and help prevent permanent damage to the quills. The best type to use is two-inch wide packaging tape, but not the plastic self-adhesive kind. You need glue-backed brown-paper tape which has to be moistened before it will stick. This is the easiest to remove (simply by wetting it again), and it won't itself cause any damage.

Choosing a Bird

Selecting a bird is, without doubt, one of the most difficult aspects of falconry, especially the first time. Most likely you will have paid a deposit (usually 10 per cent to 20 per cent of the bird's full price) and, after travelling some distance to get to the breeder's address, you will feel committed. In a sense you are since he's reserved the bird for you. But, if you don't like his set-up, or any of the birds he is offering, you have every right to back out and say 'no'. Indeed, this is your last chance to do so. If you decide to do that, you might lose your deposit, and you will surely have difficulty, at such a late stage, finding someone else who can provide you with the bird you want. Even so, if you're really unhappy, that is what you must do.

The first thing you might query is the state of the aviary itself. It will look as though it hasn't been properly cleaned for months – as indeed it probably hasn't. There will be evidence of mutes all over the place, and parts might look something like the white cliffs of Dover. But, for a breeding aviary, this is normal. If you want a parent-reared bird, no respectable breeder will enter the aviary during the breeding season to clean it out when the parents still have young to feed. If they did, it would defeat the whole object of the exercise, which is to minimise human contact.

What really matters is the aviary's design. It should have plenty of space and natural light, together with perches at different levels, some of which are under cover. Cover is essential for shade and protection from wind and rain. Open areas should be enclosed with good quality wire mesh – ordinary chicken-wire is notorious for damaging feathers and, in rarer circumstances, beaks.

First, if possible, make sure you see all the birds you're choosing from in their aviary. If they're properly parent-reared, they will not welcome your presence and will fly around the enclosure in a state of anxiety. Watch their flight. Try and make sure they don't have any essential feathers missing, and that they manoeuvre well between obstacles. In other words, satisfy yourself that they have all the physical attributes necessary to fly properly.

The breeder, or an assistant, will have to go into the enclosure to catch one of the birds, usually with a large net, but before he does he will need to know which one you want a closer look at. Point out the bird you fancy most from what you've seen already, and he will bring her out for closer examination. When he does, check in particular:

- her eyes, which should be clear, bright and alert
- her beak and cere (the waxy material surrounding her nostrils), which should be undamaged and properly formed
- inside her mouth, which should be a healthy pink
- her legs and feet, which should also be uninjured and without deformities
- major plumage – meaning wing and tail feathers.

On this last item, look in particular for evidence of fret marks (lines across the barbs of the feather which look as though they've been made with a razor blade). Fret marks (also known as hunger traces) are totally unacceptable. They mean that the hawk has either suffered a trauma or, at some point in her early life, been close to starvation. Fret marks severely weaken the feather, and sooner or later it will break off at the point of weakness.

Check also that the quills are not bent or fractured. If they are, they will stick out at an odd angle, or refuse to re-align themselves properly with adjacent feathers. Bent feathers can be straightened, but fractured quills will require a serious repair and are equivalent to fret marks. Also, check that the feather-tips of the wings and tail are all still in place. If not, it usually means that the bird has made a great deal of contact with the wire mesh or other aspects of the enclosure, which tends to break the tips leaving a 'V' shaped gap. This is by no means a serious problem, but it could indicate hyper-activity, or there could be a number of other reasons. Ask the breeder for his explanation.

In fairness, you can't expect perfect plumage on an eyass which has spent some time in a wired enclosure in competition with her siblings, and minor imperfections are inevitable. Her plumage will also look a lot worse than normal because she's just been flying around the enclosure trying to escape the breeder. Neither this activity, nor her subsequent manhandling, will do her appearance any favours. Tail feathers might also be grubby and soiled with mutes as a result of perching on the nest-ledge. But she will soon put things right once she's got a place of her own where she can bathe, preen and zip her feathers back into place.

When you've made your final choice, ask the breeder if he will fit anklets and jesses. This might as well be done whilst the bird is still cast, and it will make getting her out of the travel box much easier when you get her home. He will probably charge you for them, but it will be worth it. Alternatively, you could take a set with you.

The breeder will also have his own procedures to follow. They will incorporate getting the bird into the container you brought with you and making sure that she's secure for the journey home, dealing with any residual paperwork, and obviously accepting the balance of payment. If the breeder's paperwork doesn't include one, get a formal receipt for any money you give him. This has nothing to do with trust. It is, first and foremost, good business practice, and secondly, it will provide you with additional evidence that you obtained the bird legally if ever this is needed.

Getting the Bird Home

When you take her in the box to load her into the car, under no circumstances put her in a closed boot. There are good reasons for saying this:

1. Closed boots are not capable of being sufficiently ventilated, especially on a hot summer's day
2. Whichever car you have, there is always a chance that exhaust fumes will leak into the boot, and without adequate ventilation these could prove fatal
3. If she's confined to the boot, you can't listen out for signs of prolonged distress.

The best place to put her is on the back seat with the box wedged in somehow to keep it as stable as possible during the journey.

If you've secured either type of container in the way suggested, it should by now be fairly well blacked-out and the comparative darkness will keep your hawk reasonably calm during the journey. Even so, travelling in any car will be a totally new experience for her, and at first the noise might cause her some anxiety until she gets used to it. But once she realises that it doesn't represent a threat, she should adjust fairly quickly.

One thing she will have to deal with until you get her home is the car's movement. Steep acceleration with nippy gear-changes, hard braking, and driving fast around sharp bends will all throw her off balance unmercifully. She can't see what's happening and all she will have to aid her balance is an old piece of carpet on the floor of her box. This doesn't mean you should crawl home or drive at abnormal speeds. All it means is that you should keep your driving as smooth as possible.

Also, if it is a hot day, ensure that you have adequate ventilation throughout the car to avoid any possibility that the bird will become over-heated. This is especially important if you get stuck in a traffic jam. Throughout the journey, listen for signs of undue distress. Any bird will 'thump' the box (or crate) with her feet occasionally but, if she's really unhappy, she will thump, flutter and move about constantly. If the box is secure enough she won't come to any harm, but it might help to ease off and slow down.

The object of the exercise is to get her home in good physical shape, but also in the best possible frame of mind. You can only do that by recognising the stress she's experiencing, and showing some empathy for her situation.

Vital Homework

Introduction

There are many falconers in Britain who know their part of the countryside intimately. They know all about potential quarry, and how and where to find it. They know the significance and value of the wind for hawks, dogs and game, and the advantages and disadvantages of different kinds of terrain. They know how to select, train and work various breeds of dog; and how to use other flushing tools such as ferrets. Send any of them out for a couple of hours with an unentered hawk, and you could guarantee that he would come back with something 'in the bag'.

If, like me, you weren't born into a country sport such as falconry or shooting, you can't hope to match the fieldcraft of such people – even if you spend the rest of your life trying. It is very easy, therefore, to feel terminally intimidated by their expertise. Remember though, that they are setting the highest standards in falconry, and through them the sport itself is both ennobled and defined. It is more positive to view them as sources of inspiration and as role-models. The vast majority of practising falconers – whatever their backgrounds – never achieve the same level of skill, but the standards set by these supremos provide something for us all to measure performance against.

In learning to hunt with a hawk, your first problem will be that there is no factual answer to the question: how do they do it? You could say that they do it in the same way as an angler who looks at a river, studies its currents and eddies, then picks out a particular spot. He knows what type and quality of fish he is likely to find there, what tackle to use, and which bait will attract them most. Above all, he knows exactly how to hook them when they take his bait, then how to land them successfully. If you ask him how he achieves large catches consistently, he will probably give you an unhelpful answer – such as 'luck'. From his point of view, if you need to ask, you're not even on the same wavelength and it might take him a month to explain.

One fact is certain – you can't teach a corporate executive how to hunt on a weekend break. This is because hunting doesn't have any of the man-made rules and processes that he lives by. He would have to tap into a much deeper human self to bring him into the real world that wildlife occupies. All predators, including humans, learn to hunt through a process of trial and error. Of course, they have many qualities which evolution has given them such as instinct, speed along the ground or in the air, or the ability to use tools and brains but whatever potential their genes possess can only be realised through personal experience.

Hunting is not, therefore, just a matter of technique or buying the right kind of equipment. Far from it. For consistent success, you must firstly learn to tap into your own instincts and 'think' like your quarry. This statement might provoke another question: who exactly is doing the hunting here – me or the hawk? There is only one right answer: *you are*. If you allow your hawk to hunt for herself, you are actively encouraging her to become independent.

Obviously you want your hawk to catch quarry – indeed, the training you give her will lead her to this point – but if you also want to maintain control over her when she's flying free, you must *serve* her with it. 'Serving' means finding and flushing quarry in such a way that she has a fair chance of securing it. If you can do this consistently, she'll stick by you: if you fail consistently, she might fly off in disgust, or worse, give up altogether.

Not only must you learn to think like your quarry, you must also develop an understanding of your hawk and her needs. For example, you should be constantly asking yourself questions like: where is the wind coming from? will it help or hinder her? how far is the quarry from alternative cover? could she catch it before it gets there? if not, will I be able to find it and flush it again so that she gets another chance? Eventually answering such questions will become second nature. In the meantime the answers will depend much more on your own knowledge and abilities than on your hawk's, and even less on environmental factors.

One further point needs to be made. Shooters flush game, then shoot the quarry as it's trying to escape. But the quarry can't see the shot and is unable to take evasive action. In contrast, a pursuing hawk is plainly visible, and all prey species have a repertoire of stratagems to help them survive what is, for them, a natural event. This means that even experienced hawks often fail because the edge they have over their prey is very slight. For an unentered hawk, it is virtually non-existent, which is one reason why so many wild ones die young. You can't, therefore, expect your hawk to catch everything you flush, but there must be a balance between failure and success.

This balance is much more important for your young hawk and her confidence than it is for you. She is programmed to accept a degree of disappointment, but not constant failure. How it will work out in practice is impossible to predict with any reliability because it depends on too many variables – you, your hawk, her fitness, the quality of your partnership, the terrain, the weather, the time of year, the availability of suitable game, the type of quarry your hawk is chasing, and so on. But if she's catching nothing (even the odd mouse or vole) you have a serious problem. If she's catching ten out of ten, you're either already a supremo, or quarry is as thick as flies around a carcass. Otherwise, if you've done everything right, in her first year you should expect a success rate of something like 20 per cent to 30 per cent.

Hunting will be a continuous process of learning for both of you. You must be prepared to analyse what happens during each flush and flight and, if necessary, find ways of improving your efforts next time to give her a better chance. Your hawk will work things out in her own way, but if you don't match her by optimising your service she is likely to become too selective by refusing to pursue any type of quarry she has consistently lost. The ultimate in selectivity is when she refuses to chase anything.

All this might seem like a very big leap for you to make, but don't despair. Even as a total beginner, there is much you can do to kick start yourself into a hunting career if you are prepared to do some homework. In outline the homework programme is simple, but it requires research, legwork, and other kinds of effort on your part. In addition, it must be done before you attempt to take the exam, which is entering your hawk. You might already have heard similar sentiments expressed in relation to your own future, but in this case the life of your hawk might be at stake. If you lose her before she's been entered and isn't quickly killed by some other predator, she will most likely die by degrees through the slow process of starvation. The programme is:

1. Find out which quarry species your kind of hawk is capable of catching
2. Learn everything you can about each one
3. Find as many places as possible where they are sufficiently abundant
4. Obtain permission from landowners to hunt there
5. Reconnoitre each ground thoroughly.

Potential Quarry

To some extent, this subject has already been covered in the section headed *Hawks and Falconry*, but there is additional information specific to broadwings in the section headed *Notes on Quarry*. Alternative falconry literature might give you other ideas and, if you get an opportunity, it is advisable to read that too.

Habits and Habitats

If you have no hunting experience at all, the only learning advantage you could possibly have over your hawk is the availability of a vast wealth of stored information – books, magazines, videos, computer networks, personal contacts, and so on – any or all of which you can refer to to bring yourself up to speed. All she has is her genetic inheritance, which incorporates body design and instincts. Believe it or not, these two assets alone could, within a matter of weeks, out-perform any 'hi-tech' input you might be able to contribute.

To give yourself a reasonable chance, therefore, you must learn as much as you can about each quarry's lifestyle – in particular preferred habitats, what it eats and when, social and breeding patterns, and survival strategies when attacked by predators. There are many books available in libraries which incorporate relevant material on a factual and naturalistic basis (through field studies and the like), and they are very useful. For example, they can provide information on where to find rabbits; how to recognise a warren and judge how big it is; where the likely bolt holes are and if it is currently being used. Similarly they will help you to assess whether or not the local agricultural pattern is advantageous for hares; where they lie up in the daytime; what species you are likely to find; and how they differ from other kinds.

Such material will tell you how and where to locate potential quarry, but not how to hunt it. Curiously – even though you might expect to find guidance there – many falconry books don't cover the subject of hunting very well either (at least, from the point of view of how to do it). This is probably because it is a very difficult activity to explain, and many authors rely on anecdotes to get their message across. The main difficulty is that each flush and flight is unique. What makes them unique is not only how they occur, but also every aspect of the immediate surroundings – the wind, the nature and quality of cover, the proximity of the hawk, what kind of perch she's working from, and so on. Nevertheless, absorb as much as you can. In particular, note any differences in technique for your type of hawk, and be prepared to try them all – if they work for the author, they might work just as well for you. There is also some elementary information in the section headed *Entering and Basic Hunting* (page 150). Once you've done some homework on 'search-and-flush' theory, there is nothing to compare with the practical knowledge you can gain from experienced people going after the same quarry. These might be other falconers (if you're lucky), ferreters, rough shooters, or game shooters. You can often find such people in rural pubs which, after a hard day's hunting, are one of the best places to recount the day's events to anyone who will listen. Take some money with you, and be prepared to buy a few rounds.

The ideal preparation is to go out with one of them on a field trip. If you ever get such an opportunity, treat it like a gold-strike. When you are out there, and using your best efforts at diplomacy, find out what provoked them to make important decisions such as where to look for quarry, how to flush it, and why they took the action they did after it ran or flew. In fact 'why?' is often the most useful question you can ask, but be very careful not to overdo it, otherwise they might never invite you out again.

Locating Hunting Grounds

Ordnance Survey maps in the Explorer series (2½in to 1 mile – 4cm to 1km) are extremely useful for finding previously unknown areas and potential hunting grounds. Not only are rights of way (footpaths and bridleways) accurately marked, but also field boundaries as well as other relevant topographical features like rivers, streams and woods. If you have a dog, you can use footpaths to walk him and do a preliminary survey of the ground at the same time. Even though you must stick to the paths at this stage because you don't have permission to be on the land, a good dog will help you assess what game there is. Otherwise you will have to do the best you can from observation.

Apart from the presence of game, there are other features that broadwings need for successful hunting. The land should be reasonably open, but with plenty of mature trees, hedgerows, fence-posts, bushes, areas of rough ground and, if possible, hills and valleys. It will then provide high and low perches for the hawk to work from, cover for her quarry so that you can flush it, and open areas over which she can chase it giving you a good view of her flights. Hill slopes will provide updrafts which will enable her to gain height and do some soaring.

A common mistake that beginners make in selecting hunting grounds is that they are usually too small. They find a copse or tree-lined gully a few hundred yards long, apparently infested with rabbits, and it looks like an ideal place. In its way it is, but as soon as the hawk puts in an appearance the rabbits disappear underground and the hawk – whether visually or physically – ranges the whole area in a few minutes. A fit dog with a good nose might do it even quicker. *Remember*: hawks and hunting dogs soak up ground like a kitchen towel soaks up water.

The ground you choose, therefore, needs to be a reasonable size – say big enough to allow at least a two-hour leisurely walk, preferably via a circular route (bearing in mind that, once you are hunting, you won't have to stick to paths). You will probably take your hawk there by car, and you will want to start and finish each session as close as possible to where you parked it.

You will need to find at least three or four such places – preferably more – to give you and your hawk the best possible chance of success. It is not a good idea to hunt the same ground every day, or even every few days. Over-hunted game is easily spooked, and will dive for cover before you get anywhere near it. You might have some initial success, but you will soon get no flights at all. If you are relying on only one hunting ground, therefore, you might end up with a miserable season and an undisciplined, unpractised hawk – assuming you don't lose her in the meantime.

Seeking Permission

Once you've identified a suitable place, you need to find the landowner and obtain his permission to fly your hawk there. This sounds simple enough, but there are many complications which often make this aspect of falconry one of the most difficult and frustrating.

After spending hours, days, or even weeks selecting a hunting ground which seems ideal, you might discover that several bits of it belong to different people. Whilst there are some magnates who have bought up thousands of adjoining acres, more often than not rural areas are a patchwork quilt of landowners. Indeed, you might even find that title to a vital piece from your point of view is a matter of dispute between two or three of them. Even so, to make the ground viable, you must get permission from all its owners. If you obtain permission from only three out of four, but decide to hunt there nevertheless, you could end up in trouble if your hawk catches quarry on land belonging to the fourth. As Sod's law has it, this is highly likely at some point, and you will then be guilty of poaching.

The first step in seeking permission is to knock on a few doors. Obviously if there is a farmhouse or a laird's castle in the middle of the patch you're interested in, this will be your starting point. If the landowner doesn't live there, the occupier should at least be able to tell you who he is and where you can locate him. Otherwise, anybody working on the land will be a useful source of information. Face-to-face contact with the owner is preferable, but if he lives in another county you might have to resort to the phone or a letter. Of these, the phone is better, mainly because anything other than vital correspondence is easily put aside.

When you establish contact, things are not necessarily straightforward either. In effect, you are asking each landowner to give you a favour. Ideally you want unrestricted access to his land, and to pocket any game your hawk catches even though legally it belongs to him because you caught it on his ground. It isn't common practice for landowners to charge falconers for their activity (unless you're planning to hunt grouse), but this means that there isn't much incentive for him to agree.

Of course, he will welcome the fact that you might catch a few 'vermin' like rabbits, squirrels, rooks or crows, but he could be using part of the land to breed pheasants or partridge to shoot in the season. Even if he isn't, he might have valuable livestock to worry about, such as lambs and chickens. He knows that all of these are vulnerable to large aggressive hawks like broadwings. Your simple request could, therefore, present him with a problem he would much sooner do without. Ironically, the more he is in favour of falconry as a country sport, the bigger his problem might be. If he's totally against, he will refuse right away. If he's in favour, he will have to assess the risks involved in giving you permission.

You have to ask yourself: why should he? And there isn't an encouraging answer. You are entirely at his mercy. If he refuses, you must accept his decision graciously whatever his reasons, then thank him for listening and go on your way. *Remember*: you have nothing to sell, and if you attempt to create a sales pitch – or you come across as too pushy in some other way – you will destroy your chances forever. If you deal with him sensibly, there is a good chance he might change his mind at some future date, especially if his neighbours agree to give you access to their land.

If, as is likely, you are a total stranger to him, the only thing that could possibly allay his fears are your credentials. For example, if you live locally, he is much more likely to be receptive compared to someone who comes from a hundred miles away. Obviously if you have mutual friends or acquaintances, this fact could influence him greatly. Similarly, if an adjacent landowner has already given permission, this can also be persuasive (provided that they are not deadly enemies). In the end, though, you must convince him that you are a genuine and responsible person and, from his point of view, harmless. In this respect, seeking permission is itself a responsible act, but proof of membership of recognised falconry or other field sports clubs can also go a long way to eliminating suspicion and building trust. Even snapshots of you and your hawk can help because they are evidence that you are what you say you are.

Once you have the landowner's agreement, make sure you know exactly where his boundaries are. An Explorer map of the area will enable him to point out which fields and other topographical features are his. Just as important, it will make it easy for him to indicate which areas he wants you to leave alone, such as those containing breeding pens. He might also insist that you avoid any fields with livestock especially if you have a dog. It goes without saying that you must respect his limitations. If you don't, not only will he withdraw his favours, neighbouring landowners will probably follow suit.

Another possible complication is that the landowner might already have given hunting rights to someone else. Usually this will be a group of people who shoot pheasant or partridge as a sport. The problem is that they pay the landowner for the right to breed these birds on his land, and to shoot them in the season. Whilst he might not personally be against you flying your hawk in the same area, he will not want to risk losing this custom and will refer you to the shoot organiser, making your access entirely conditional upon his agreement.

Rearing large numbers of gamebirds each year can be an expensive business. In some cases, expensive enough to justify creating syndicates to spread the costs, and employing gamekeepers to minimise losses. Such costs are additional to any charge that the landowner might levy for the use of his land. These people know full well that hawks and gamebirds don't mix. Indeed, if native hawks weren't legally protected, they would eliminate every one of them straying into gamebird territory by whatever means necessary. For them, no kind of hawk is tolerable. Even the diminutive sparrowhawk will take young pheasant poults from a breeding pen because, in this early stage of life, they are easy prey.

It is completely unrealistic, therefore, to expect gamebird shooters to allow your hawk anywhere near their breeding and hunting grounds whenever you feel like it, whether you're a total stranger or not. Even if you can convince them that she isn't likely to catch many, hunting there, especially if you use a dog, could spook the whole batch sufficiently to spread them far and wide. That in itself could have disastrous consequences for their shooting activities.

Given this gloomy scenario, you have only two options. Either you accept defeat and find somewhere else, or you offer to become part of the syndicate by paying for x number of gamebirds to be reared each year. If the organiser has any sense, x won't represent the number your bird is likely to catch, but the number he thinks the syndicate will lose by your presence. In the end what you negotiate will depend partly on your financial circumstances, but mostly on how much you think you need that particular ground.

Assuming that you achieve success in obtaining flying grounds, the best way to show your appreciation for a landowner's favour, deal with difficult situations, and promote your own cause for the future, is by generating as much goodwill as possible whenever you can. For example
- by avoiding any areas the landowner (or shoot organiser) has asked you to leave alone
- by inviting him out with you and the bird on occasions – if he's interested enough (and has the time)
- by reporting such things as broken fences or gates, and escaped or injured livestock
- by giving no-one any reason to complain about your presence, such as engineering a successful flight in full view of a family's back garden
- by occasionally giving the landowner (and shoot organiser if there is one) a token of your appreciation – such as a decent bottle of whisky or port, say, at Christmas time.

Reconnoitring the Ground

Once you've obtained permission to be there, you should do a thorough survey of the ground before you attempt to fly your hawk – for two reasons. Firstly, because you need to get a more accurate picture of what kind of game the ground supports and in what numbers. Secondly, because you need to locate and memorise access points between significant topographical features such as rivers and hedgerows.

If you've done your homework on quarry species and their habits, and if you've chosen your ground well from walking surveys, you shouldn't experience much trouble with the first.

Nevertheless, it pays to do some dress-rehearsals at flushing game. Analyse what happens. For example:was the flush an accident or truly engineered by you? where did the quarry go; and why? could you locate it a second time and flush it again? during its run or flight, was it forced to cross open ground? where was the wind coming from? did the wind affect its run or flight in any way? where would you have wanted your hawk to be? why? and how would you have got her there?

Hawks don't recognise hedges or fences, except as potential perches, and there is nothing more frustrating than seeing yours connect with quarry in the next field with a thick hedgerow between you and her and no way through in sight. It follows that you need to find out beforehand where the nearest gap or gate is. If the gate doesn't open (a common feature in the countryside), you can climb over, but if you intend to use a dog, what about him? Fences are also scalable, but again many are built to be sheep-proof, which means that any dog larger than a Jack Russell terrier will also be closed in. If he can't (or won't) jump the fence, how will you get him across?

Some of the worst access problems are caused by small rivers. In the summer they might look fordable at many different points, even with walking boots. But in autumn and winter – the flying season – they are an entirely different proposition. Whatever their width or depth, they won't deter your hawk who is just as likely to chase game on the opposite bank as she is on yours. If you manage to flush moorhen, coot or mallard off the water, they will fly away from you, perhaps over to the other side. If there are no bridges you might have to wade in to reach a hawk who has connected with quarry on the far side, even if the water comes over the top of your boots. If you are not prepared to put up with this, you will either have to wear waders, or avoid the area altogether when the river is too high.

The same applies to ponds and lakes, both of which can fill up alarmingly in winter months. If you intend to hunt one of them for water birds, make sure that you can actually get round the whole perimeter first or, if you can't, that you know exactly where the impassable barriers are. Bear in mind, though, that in the depths of winter, vegetation everywhere is much thinner, and some of it – for example nettle and bracken – dies back completely. What looks like an impenetrable jungle in the height of the summer might look very different towards the end of the flying season.

PART 3

Training And Flying

Training: *Introduction*

Although the training regimes of longwings, shortwings and broadwings have a great deal in common, they diversify in the later stages especially in the use of lures. What follows is a programme formulated specifically for broadwings, which are the hawks most suitable for beginners who don't have frequent access to an experienced mentor (see the section headed *First Birds*). It is not, therefore, a programme wholly appropriate for other kinds.

Training broadwings incorporates several distinct stages which are mostly progressive. By this I mean that the hawk can't move onto stage *b* until she has thoroughly mastered stage *a*. Each step uses and builds on skills and responses she has learned in previous lessons, and exactly how this works will be explained fully in later sections.

Bear in mind that your first bird will be captive-bred. Without you or some other falconer she would be given no chance to fly free and do what she was designed to do – hunt and catch wild prey in a natural environment. Giving her the opportunity to gain such a high quality of life must be your ultimate goal, *but she will need the discipline of falconry training to achieve it.*

This means:

- reducing and controlling her food intake to develop a consistent response to you
- controlling her degree of liberty until she can be trusted to use it in a disciplined way
- realising and developing her inherited skills.

During training and on the whole, throughout the flying season the process involves giving her much less food than she wants. You might consider this a harsh regime, and experience some emotional stress as a result especially in the initial stages. But the *only* other options are to keep her tethered to a perch, or untethered in a wired enclosure, for the rest of her life. If, out of misguided sympathy, you decide to release her before she's learned to catch her own food, she will surely die.

As captive birds themselves, her parents were in no position to teach her how and what to hunt. She is unlikely to learn this on her own. Although much of what all hawks do can be regarded as 'instinctive', wild parents deliberately present their offspring with hunting opportunities to 'switch on' these reactions. Before that, they reduce their food intake drastically. This provides fledglings with the motivation to accept such opportunities so that ultimately they are able to shift from a state of dependence to one of independence. In addition, parents might actively assist their fledglings in catching prey until they develop the skill to do it on their own.

As a would-be falconer training a captive-bred eyass, you are taking on a similar role. The only difference is that you are not training her to become totally independent. What you *do* want is for her to fly and hunt when and where you choose, and still come back to you.

Wild or otherwise, any young hawk's first year is a period of learning. Once she is fully-fledged, it is devoted to developing the skills required to fly in natural conditions and discovering her inherited prowess at catching live food. But, as a falconry bird, your hawk must first learn to accept a situation neither her genes nor her instincts equip her to deal with – living and working with a human being. Ultimately this will help her because it will ensure that she doesn't starve, but she is unlikely to appreciate that. In the meantime, it will put an extra burden on her learning.

Whatever type or quality of bird you own, your primary objective must be to have her fully-trained and *entered* before the end of her first year. Indeed, it would be preferable if she had caught several heads of quarry by then. The confidence this will give her, and the commitment to chasing game it will develop, will be qualities she will carry forward into adulthood the next year. More importantly, in second and subsequent years, her capacity to learn new things will be much reduced. If she isn't entered on a variety of quarry as an adolescent, your chances of developing her full adult potential will also diminish.

For a captive-bred eyass – especially your first – the training schedule can be both tight and demanding. Although your hawk will probably hatch in May, you won't be able to collect her until the end of July at the earliest. Indeed, if you've decided on a Harris' Hawk, the breeder might not be prepared to release her until late September. Whenever you acquire her, training to the point of free flight could take two to three months.

This means that it might be well into November before she is ready to be entered. You will then have the problem of pitting a complete novice – one that is still learning to fly in natural conditions and has no hunting experience – against fit and healthy game in the worst of winter weather. From November onwards, the abundance of quarry (such as rabbits) declines significantly partly because the first frosts weed out the weakest, and partly because other predators, such as foxes, start to make a real impact on their numbers. Only the healthiest, fittest, and smartest survive. In addition, the weather could be so bad that you might not be able to take your hawk out for days at a time without the risk of losing her, which means that it will be difficult for you to get and keep her fit enough to catch any kind of quarry, so compounding the problem.

Nature never makes things easy for young hawks, but the breeder's intervention, and yours by spending time taming and training her, make things even more difficult. This is because it denies her flying and hunting experience at a time when there are still young and inexperienced quarry-species available – namely, well before winter sets in.

In April your hawk will start to moult and, if you want her to grow strong and healthy feathers as quickly as possible in time for the start of the next season, you will have to feed her as much as she wants to bring her back to top weight. You won't then be able to fly her at all. In any event, the start of the moult signals the end of her first year and the beginning of maturity.

The time-frame for achieving your objective is, therefore, much shorter in practice than it might seem to be at first sight. Nevertheless, even with the worst scenario, there should be time enough if you approach her training in a sensible way and choose suitable weather and hunting grounds to maximise her opportunities. The next few sections describe ways of achieving that.

Training: *First Steps*

Introduction

In the first stages of training you are trying to achieve two things

1. To man (or tame) your hawk
2. To persuade her to eat off the fist.

'Manning' is the process of familiarising her with human beings and their environments, mainly by perching her on the fist, then carrying her around for long enough to overcome her fear through frequent exposure. Getting her to eat from the fist is also a significant step because it demonstrates that she has overcome her fear sufficiently to respond to further training.

Both are of vital importance. Until a hawk is willing to take food from you on a hand-to-mouth basis, you can't train her to do anything. And she won't accept food in this way until either hunger drives her to it, or she has learned to have confidence in you. Manning and fist-feeding are therefore inter-dependent, and they are the basic foundation on which future training and ultimately the hunting partnership are built.

The procedure I recommend in this section differs from long-established techniques. It is different because it makes use of *confidence* to motivate a hawk to overcome her fear rather than *hunger*.

There is no doubt that the quickest way to man a hawk, and reduce her weight significantly, is to deny her any food until she is willing to eat it off the fist. This method works because it is based on the certain knowledge – gained from hundreds of years' experience – that *no hawk will starve herself to death by refusing food when it is there for the taking*. Spurred on by hunger, she will conquer her fear and she will eat. Hunger is, therefore, the tool that the vast majority of falconers use to achieve this initial breakthrough. With this method, even the most fearful of broadwings will eat from the fist within a week. Some might take only two or three days.

But, as an alternative strategy, you need to know that it is entirely possible to
- man *any* broadwing *when she is at top weight*
- get *any* untrained broadwing feeding off the fist *when she is at top weight*.

Denying food until the hawk complies is not, therefore, an essential pre-requisite for conquering her fear. The fact that no hawk will deliberately starve herself to death might be irrefutable, but it is actually irrelevant to the manning of a hawk. Much of a hawk's fear can be overcome simply by developing her confidence – confidence that neither you nor her new environment are a threat to her. When she has *enough* confidence, she will eat off the fist even at top weight. She might not eat as much as she would alone in her quarters, but the fact remains that she will make this vital initial response *because she is learning to trust you*.

Gaining a hawk's confidence sufficiently to get her feeding off the fist might take longer from start to finish than denying her food until she does, but ultimately it works at least as well. Indeed, I believe (based on empirical evidence) that it
- produces steadier and better-mannered hawks
- reduces the chances of them becoming persistent 'screamers' (see the section headed *Buying a Hawk*)

- makes it possible to fly them at a higher weight than they might otherwise without jeopardising either quality of response or commitment to catching quarry.

At the very least, it halves the initial stress a hawk has to go through. With traditional methods, the stress is a dual one: the first caused by having to perch uncomfortably close to a human being; the second by having – at the same time – to go without food until she accepts the first.

Another way of gaining a young hawk's confidence is described first in the epilogue of T H White's book *The Goshawk* (1951), then in Doctor Nick Fox's book *Understanding Birds Of Prey* (1995) – see the section headed *Helpful Literature* page 242. Both advocate a gradual invasion of the hawk's personal space until confidence is gained, rather than an abrupt and sustained invasion by carrying her on the fist from day one of training. Although this method is obviously feasible, I haven't yet had an opportunity to try it and I can't, therefore, offer any comment on its effectiveness, or provide any indication of time scale.

Procedure

There is no doubt that manning *any* hawk – in particular short and broadwings – is a tedious business, especially when you've done it several times before. But there isn't a substitute and there are no short cuts. Once a bird is flying free, it is virtually impossible to improve her social behaviour through further manning. By then habits are firmly ingrained and it is too late to change them. Any badly-manned hawk is a pain in the neck to carry, as well as an embarrassment when she is around other people. So, boring and time-consuming good manning might be, but you *must* devote the time and effort required to achieve it.

In common with all other animals (including humans), hawks fear the *unknown* which, for those reared in sheltered aviaries, amounts to virtually everything. They know very little about the world outside, and any new experience can provoke fear and panic. You will be very lucky if these new sights and sounds merely excite your bird's curiosity: she is much more likely to view them as potential threats. Her reaction to any perceived threat will be to get as far away as possible, which means that she will bate off the fist frequently if not constantly.

Although the analogy could be considered extreme, it might be useful to view her as a Martian visiting Earth for the first time. If she's been reared exclusively by her parents, even people will be alien to her. She will certainly know nothing about cats, dogs, ferrets, sheep, horses or cattle, not to mention vehicles, houses, rooms, doors, windows, stairs, lawnmowers, hosepipes (which resemble enormous snakes), or any of the other paraphernalia found in and around human habitations.

Remember also that this is likely to be the first time she has been on her own, parted from the company of her parents or siblings. The vast majority of wild hawks go through this process, but they usually choose to do it themselves when they feel capable of becoming self-sufficient or (more likely) when they are driven out of the territory by long-suffering parents. Your eyass has had no such experience – neither the luxury of a natural environment, nor the parental tuition which would make going-it-alone feasible.

All this adds up to a need for empathy and caution in the manning process. *Gradual* exposure to new things is much more effective than blitzing a hawk with everything on the first day. All that will do is to incite blind panic and take you at least one step back.

Most falconers these days give a newly-acquired hawk time to settle down before attempting to man and train her – usually one to two weeks. This helps the bird to get used to her new situation, including the restraints imposed by her tethering equipment. Throughout this period they give the hawk as much food as she wants, by providing it in her quarters and allowing her to eat it at her leisure. This also enables them to ensure that she is a top weight by the time that serious training begins, which makes it easier to estimate flying weight (see page 96 *Weight and Condition*).

However, this 'settling-in' period can also be used to man the hawk, starting as soon as she is taken out of her travel-box and tethering-equipment has been fitted (see page 89 *Handling Hawks*). Firstly, by trying to get her perching on the fist. She will not, of course, stay there. She will dive off flapping her wings furiously to get away and she will end up hanging upside down. Don't panic. Keep your gloved hand parallel to the ground, then lift her back onto the glove.

At this early stage, you can't expect her to co-operate. She has never perched on a gloved hand before, and she will resist doing it now with all her guile and energy. Even when you lift her back, she might close her feet and refuse to grip or balance there. Now, and over the next few days, you can help her to accept the fist by not actively *provoking* bates:
- avoid making sudden body movements, in particular with your free hand
- avoid direct eye-to-eye contact which, at this stage, she will interpret as a threatening gesture
- resist any temptation to stroke her to calm her down
- when you need to put her back on the fist, handle her gently and sympathetically however frustrated you might feel.

After a few bates she might stand on the fist, but with her mouth open and wings and tail fully spread. Usually this means that she wants to get her breath back (bating takes up a lot of energy, particularly for an overweight and unfit bird). Once she's recovered, she will probably dive straight off again. It will take several days to get her standing on the fist without constant bating, and for her to learn how to fly back on without assistance. In the meantime, you will have to replace her each time she bates.

Don't prolong this first session unduly. If she refuses the fist even temporarily after ten or fifteen bates, she's unlikely to do it at all that day unless you physically wear her out. If you do persist, you will simply multiply the stress she has already suffered through travelling and being manhandled, and the experience may even become counterproductive.

Put her in her overnight quarters and leave her alone. She probably won't be interested in eating because her high weight, combined with the stress she has suffered, will eliminate any appetite she would otherwise have. But leaving a familiar kind of food in her quarters might at least reassure her and help her to settle in. What she hasn't eaten by the next day, make sure you dispose of – old food should never be left to rot.

From now on you can help her to deal with the unknown by
- establishing daily routines
- limiting her new experiences to two or three a day.

Familiarity is the antidote to the unknown and with set routines a young hawk will quickly learn to anticipate events and become less fearful. It doesn't really matter what these routines are as long as you stick to them, at least for the first few days. For example, you could bring her out of her overnight quarters each morning, walk her around on the fist for a while, then weather her on a bow-perch on the lawn. The same routine can be repeated a couple more times over the course of the day. The essential thing is to give her a *pattern of activity* she can learn to predict.

This all sounds very straightforward, but in practice it isn't. The first thing you might notice – even after a few days of manning – is that, when you go into her quarters to collect her each morning, she behaves as though she's never seen you before. She will bate furiously away from you, thrashing the floor with her wing and tail feathers. This is because overnight she has, in effect, reverted to a wild state. Gradually this reversion will diminish in intensity, but will probably continue until she is eating happily off the fist and has progressed some way through her training.

Over the first few days I usually spend a great deal of time carrying a new hawk, partly because I like doing it, and partly because it is the most effective way I know to man one. Being careful not to over-exposure her, I aim *eventually* to be able to carry her anywhere.

I watch television with her perching on the fist, read a book, play on the computer, take her to meet the neighbours, sit in the garden, and so on. Gradually I carry her further and further afield, walking her through the village so that she gets used to passing vehicles as well as curious people, and through the fields with the dog giving her some exposure to other animals and the wider world.

Whichever activity you undertake with her, you need to be able to manage it *competently* with your free hand. Opening an ill-fitting gate from one field into the next, for instance, can be a real trial, but trying to climb over it with a large unsteady bird on the fist is even worse. If you don't handle such activities competently, you will simply provoke unnecessary bates which will neither allay the hawk's fears nor endear her to being carried.

Weathering a hawk on a bow-perch out in the open is also valuable in manning terms. At first, put her in the most secluded part of the garden where she is likely to see only irregular and distant human activity. As her manning progresses through carrying, you can weather her in more exposed places – for example, closer to the house and eventually in the front garden where she will be exposed to passing traffic as well as curious neighbours.

When you start tethering her outside, don't expect her to stand nicely on her expensive perch. Even if you manage to get her on it, it is highly likely that she will bate off it within a few seconds. Once off the perch she will not, at first, hop back on. Leave her to work things out for herself, and in time she will learn to use it. Meanwhile, tether her as tightly as possible by which I mean give her as little freedom as you can within the limits of the jesses and leash. This is a *responsible* act, not a cruel one. Hawks have been known to break a leg bating off a bow-perch because their equipment has given them too much leeway. The further it allows them to fly during a bate, the greater the acceleration they can generate, and the greater the stress on their legs when they are eventually pulled up short. Your hawk should be able to reach the ground comfortably from the apex of the perch, but go no further.

Whenever she is tethered to an outdoor perch, don't leave her unsupervised for long periods. You will need to check occasionally that her leash and jesses haven't become entangled and that they are still secure; and be aware of possible interference from other animals or curious neighbours. Even occasional checks like this are beneficial to her manning, but be careful not to incite a bate by going too near if it isn't necessary.

Continue this pattern of activity for the next few days, introducing her to more new sights as you carry her around. In the meantime, give her an over-generous amount of food to eat in her quarters when you tether her there at the end of the day. You will soon learn how much she's eating by observing how much she leaves. If she eats it all, you're not giving her enough. At this stage you need to give her *more* than she apparently wants, even though this means you will waste some. A surplus of food will do much to settle her in, and it will enable her to reach or maintain her top weight.

Within a few days she will become more accustomed to balancing on the fist when you walk, and she will learn to fly back on when she bates. She will still bate, in particular when she comes across a new sight or sound, but for most of the time she will appear reasonably comfortable (if alert). You can tell whether this is so from her demeanour. She will stand on the fist with her wings and tail folded in neatly, and her attention will be focused less on you, more on the things going on around you.

At this stage you can introduce food to the fist. This is best done towards the end of the day when she is most used to being fed. To increase your chances of success, sit quietly with her somewhere outside (or inside if it's pouring with rain) where there is the least number of distractions. Grip a whole day-old chick between the first finger and thumb of the glove. She certainly won't accept it yet, but it will encourage her to view the fist as a pleasant place to be and it will introduce a connection between glove and food. Tempt her as much as possible by using a combination of tactics:

- coax her to concentrate on the food by occasionally tapping or stroking one of her feet *lightly* with a finger of your free hand (this should prompt her to look down at her feet)
- roll the food between the gloved finger and thumb (this cons her into believing the food is alive, and it should have a similar effect to foot tapping)
- roll the fist *gently* backwards and forwards if she seems to lose interest. This also re-focuses her attention because she has to shift her feet to stay balanced (but don't overdo it, otherwise you will provoke a bate)
- break open the yoke-sac of the chick just enough to allow the fluid to ooze out (most broadwings positively *relish* egg yoke)
- if the sight of the yoke doesn't impress her, lift the chick up to her beak and dip the tip of it into the yoke. Sooner or later she will lick it with her tongue, then she might be tempted to draw out the whole yoke-sac. If she does, slowly bring the chick back down to the fist so that the next mouthful – if she takes one – will be off the fist.

It may take a few days to persuade her to eat confidently from the fist, but don't be too anxious and give her time. If she is unwilling, continue providing her full supply in her quarters. Once she has taken her first food off the fist, and eaten as much as she wants, give her the balance of her normal intake in her quarters again.

The next day, just before you intend to feed her, weigh her and make a note of the result. From this point on, feed her *exclusively* on the fist. She will only eat enough to satisfy her immediate hunger, which won't be anything like the amount she has previously consumed. Which means you will begin to reduce her weight.

At first, she will take her time and it might be several minutes before she makes up her mind to eat. But what you now have to aim for is *instant response*. In falconry terms, 'instant' means within a second or two, and it is this quality of response which will drive her training forwards enabling you to move from one stage to the next.

Bear in mind, though, that response is governed by three factors:

1. Hate
2. Habit
3. Hunger

Hate is about her attitude towards you which is what manning is designed to overcome, but even a well-manned and experienced hawk will always retain an element of it. Even so, its dominance over her behaviour will decline as training progresses. On the other hand, the importance of habit will increase throughout her training and beyond into her hunting career. Once she is in the habit of undertaking a task – such as flying to the fist – she will do it much more readily. Finally, hunger provides the consistent motivation for dominating her hate and developing the habits you want.

At this stage, her hate will still be at a high level, no habit has yet been established, and she certainly isn't hungry enough. Her food therefore needs to be cut back to bring about a steady reduction in weight, and weight-reduction should continue until you achieve a satisfactory response. Her response will be satisfactory when she begins feeding the moment food is presented to her.

How long this will take is variable (see the section headed *Weight and Condition*) but, in view of the importance of food to the hawk's psyche, it is preferable to feed her *something* in the course of each training day – even if her response is very slow. There should be a large enough margin in her daily requirements to reduce weight significantly without the need to withhold food altogether. If she gets to eat something, she might not be satisfied, but she will be a lot less anxious than she would be otherwise. It is also of vital importance to weigh her every day just before feeding so that you can accurately gauge her progress.

One other aspect needs to be considered at this stage – hooding (see the section headed *Hawk Furniture*). Once she is fairly comfortable being carried around on the fist, and at about the same time as food is introduced to the glove, hood training should also begin if you intend to use one.

Broadwings are not easy to train to the hood, and they don't take to it anything like as readily as longwings. Getting them to accept a hood whilst perching on the fist, and without provoking a bate, takes a high level of manual dexterity. The aim is to slip the hood over the hawk's beak and head before she has time to protest, and this requires a swift and very precise scythe-like movement of the hand. If this movement is hesitant or inaccurate she will bob and weave, which makes settling the hood over her head much more difficult to achieve.

The problem is that if the job is consistently botched, it is highly likely that the hawk will become 'hood shy' which means that she will quickly learn to hate all hoods and will bate just at the sight of one. Also, if she bates once the hood is on her head, and succeeds in throwing it off, she will bate every time to get rid of it. *Remember* that you cannot force a hawk to accept a hood – she has to be *trained* to accept it.

The method is very straightforward and, like manning, it simply involves increasing exposure to the hood. Also, it is better to do this sitting down with the bird rather than walking around with her to minimise the risk of a bate. The first day you decide to use the hood, slip it on, then slip it off immediately. The next day, slip it on, leave it for two or three seconds, then take it off again. Over the next few days, keep it on for progressively longer periods, but without doing up the braces. Once you can keep the hood on for several minutes, start doing up the braces – again in progressive stages.

Hood training will proceed through most of her training, but by the time she's flying free she should be hood-trained.

Training: *Up to Free Flight*

Introduction

When your bird is eventually out in the fields flying free, the level of control you have will depend entirely on her willingness to return. If she won't return, you can consider her lost. Developing this habit – from any distance, and in a variety of circumstances – is the primary objective of the next few lessons. In effect they bring about the transition between control through tethering, and control through disciplined free-flight.

Manning, and in particular the search for her flying weight, make a vital contribution to achieving this objective. Both might have to continue through much of this 'middle-order' training.

Ground Rules

First and foremost, there is no timetable to work to. Basic training takes weeks rather than days, but exactly how long is dependent on many things – the kind of hawk you are trying to train; how 'fat' she is when training begins; how you manage weight reduction; and so on. Time itself is not important. What *is* important is moving on to the next stage at the *right time for her*. She can't progress to stage two before she's mastered stage one, but once she has, don't hold her back.

The 'trick' of falconry training (if there is one) is, first of all, to get instant response, then maintain the hawk's weight at the level which provoked it. If her response genuinely deteriorates, weight should be reduced gradually until quality of response is restored (but see the section headed *Weight and Condition* for the complications).

However, even if your hawk's weight is at the optimum level, she will only give you an instant response

- if the lesson itself is within her capabilities, and
- she has the confidence to do it.

No bird will come to you instantly until she is confident that she can do what you're asking, however much she might want the food you're offering. Building confidence in her own ability step by step is, therefore, a major aspect of this middle-order training. Remember also that you are training a captive-bred eyass. She is certainly fully-grown, but she has no experience of flying in natural conditions. In fact, later on when she's working with the creance, you will be asking her to fly further than she's ever flown before.

Any experienced broadwing flying from one perch to another will take off, skim the ground, then rise up to the next perch. Furthermore, she will take off into the wind because an upwind take-off gives her immediate lift. If you want her to come downwind (which means with the wind blowing from her to you), she will initially fly away from you. Then she will bank round and fly towards you with the wind behind her. Downwind flight gives her much more impetus, but it requires a lot of flight control, particularly in landing.

Such a standard of flight is beyond an eyass whose experience has been limited to flying from one end of a sheltered aviary to the other. It would be like expecting someone to pass an advanced driving test while they're still learning how to drive.

When you call her off a training perch for food, even in favourable weather conditions, she is most likely to take off, fly upwards, then drop down onto the fist – the exact opposite of a hawk with experience. She might be able to handle downwind flight in a light breeze, but it's unfair to expect much more than that at first. Even then she could overshoot, or at best, 'thump' the fist with unexpected force because she's misjudged her landing.

You must, therefore, take weather conditions and her inexperience into account when you're trying to fly her any distance, especially in the early stages of creance-training. It is patently unfair to punish her (by reducing food intake) because she lacks confidence, hesitates, and ends up not giving you the instant response you're seeking.

With practise she will teach herself to fly, but in the meantime, you must give her every chance to succeed with each new lesson. For example:

- make sure you choose a training ground where you can call her to you into any wind
- never attempt to fly her in a high wind or a raging gale – she will simply get blown away and lose any confidence she might already have acquired
- avoid flying her in heavy rainfall – juvenile plumage is not very waterproof, and the wetter it gets the harder it will be for her to fly at all
- even if she does delay her response in what you consider to be satisfactory conditions, think about what else might explain her 'bad' behaviour before you decide to reduce food intake.

Having said that, be as objective as you can and don't be tempted to make excuses for her.

Within a relatively short time you will be flying her with the aid of a creance. For this to be successful and trouble-free you will need:

- at least fifty yards of clear flying space – in other words, space through which she can fly in a direct line from her training perch to you without having to dodge obstacles like trees, bushes or buildings on the way
- obstacle-free ground for the creance to trail over – creance line is very easily-snagged on such things as hummocks, tussocks of grass, weeds, fallen twigs, branches, stones, or any other irregular object you are likely to find on the ground.

The ideal surface is a level, fifty-yard close-mown lawn, but most of us don't possess such a luxury. The next best thing is a football or rugby pitch, but if there isn't one nearby any flat closely-cropped field will do. It is well worth taking the time to seek out suitable ground within reasonable walking distance (*and* getting permission to use it) well before you start creance-training. The better this surface is the less frustration you will experience trying to sort out a snagged line with a hungry bird waiting for your next call. Much more importantly, the less her confidence will be undermined by not reaching the fist because she has artificially been pulled up short.

Alternatively you could set up a 'static' creance as described in the section headed *Training Equipment*, but for this to work you will need permission to use the land for as many days/weeks it takes to get the hawk flying free. This is because the static creance is not designed to be portable. However, the advantage of this arrangement is that it overcomes the need for a good surface because the creance does not make contact with the ground. So it can be made to work anywhere that there is clear flying space in a straight line from the bird to you.

From now on your bird should be fed small pieces of food at a time, for two reasons. The first is to enable you to repeat the lesson, or move onto the next, without exceeding the rations needed to keep her weight stable. The second is that smaller 'parcels' of food like this will help you to refine her food requirement as she starts to use up more energy. Small each parcel might seem, but for her each represents a significant proportion of her food requirement, and each will have an effect on her weight.

Finally, it is good practice to start a new training session where you left the last. For example, if yesterday she ended up flying ten yards, start today's session with the same distance, *then* increase it. This reinforces previous lessons, builds her confidence, and motivates her to try greater things.

Procedure

For some time now her food ration has been eaten while she's been perching on the fist. The next lesson involves getting her to *step up* to the fist for a piece of food from a different perch. 'Stepping up' is the first stage in training her to come to you for food, and it is this movement which will be developed in later lessons.

Prepare her rations, then collect her as normal. Weigh her, then take her to a suitable perch – the back of a chair you've been using so far, a fence post, gate, or anything else that she can comfortably stand on. Ensure that the leash is secured to the glove ring, coil any loose portion of the leash around the third and fourth fingers of the glove, then back her onto the perch.

Once she's perching, place a piece of food between gloved finger and thumb and place it roughly level with her breast. She will bend her head to grab the food with her beak. Keep a firm hold on it so that she can't take it off you, and keep your hand in the same position. She should step onto the glove to get a better grip.

If she just tugs at the food without stepping up, *don't* let her take it from you. Instead, let her lift your hand as she tugs and she will then step up – which is the only way she can gain any control over what happens to the food. Repeat this exercise, refining weight if necessary, until her rations are exhausted or she steps up as soon as a piece of food is offered.

Once she's stepping up confidently and instantly, movement towards you is developed by getting her to jump to the fist. The method is similar. Make sure the leash is secured to the glove-ring, but otherwise leave it loose so that you have some distance to work with. Ensure also that her jesses are hanging *in front* of her feet to avoid any possibility that they will become snagged on the training post when she launches herself.

The object of this exercise is to get her to come further than she can get by stepping up, but not so far that she has to fly. Bear in mind that some of these birds (particularly Harris' Hawks) have long legs, and their true length is not evident when they are standing on a perch. You will need to offer the food about twelve inches or so from her breast to avoid the embarrassment of seeing her grab it with a foot while she's still standing on the perch.

From now on, whenever you hold out your fist to offer food, keep your arm fully outstretched at shoulder height and parallel to the ground. It should be positioned *across* her likely flight-path – as if it were the branch of a tree – *not* along it.

At first she might hesitate to make the jump, but after she's achieved it once or twice she should come immediately. When she's doing that consistently, increase the distance to leash length (or what remains of it, allowing for the knot securing the leash to the glove). Again, repeat this exercise until she's mastered it and you are satisfied with her response.

The next development makes use of the creance, which replaces the leash and enables you to keep her under control for increasingly longer distances. The traditional creance is by no means an easy piece of equipment to use. For one thing, you will need to swap her mews jesses for field jesses with punched holes to take the line (see page 69 *Hawk Furniture*). This is to ensure that, if she veers off and lands in a tree, the chances of her snagging her equipment are minimised. Furthermore, when you switch back to the leash at the end of the training session, the jesses will have to be swapped over again.

Although you might find this an irritation, don't be tempted to attach the creance to mews jesses. If she flies into a tree and becomes entangled, not only will you destroy a great deal of her confidence, you might be jeopardising her safety which must always be paramount. If she's really stuck, you will have to climb the tree to rescue her. Reaching her might be easy enough, but climbing down a tree with only one free hand because the other has a large frustrated hawk perched on the fist is a nightmare.

Both of you need to get used to inter-changing jesses anyway, and this is the time to start. For her it will eventually become just another routine and in time she should learn to stand on the fist patiently while you carry out the operation.

The procedure is as follows:

1. Put both jesses in the normal glove-lock position, then remove the leash and swivel
2. Push the little finger of the glove through the slit cut for the swivel on one of the jesses, then free the other from the glove-lock
3. Take hold of the button-knot of the free jess, then pull it out of the eyelet in easy stages by pushing your finger and thumb against the eyelet, pulling the jess through at the same time
4. When it is clear of the eyelet (and put away for later use), push the point of the replacement jess through the eyelet, then gradually feed the jess through in the same way
5. Put the new jess in the glove-lock position, then repeat the whole procedure to replace the remaining jess.

At any time your bird could protest by lifting and stamping her foot on the glove, but let her settle again, then continue the manoeuvre until both jesses are secure.

Take out the creance and unravel a few yards. If your bird has never seen it before she might bate, but put her back on the glove and persist. Thread the end of the creance line through the hole in each field jess without unlocking them from the glove, then tie them both together with a falconer's knot. This is rather like trying to thread a needle with one hand and cold grey weather makes it even more difficult to manage. But don't be tempted to botch the job – the life of your bird might ultimately depend on this knot, and such a risk is never worth taking. If you're using a static creance, first attach the field leash to the jesses as described above, then to the welded ring on the creance line with another falconer's knot.

Once she's attached to the creance, put her on the training perch. Take account of wind direction, and make sure her jesses are to the front. Run three or four feet of line through the glove, then loop it a couple of times round the little finger of your gloved hand. Drop the rest of the creance on the ground and put your foot on the stick. Place a piece of food on the fist and call her to it. With the static creance, you won't need to control the line in this way: simply move a few feet away from her and call her.

When she's coming this distance instantly, double it. The objective is to keep increasing distance until she is flying the full length of the creance-line, but don't initiate *any* increase until you get an instant response.

Creance-training will help you to hone her weight, but don't forget, she's also still building up confidence and learning how to fly. With some birds, it might take several days to get them coming three or four yards. Then the penny seems to drop (helped by proper weight-control) and in half that time they are flying the full length of the line. So don't be tempted to increase distance too soon. *Remember* it is *quality of response* which must drive her training forwards, whatever stage she's at.

Once she's flying twenty yards or so reliably on the creance, she no longer needs to be tethered to a bow-perch in her weathering. If you have a weathering large enough (see the section on *Hawk Quarters*), and you can rig up a perch she can roost in, let her loose in there overnight and during the day if the weather is too bad to put her out on the lawn. Even in a restricted space, it is amazing how much hawks can move around, and most of them are much better for having this freedom. For a start it relieves boredom, and gives them the potential for some exercise.

There are three additional things you may need to deal with during creance-training:

1. At some point your hawk might want to fly back to her training perch instead of being carried there
2. When she's flying to you some distance, she might suddenly change direction and veer off somewhere else
3. She might decide to come to you *before* you are as far away as you want to be, and *before* you've called her to the fist

If she wants to, let her fly back to her perch, and encourage her to do so from that point on. This is another sign that the penny has dropped and she knows what she has to do to get her food-ration. Letting her get on with it will confirm this, and help to boost her confidence.

However careful you are it is probable that she will veer off at some point in creance-training. There could be any number of reasons – an unexpected gust of wind which blows her off course, something else in the environment which scares her in mid-flight, a sudden panic attack or loss of confidence for no obvious reason, and so on. Whatever the cause, this shouldn't be a problem with the static creance if the anchoring rod is fixed in the ground securely enough but, with a traditional creance, the important thing to remember is: *keep firm control of the line*. Then,

- **If she lands on the ground**, recovery is relatively easy. Walk towards her gathering up the slack on the line as you go. When you get near to her, move in slowly and as low down as you can, then pick her up onto the fist again by the jesses. Keep control of her on the fist, and take her back to her training perch (or let her fly back if you are confident that this is where she intends to go).
- **If she lands in a tree, or some other high perch**, the procedure is less straightforward. First, take up any slack in the creance-line and keep it taut. This is to stop her flying on somewhere else, which will only aggravate the problem. If the line itself hasn't snagged, reel it in slowly but firmly until she's dislodged – once the line starts to put pressure on her jesses, she will move towards you to ease that pressure. Eventually she will have nowhere else to go and she will fly. When she takes off, keep reeling the line in carefully until she lands on the ground. Then move in slowly as above.

If the line *is* snagged, call her back to the fist for food (a large tempting piece if necessary). As soon as she takes off, release the creance-line and let it flow freely. Hopefully her flight will bypass the snag, but if it doesn't, her weight and power should enable her to drag the line far enough to enable her at least to reach the ground. Move into her as quickly as possible. Give her the food on the fist and, while she's preoccupied with this, untie the creance-line from her jesses. Keeping the jesses firmly 'glove-locked', pull the creance free from the obstruction, then re-attach it. Once she's back on her training perch, give her time to settle, then carry on as normal.

Dealing with birds that fly to you too soon can be a problem, and there are divided opinions about the 'correct' solution. It usually happens when a bird is close to flying the full length of the creance, and it is another measure of her 'keenness'. The opposing arguments are as follows:

1. Such behaviour amounts to disobedience, and *obedience* is what you've been trying to achieve ever since the start of her training. Walk her back to the perch and try again. If this doesn't work, get an assistant to walk her back to give you time to get far enough away.

2. This is *precisely* the behaviour you want to develop when she's flying free and you're trying to get her to 'follow-on'. If you discourage her you might give yourself problems later on when you want her to duplicate this behaviour. In effect, you will be teaching her to abandon the habit by convincing her it's a waste of energy.

I agree with the second argument. First of all, where hawks are concerned, it is more helpful to think in terms of *response*, rather than *obedience*, which implies a higher level of communication than they're capable of. You couldn't, for example, tell a hawk to go back to the post she just came from and wait for your call, even though something similar is possible with a dog.

The fact is that, in coming before you call, she is – in her own way – responding to you, and her response is positive. She's reacting to the sight of you walking away with her food-ration, and she wants nothing more than to stay in touch so that she's close by when you do call. If you prefer to be anthropomorphic about it, she's trying to say: 'Look! I'm here! *Notice* me – and please give me some more food!'

The length of a creance-line is usually fifty yards, but there is nothing sacrosanct about this distance. If she's waiting until you get significantly over thirty yards before she comes of her own accord, that will do. Move on to the next stage of training – flying to a swing lure. If she's only allowing you to get as far as ten or fifteen yards, it is probable that her weight has been cut too low and you can afford to raise it (see the section headed *Weight and Condition*).

When she's flying the full length of the creance (or thereabouts), it's time to introduce a lure. At this stage her flying weight – for training purposes at least – should be apparent, and you will have a good idea what margin there is *above* flying weight before her response starts to deteriorate.

Remember: you are still trying to develop her willingness to return, and the lure to use for this purpose is a *swing* lure which, for broadwings out in the field, is primarily for long-distance retrieval (see the section headed *Training Equipment*). It can also be used to signal the end of flying for the day, or as an attempt to get her back in an emergency.

For any of these to work properly you have to get her to associate the swing lure with a generous portion of food (but still within her normal ration). It is advisable to use it only once in any training session and preferably at its conclusion. If you use it several times, you run the risk of your hawk becoming 'lure-bound' – meaning the only thing she will ever chase is the lure itself. This is especially true of common buzzards.

Until she's familiar with the lure, hold back a fair proportion of her ration (say, a third) to use with it. Also, for the first few days, 'garnish' the lure (which means tying a piece of food onto it – such as the leg of a day-old chick) to get her to associate it with food. Do this before you take her up for training, then put the lure in your bag (or hawking vest) ready for use later in the session.

The lure-training model goes as follows:

- collect your bird as normal, and fly her on the creance three or four times over the full distance
- get her back on the training perch, then take the lure out and drop it on the ground a few feet in front of her. When she sees the food, she will fly onto the lure
- 'tweak' the lure a couple of times to make sure she's gripping it properly with her feet, and let her eat
- when she's eaten this small offering, put your foot on the lure-line twelve inches or so from the lure itself, then throw a large piece of food (such as the body of a day-old chick) to one side on the ground. It should be far enough away to force her to choose between the lure and the food. Given time, she will release the lure and jump onto the food

- while she's occupied with feeding, put the lure away again
- as soon as she's convinced that there's no more food on the ground, she will look around wondering what to do next. You should then be able to collect her up again with another piece. Give her the rest of her rations (if any) off the fist, and put her in her weathering.

Simple and straightforward, but unfortunately things don't often work out this way.

In all probability she will be too nervous to fly down to the lure, even though there can be no doubt that she's seen the food. First, try twitching the lure a couple of times to make it move, and encourage her vocally. If this doesn't work, the only other solution is to take her to it. She might then jump onto the ground beside it. If she does, let her be and give her time to work things out. She will try to take the food without stepping onto the lure but, if it's been tied on properly, she won't succeed because the lure will move towards her each time she tugs. Eventually she will jump onto to the lure to keep it under control while she eats. Once she's eaten from it, she should be less nervous next time.

Another possible response is that she will jump straight onto the lure as soon as she sees the food, then try to fly to a nearby perch with it. If you allow her to do this, she could end up 'carrying' (flying away with) quarry out in the field. This means you won't just lose the quarry – which she will consume high in some quiet tree out of reach – but possibly also your bird. Once she's eaten her fill, you won't have anything to offer to induce her to return. The solution is simple. Put your foot on the line as soon as you drop the lure in front of her. She can't then carry it away, and she'll get accustomed to not doing so.

As with earlier creance-training, gradually increase the distance she has to come to the lure but again, don't initiate any increase until her response is satisfactory. When she's flying ten or fifteen yards consistently, the lure no longer needs to be garnished so long as you continue to give her a generous portion of food once she's 'caught' it.

At twenty yards or so, swing the lure three or four times before dropping it onto the ground to get her to associate it with movement. A hawk's vision is especially attuned to motion, and out in the field she will be able to see a swung lure from a long way away.

Once she's flying to the swing lure the instant it appears, she's ready to fly free.

Training: *Flying Free*

Free flight is by no means the end of training, but it is the beginning of the end. Getting a hawk to this stage is, in itself, a major achievement especially for someone who has never done it before.

If there is a problem, it probably lies in the fact that you won't want to let her go and you will find all sorts of reasons to delay the day it happens – you don't like the look of the weather, or you didn't think her response was *quite* right the last time you flew her, and so on. More fundamentally, you might be worried about what to do if she did fly away – how would you find her, and how would you get her back again?

You might be right to be apprehensive, but you don't need to be too worried just yet. At first, when you take her off the creance, she will be blissfully unaware that she is actually free. Why would she want to fly off anyway? If you've got her weight right and her training has gone to plan, the only thing she will be interested in is where you are because you represent her food supply. Indeed, since you acquired her, you've been her only source of food. Problems (if there are any) are more likely to come later when she's in the habit of flying free and catching game, and by default you relax control over her weight, or you fail to serve her adequately.

For her first free flight, the best place to begin is where you left off with creance-training. As with past days, consider the weather conditions, then place her on her usual training perch – this time without attaching the creance-line. As a precaution, switch her mews jesses for plain field jesses (see the section on *Hawk Furniture*), and use these from now on whenever you fly her free.

Call her to the fist from fifty yards or so and she should come to you as normal. Give her a few more flights, then call her to the swing lure as normal. Feed her the rest of her rations (if any), and put her back in her weathering as normal. In other words, carry out exactly the same routine as the day before, but *without* using the creance. If all this goes without incident (as it should), at least you know that she *will* return to you, even though she's free to fly off somewhere else if she has a mind to.

Flying free is a big milestone, but there is still much more work to be done. For both of you free-flight training is likely to be the most difficult and testing so far. For a start, it incorporates three new elements:

1. Getting her used to flying in and out of trees
2. Persuading her to 'follow on'
3. Using a quarry-lure to encourage her to chase ground game.

In working through this programme, she will use increasingly larger amounts of energy, which means you might have to revise previous ideas about her food requirements just to keep her weight stable. Then once she starts to get used to this 'independence', in particular when she's in hunting mode, her quality of response might deteriorate, and you may well find yourself having to revise your notion of her flying weight. Finally, she will be exposed much more to the sort of weather conditions which influence flight. At first they will exaggerate her limitations, but later, when she feels more able to cope with them – and starts to enjoy them – they might give her an incentive to take her liberty permanently.

There is no doubt, therefore, that free-flight is a risk, and nobody can guarantee that you won't lose your bird. But, with good basic training and proper weight control, the risk is a calculated one and the likelihood minimised. In the end, these assets are the only insurance you have against this eventuality.

Flying In and Out of Trees

This part of the programme might surprise you. But remember, your bird is captive-bred. She will certainly have seen trees before but, unless she crash-landed in one when she was flying on the creance, so far she won't have used one as a perch. For a bird as big as a broadwing, manoeuvring through branches to find a suitable landing place takes skill and has to be learned.

If you just let her go in an area where there are many trees, she is most likely to circle around looking for somewhere familiar to land – a fence-post or a gate, depending on what she's used to. What she won't do is make for the nearest tree. If she can't find anything familiar, she'll keep circling, becoming more and more confused and frustrated, until you put up your fist or she gets fed up and lands on the ground. Her demeanour will then convey the message: 'what the hell are you expecting me to do?'

Experienced falconers 'cast' their birds into trees, and they can do this with some precision. Casting simply means launching the bird off the fist in the direction you want her to go. Some can cast their birds in such a way that they not only land in the target tree, but also on the target branch. *Now is not the time to attempt this*, nor anything like it. You might eventually want to learn, but if you do you should start with a fully-trained and seasoned bird, *not* an eyass with little or no experience of landing in trees.

The first step is to find a low branch that you can back her onto without over-stretching. In fact, for the early days of free flight, it pays to reconnoitre available trees before you begin these training sessions to see which ones you can easily utilise. If they're in a line (for instance, bordering a field), they will also be useful for 'follow-on' training later. Then you won't have to change venues when she's ready to advance her training.

Back her onto a suitable branch, then move away thirty to fifty yards keeping as clear a line of flight between you and the hawk as possible. When she's on the branch, she might want a little time to look around and assess the situation. Let her do that, and don't attempt to call her until she's facing you and you're sure she's ready. When she's ready, call her to the fist as normal. After she's eaten the food, walk her back towards the line of trees. Most likely, she will take off and land on the same branch of the same tree. This is because you've given her an answer to the question: 'what are you expecting me to do?'

Move up the line of trees so that she has to come to you at a more acute angle, then call her again. When she's eaten, walk further up the line but towards the trees again. If she takes off of her own accord, let her go. Hopefully she will land in a different tree because it's nearer to you than the previous one. If she goes back to the same branch, call her again. Then, when she's eaten, take her and *plant* her in a different tree closer to the forward line you're taking. Eventually she will get the message, and she will fly back to any tree with an obvious perch which gives her a clear view of your movements, and is consistent with your progression along the tree-line. When she's nearing the end of her food ration, call her to the lure and take her home.

Continue calling her out of different trees for the next three or four days to give her practice and develop her experience. When she lands on the fist, don't attempt to take up her jesses, and let her fly off again at will once she's finished the piece of food. End each session with the swing lure. To add a bit of interest, and improve her footing ability, try getting her to catch the lure in mid-air. In other words, instead of just swinging the lure and dropping it onto the ground as usual, throw it up in the air and out to one side while she's still a few yards away.

Following On

In falconry terms, if 'waiting-on' (taking station high overhead) is the speciality of longwings, 'following-on' from tree to tree is the speciality of short and broadwings. But, whereas a falcon may stay overhead for up to twenty minutes, a fit hawk following-on can be flown for two or three hours at a time, depending on her degree of fitness. During this time-span you should only need to carry her on the fist to and from the hunting ground which could incorporate a circular route extending several miles. Always assuming you've trained her well, she should follow wherever you go leaving you free to flush game and enjoy her flights.

Following-on is a technique which exploits the hunting tendencies of accipiters, and to a lesser extent buzzards. Accipiters naturally work from trees, and buzzards can be persuaded to do the same, even though in the wild their first choice might be to soar.

Training a young broadwing to follow-on is by no means easy. When they are not soaring, they prefer to *still-hunt* like goshawks, which means perching – perhaps for half an hour or more – in a tree waiting for prey to pass by. Eventually they will move on if they have no luck but, as soon as they land in a different tree, they will use the same tactic. There is nothing more boring than waiting for a hawk to move on, and this can't be regarded, by any standards, as an acceptable performance for a falconry bird. Following on – which is actually a speeded-up version of still-hunting – does not, therefore, exactly mimic the hunting style of broadwings, but most will slot into the habit given the right encouragement.

The object of the exercise is to keep the hawk moving *in the direction you want her to go*. Ultimately this is achieved by flushing quarry for her consistently and frequently enough to persuade her that there is no point in waiting around on the off-chance that it will eventually pass by. In other words, from her point of view, your activity presents her with a much better chance of success.

The problem lies in the word 'persuade'. There are only two reasons why any hawk would be convinced that it's in her interests to follow you

1. She knows you have a food supply, and she knows that sooner or later you will offer her part of it. Consequently she wants to keep you in sight, and be close enough to reach you when you call her to the fist

2. An experienced bird will appreciate your value as a reliable source of food, but she also knows from previous hunting trips that you will flush game for her. She much prefers to chase that than come to the fist just for a morsel. In this case, she wants to stay close so that she's in a good position to catch the quarry when you flush it.

The motivation for following-on is therefore very different for an experienced bird compared to an eyass not yet entered. The first sees you as a *working partner*, the other simply as a reliable but a receding food supply.

Depending on how often you hunt, and how successful you are at locating and flushing game, a good hawk will learn in a season or two to fly ahead of you. First she will let you walk past to confirm your direction, then she will fly on. This is because she's learned that, when you do flush game, it usually moves away from you and, if she takes up a forward position, her chances of success are maximised.

Obviously your ultimate goal is the follow-on pattern of a seasoned hawk, but you are not likely to achieve this with a juvenile bird, at least for the first months of free-flight. Consequently, you will probably have to live with her lagging behind to some extent or, put another way, indulging her natural inclination to still-hunt. However, *you must not* allow this inclination to develop into a regular habit. The habit you want her to develop is to *follow you*, however reluctantly at first.

You might want to ask the question: why can't I just take her out where I know there are plenty of rabbits, carry her on the fist, and when I flush one, let her go? You can, but there are three problems with this approach at this stage in training

1. Before she makes a serious attempt at any quarry, she needs to build up fitness and flying experience
2. She needs to develop at least a minimal amount of skill in catching a moving target
3. She is unlikely to recognise rabbits (or any other quarry) as potential food.

Even if she is willing to chase rabbits, without 1 and 2 she will consistently fail, and constant failure will destroy her confidence – possibly to the extent that she will refuse to chase quarry at all.

Basic follow-on training, therefore, attempts to develop the habit of following you even though she won't yet see the purpose of it; through that, get her reasonably fit and competent at flying; then give her some practice at catching things that move. The standard training model goes as follows:

1. Take her out to her free-flight training ground, put her into a tree, let her settle, then walk away
2. Without raising a fist or showing any food, call her after you've gone thirty or forty yards, but using a different call to the one you've used so far to bring her for food
3. When she flies, keep your fist by your side and keep walking. She will see that there's no food-offering and veer off into a nearby tree
4. When she's settled again, call her down for a piece of food
5. Continue this pattern over the next week or two, *gradually* increasing the number of times she has to follow-on before calling her to the fist for food.

This basic model works as well as any other. But you will get varying levels of compliance, not only from different species of hawk, but also from individuals of the same kind.

For example, instead of veering off into the nearest tree when you walk away for the first time, some hawks will choose to land on you, or on the ground beside you. If either happens, get her back into a tree as soon as possible – even if you have to 'shoo' her, or pick her up off the ground and throw her – without offering any food. If you *do* give her food, you will be signalling that she's done the right thing. Once she's in a tree and settled, call her to the fist for a piece of food and start again.

By all means try developing a follow-on call, and good luck to you if it works. If you've already established, say, a single-note whistle to bring her for food, you might try two notes in rapid succession for the follow-on call. However, in my experience, success is variable. Despite what you might read elsewhere, it is an unusual hawk which consistently distinguishes between one kind of call compared to another. Frankly, if the hawk hears the whistle – whether it comprises two notes or one – she is most likely to read it as a call for food and take off with that expectation. Before long, she will look to see if you are actually *offering* food before she takes off. If you are, she'll come; if not, she probably won't.

Whatever else you do, *don't* be tempted to offer food to get her to follow on, then take it away by dropping the fist before she reaches you. If you do, she will feel cheated, and it will undermine any trust she has in you. *Whenever* you offer food you must let her have it. She might, however, respond to an empty fist held up, and then dropped once she's in the air. She might also be provoked by the sight of you fumbling around in your food pocket. Although she is unlikely to be fooled on a long-term basis, both con-tricks are worth a try in the early stages and could help to get the follow-on habit started.

If you decide to cut her weight in an attempt to improve her follow-on response, be careful. You could get one of two unwelcome reactions:

1. She might start to harass you for food by 'buzzing' (flying close by your head or some other part of your body), and landing on the ground beside or in front of you
2. She may be more aggressive than that, for instance, by trying to 'thump' you with a foot as she buzzes just to get your attention and let you know it's time you fed her.

Nevertheless, *careful* weight-reduction might be the only way you can obtain a level of response which enables you eventually to take her for walks over a reasonable distance (meaning, say, four to six follow-on flights before she gets a piece of food). But if you have to *continue* reducing weight to achieve this, you must keep a lookout for signs of low condition (see the section headed *Weight and Condition*).

Two other things might help to improve her follow-on response until the habit has been established:

1. Keep your walking pace *leisurely*. When she lands in a new tree, she will want time to look around, perhaps even swap branches to give her a better view of things. Only when she's done that will she turn her full attention to you again. If you're already two hundred yards away, she will simply feel daunted and be undecided about what to do
2. Don't expect too much from her too soon, for instance by flying her over two fields one day, then two miles the next. All this will achieve is to wear her out, then she *will* lag behind. Build up the amount of work she has to do *gradually* over several days.

Out hunting with her, your pace will be leisurely anyway, and her early free-flight training should reflect that. You will be stopping every few yards to poke around bushes and other cover to try and flush game. She, in turn, will need time in each tree to survey the ground below and around to see what she can find for herself. If you attempt to take even a seasoned hawk on a route march over several miles, you would be wasting your time – she will insist on hunting and covering the ground properly anyway.

All you're trying to do by getting her to follow-on is to give her a sense of direction – in other words you're saying: 'this is where I want us to go, and this is the ground I want us to cover'. Ultimately, the more game you produce for her to chase, the more enthusiastic she will be, but she will only develop enthusiasm *after* she's been entered and learned to hunt successfully.

Right now, you're expecting her to follow simply because you've got food. What's more, she's spent however many weeks flying a few yards to get it, and suddenly you want her to cover many times the distance. As the days wear on, she has to keep flying further and further for no additional reward – indeed, she's just as hungry as she ever was. Perhaps you could forgive her for harbouring slight feelings of tiredness and resentment. In the end though, she *will* come because she *has* to if she wants the food at all, and you will have to persist and work at it.

Using a Quarry Lure

Once she has started to follow-on, however tentatively, it's time to introduce the quarry-lure (see the section headed *Training Equipment* for a full description). Usually it resembles a rabbit, but its purpose is to encourage her to chase and catch *any* ground game. Believe it or not, she has probably never seen a rabbit in her life, and even if she has, she will certainly not have thought of it as food. First of all, therefore, you need to get her to associate the quarry lure with food, then give her practice at catching a moving one. Once the association is made, and she's catching the lure consistently 'on the run', securing the real thing is only a step away.

To begin with, the procedure is very similar to training her with a swing lure. Again it is advisable to use the quarry-lure only once in a flying session so that there's no danger of her becoming 'lure-bound'. For the moment, therefore, replace the swing lure with the quarry-lure at the end of each session.

First, get the hawk settled in a tree, then drop the garnished lure on the ground below her. Make sure the food is visible, and give her time. If you're lucky, she will jump straight onto the lure and take the food. Otherwise, she might be interested but show no inclination to leave the tree branch, or she will take off and land on the ground beside the lure.

If she stays on the branch, twitch the lure a couple of times (by pulling on the line) to make it move. If this doesn't impress her, call her to the fist with another piece of food and, when she's finished that, *plant* her on the lure. If instead she takes the other option and lands beside it, let her be for the moment. When she's plucked up enough courage, she will try to eat the food, probably without jumping onto the lure. But if you've tied it on securely she won't be able to do that because, without using her feet, she can't control it. She should then climb on to gain control.

Whichever way she ends up on the lure, after she's eaten the garnish, throw a generous piece of food to one side far enough away so that she has to jump off the lure to retrieve it. This procedure attempts to convince her that ground game is worth expending energy on because you will give her a big reward if she catches it. It is this idea of 'fair exchange' which, in the field, will enable you to get her off game easily, put it in the bag, then carry on flying without any reduction in the hawk's response or motivation. Keep doing the same thing over the next few days until she comes to the lure as soon as it is dropped in front of her. Once she's achieving this consistently, it no longer needs to be garnished.

Now you can start dragging the lure as soon as she takes off so that she has to catch it on the move. If she lands on the ground, keep going but not too fast. She might run to catch up with it, or take off and attempt another landing. Either way, *don't* give her any reward until she's secured it properly. If you do, she won't hold onto the real thing.

Eventually she will outgrow any apprehension she might have and learn to judge her landing precisely. When she's able to do that, increase your pace a little each day until she can catch the lure easily when you're running at full speed. It also helps to vary the location in which you make use of the lure.

Quarry lures can also be used to sharpen up a hawk's follow-on response, but for this you will need to pre-prepare. Before you take her out, hide the lure in the undergrowth somewhere along the route you want to take that day. When you arrive later with the hawk, drag the lure out of its hiding place and run away with it. If you want to make things really interesting, get a hidden assistant to run with it instead. In this case, attach the lure to a creance-line so that there is plenty of distance between him and the lure and, if possible, get him to drag the lure *away from you* so that it behaves in a similar manner to flushed quarry. Both will help in persuading the hawk to keep up with you and keep her attention on you.

If you intend to train your hawk to respond to an emergency whistle (see the section headed

Personal Gear), this is also a good time to do it. As with both types of lure, the secret is to get her to associate it with a generous portion of food. Don't use the whistle too often – once or twice per session is enough until she has learned to respond. The method is simply to hold up (say) the body of a day-old chick in the glove and call her to it using the new whistle, then give her a similar offering *every time you use it*.

When she is catching the moving quarry-lure consistently from wherever it appears – and she is responding to the emergency whistle if you are using one – she is ready to be entered. However, there is one other short but vital piece of training which should be addressed first – namely, transport to and from suitable hunting grounds.

Car Travel

Unless you live on a landed estate with suitable hunting grounds on your doorstep, or you have permission to use many acres of suitable ground within walking distance, there is yet another aspect of training which needs to be addressed – car travel. These days, transport to and from suitable sites is usually accomplished by car, and your hawk will need to become accustomed to riding in one.

For the bird, initial adjustment can be difficult, depending on how it is managed. At first, hawks will panic at the noise and they don't like the vehicle's movement – especially during braking, acceleration, and negotiating bends. And they don't like other vehicles behind them or going past them. So if you just stick one tethered to a portable bow perch in the back of your estate car and hope for the best, she will bate incessantly. Hawks do not understand glass, so in their panic they will make straight for the nearest window in a bid to escape. When you get to your destination, your bird's plumage will be in a horrible mess, she will have used up much of her energy, and she will be in a foul temper.

Car travel is a bit like initial manning – hawks need *gradual* exposure to it. If you manage it right, your bird might actually learn to enjoy it. There are basically two ways to overcome the initial trauma and stress of travelling:
1. Hood the bird
2. Put her in a box.

Obviously hooding is only feasible if the bird is already hood-trained (see the sections headed *Hawk Furniture,* and *Training: First Steps*). Hooding is always a good control-option to have because it calms the bird down like nothing else. If you choose this option, you've already done all the initial training required. All you need to do now is hood her, then tether her to a suitable perch in the back of the vehicle.

As far as boxes are concerned, there are basically two types – pet-carriers, and so-called 'giant' (or 'modified') hoods. If your bird hasn't been hood-trained, you will need one or other of these. Pet-carriers are available commercially, but a 'giant hood' you will have to make yourself.

Pet-carriers are actually designed for four-legged animals which can walk in and walk out. The type of carrier illustrated opposite is very common and obtainable in many pet shops.

These carriers are made of moulded plastic. They're lightweight, tough, durable, and easy to clean. The top and bottom halves are held together by retaining screws so that the whole thing can be taken apart for cleaning. The door is made of plastic-coated mesh, and there is ample ventilation. It is also easy to train a bird to go into and come out of one without the need to cast her.

To persuade her to go in, first place the carrier on a table or similar surface and place an old piece of carpet inside to give her something to grip with her feet. Open the door, then throw a piece of food inside. She may hesitate at first, but give her time. If she refuses, carry her to the lip of the door-frame and get her to step onto it if you can. If she's really stubborn and still refuses, try placing the carrier on the ground. She might amuse you by walking around it a couple of times to see if she can get to the food another way, and then go in. If not, you might have to resort to placing a trail of small pieces leading from outside the door of the crate to just inside.

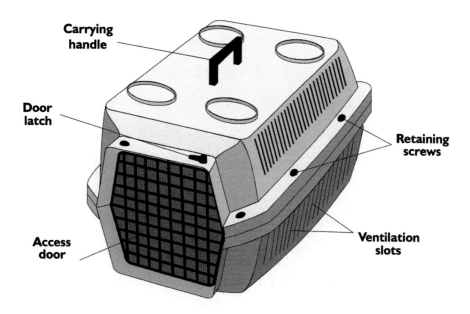

Then progressively place the food further and further towards the back of the crate until she has to go all the way in to retrieve it.

Once she's in the crate, leave the door open and let her finish the food. When she turns towards you expecting the next piece, call her back to the fist. Repeat these exercises until she's going in and coming out without any hesitation.

The next step is to close the door when she's inside, then pick the crate up and carry her around for a while. Open the door again, and call her back to the fist for another piece of food. Continue this procedure until she is totally familiar with the crate and being carried around – to the extent that she shows no anxiety at all.

This might take several days, but if this is the option you choose, it is well-worth taking the time and trouble. For her, being carried in a car as opposed to by hand is only another small adjustment to make. Even so, when you first load the crate into the car and drive away, take things *slow and easy*, and don't drive too far. You can then gradually increase speed and the distance travelled until you can drive normally wherever you want to go without her showing any signs of distress. It will also help her to accept car travel in the crate if you can use this part of training to take her to and from a flying ground. She will then associate travel itself with something worthwhile – getting her food ration, or later on, going out hunting.

However, there are two major problems I've found with carrying hawks around in crates like this:
1. A certain amount of food has to be held back to make it work
2. The bird is free to move around within the confines of the carrier.

You will need to reserve one piece of food to persuade her to go into the crate, and one to get her out again. You will then have to repeat the process at the end of her flying session. This cuts the amount of food you have to work with in the field without exceeding her rations, and therefore reduces real flying time. Also, the fact that she can move around inside the crate doesn't do her tail plumage any favours and it can end up in a real mess before you even start flying. The problem is that you can't black the crate out fully. The mesh door can be light-proofed with a piece of black bin bag or cardboard cut to shape, but it's difficult to deal with the ventilation slits – the more you interfere with these trying to cut out light, the less air you give the bird.

The 'giant hood' is an American invention and increasing in popularity here. If it's made well, it is capable of being blacked out completely and restricts the hawk's movements – not only because she is 'hooded' and therefore less anxious, but also because she is tethered. The basic idea is illustrated below.

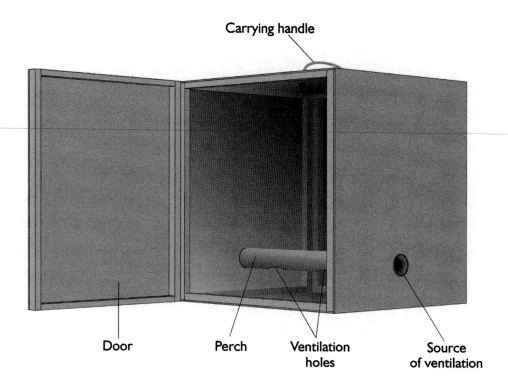

Carrying handle

Door   Perch   Ventilation   Source
                             holes   of ventilation

In this example, the perch is made of plastic pipe – the type used by plumbers for under-sink drainage is ideal. It needs to be hollow to provide ventilation inside the 'hood', and this is achieved by drilling holes on the underside of the perch which admit air into the interior. Cover the standing area of the perch if you want to – with Astroturf, carpet, or leather – but bear in mind that the hawk will not develop bumblefoot by perching on a piece of smooth plastic pipe for a few minutes, or even two or three hours.

The door is the element that needs most attention. You can never block out every ray of light in a box like this, but it should be blacked out as much as possible, which means that the door needs to be close fitting. Door furniture (hinges, latches, etc) can militate against this so choose them carefully and construct the door as best you can. Flush hinges, and two or three fastenings (top and bottom, or top, bottom and centre) work best because they help to nullify any warpage in the door which would otherwise admit light. Also a simple carrying handle on top will increase portability.

This device works very well, and there is no additional training needed to get the hawk to use it – you just back her onto the perch as if you were putting her into her weathering, secure the leash, then close the door. The leash can be tied to the perch with a standard falconer's knot, or to a large staple driven into the inside framework of the box. Some people secure the leash outside the box by drilling a hole in the side, passing it through, then securing it to a staple in the same way. This allows them to take control of the leash before the door is opened. However, any holes drilled through the box are going to allow light through, which tends to defeat the object of the exercise.

All these methods of transporting birds can be used on a permanent basis. Indeed, some falconers much prefer to use the 'giant hood' instead of hooding the bird on a perch simply because it doesn't cause distraction to other motorists who might see a hooded bird in the back of a vehicle. However, once she's used to travelling in a car she should adapt to perching unhooded on a portable bow-perch or the back of a seat without any difficulty – especially if she has already been entered. This is by far the best method of transportation in my opinion, because the hawk can maintain an interest in the journey by looking out of the window, even spotting potential quarry on the way. She might be an object of curiosity for other motorists, but that's no different to seeing any other unusual or interesting cargo on the road.

Clearly, though, not all kinds of vehicle are suitable for carrying hawks in this way. For example, a two-seater coupé sports car with only the back of the passenger seat as a potential perch is asking for trouble. If the hawk bates for any reason, she will seriously interfere with your driving. Unless you can devise some new method of tethering your bird properly on a back seat, even standard saloon cars or hatch-backs are unsuitable for transporting large hawks, except by carrier or giant hood.

The best vehicles for tethering broadwings to a perch are vans, estate cars, or larger 4 x 4s, all of which have a floor area at the rear on which you can place a portable bow-perch without any danger of interference. Of these, estates and 4 x 4s are preferable because they also give the hawk a view of the outside world in transit.

Entering And Basic Hunting

Introduction

'Entering' is, unequivocally, about catching something with your newly-trained hawk. Chasing and securing natural prey will give meaning to her life because, in the process, she will be presented with problems and challenges that her particular species has evolved to overcome. She will have to use her brains as well as all her physical attributes to succeed consistently. Regular success will ensure that she develops into a confident and competent bird of prey. A hawk that can't catch its own food is worth nothing to nature, and in falconry terms she might as well live in a zoo.

When she catches her first head of quarry she will know immediately what life is all about, and she will want to do it again and again. For her, hunting will become of paramount importance. In addition, entering a first hawk is central to your own identity as a falconer. But one catch is not enough: it will neither satisfy your hawk, nor merit the title of falconer. After her first, if you haven't got your hunting organised into an effective partnership, she is most likely to take control of her own future by abandoning you and relying on herself. Entering is, therefore, a risk as well as a necessary step for both of you.

Four things are required to get a hawk entered *and* provide the foundation for a long-term partnership:
1. She needs to be flown in an area where there is plenty of appropriate quarry
2. You need to flush the quarry for her to chase — *and she must see that you flushed it*
3. She needs to catch and secure it
4. Once it is secured, you need to reward her by feeding her as much as she can eat *on the spot* – preferably with part of the animal she has caught.

If you reward her with an abundance of food the first six or seven times, she will become totally committed to the pursuit of game. And once she associates your activity with its appearance, she will learn to see you as useful and be much more willing to follow.

Feeding her up when she succeeds means you will have to abandon the flying session from that point on – and for the next two or three days until she's back to flying weight – but it is well worth the sacrifice. These will be the largest amounts of food she has received from your hands since she first ate from the fist, and this action more than any other will get the message across. Once she is succeeding regularly, you can then move onto catching several heads of quarry each session without losing her motivation or enthusiasm.

Preparation

The use of dogs and ferrets is covered later (see the sections headed *Hunting Aids*), but assuming you have neither for the moment, a stout walking stick is an invaluable tool. It is used primarily to beat hedgerows and ground cover to help flush out game, but it is also an aid to climbing steep and slippery banks (especially with a bird on the fist); beating your way through brambles, nettles, bracken, and any other obtrusive undergrowth; climbing over unyielding barbed wire fences; acting as an insulator when you want to get over an electrified fence; and above all, something to lean on when you need to regain your breath.

It helps if the stick has a crooked handle which can be hooked over your arm (or a gate, or some other convenient place) when you need your free hand to do some work, such as feeding your hawk. Bending down to pick a stick up off the ground when feeding is over is both irritating and awkward – especially if she is still on the fist. An alternative is to have the stick carved into a point at its bottom end so that you can push it into the ground out of the way.

When you decide to go out on your first serious hunt, you will need plenty of food for the hawk, which means at least double her normal rations. This is really a fall-back measure. When she catches her first head of game you should use part of the quarry to feed her up on the spot but, for a variety of reasons, it is always useful to have an extra supply of food. For example, if she finds a piece of carrion stashed in a tree-fork by a wild buzzard, and you've only got one piece of her normal rations left, you will have a problem. It might take lots of food to tempt her back down again. It helps to keep this additional supply separate so that you can keep track of, and control, her intake if she catches nothing.

Some young broadwings – notably Harris' Hawks – will chase almost anything that moves, including such unpalatable items as stones or apples accidentally kicked along the ground. Where wildlife is concerned, they might have a go at any kind of bird from a wren to a buzzard, or mammals from shrews to deer. If you're lucky enough to own such a bird, *never discourage her*. Often such sorties end in failure, but chasing *anything* wild will improve her fitness, speed, stamina, footing ability and flying experience. She will soon learn which of them is too big, too small or too fast – in other words, what merits using her energy resources. Indeed, she has to go through such a learning process if she is to become a successful hunter, and you should allow her enough freedom to work these things out for herself.

Your role is to choose and cover the ground you want to hunt, and make every effort to find and flush quarry for her. The training schedule she has just gone through gives you the flexibility to use two different hunting methods – *follow-on* flights, and *off-the fist* flights.

Follow-on Flights

This technique is used in wooded areas where there are plenty of trees for the hawk to work from. Ideally of course, she should fly on *ahead* of you because quarry, when it is flushed, mostly breaks away from you. Obviously, if she's ahead, there is a good chance it will be moving in her direction. In addition, the higher she is in a tree, the more she will have the advantage of speed and surprise.

An unentered eyass is unlikely to use height or forward perches at first since they both involve skills acquired through experience of abortive flights. More likely, she will lag behind using fence posts or low branches, and you might have to take things much slower than you would like. However, don't let her lag behind more than fifty to a hundred yards. If she's still sitting in a tree when you've gone this far, wait for her.

Although this behaviour is not acceptable on a long-term basis, at this point *you are trying to get her entered*. If, through impatience, you call her for food, or you return to her to do the same thing, she will end up training you. On the other hand, if you walk on, you will lose touch with her, which means you will also lose control. It is best to adopt the attitude: 'OK. If you think you can do better, get on with it'. If she does find something and connects, you will still be close enough to see it and take charge. If she doesn't, she will soon get bored with waiting for her rations, and she will fly towards you.

Unfortunately there is nothing you can do to teach your hawk about the benefits of height – she will either learn this from experience, or she won't. But it will help to encourage her if there are plenty of tall trees around and you include them in your itinerary as much as possible.

This can be nerve-wracking to do initially. It is easy to feel a sense of panic when you see your first newly-trained hawk launch herself into the top of a massive oak completely out of sight, then still find the courage to walk on. But you must show some trust in her (as well as faith in her training) and take the risk, otherwise she can never fully develop as a falconry bird. Remember also that, when she lands in a tree she will want some time to survey the ground. She may even 'ladder up' branches to gain height and get a better view – the higher she is the further she will be able to see. A hawk's vision is several times better than our own, and she will be able to spot things completely hidden from you.

Hawks also seem to *sense* when there is game around, so watch her demeanour if you can see her at all. For example, if she is looking down at a particular spot studying it intently, with a still head and hunched-up appearance, this is usually a sign that she thinks there is something there. She might have seen a slight movement in the undergrowth, or heard a rustle, and is waiting for confirmation before she commits herself to an attempted strike. If she gives you such a positive cue, concentrate on the area and try to drive any possible game *towards* her position rather than away from it. If there is nothing there, your activity will confirm it for her, as well as satisfying yourself.

Above all, take your time and work the ground thoroughly before you move on. This might mean slow-going at first, but it is totally pointless and even worse, a waste of a golden opportunity, to flush a rabbit from a hedgerow when she's still two hundred yards behind. Remember: *the further you are apart, the less of a working partnership you can develop*. To maintain control, you must be aware of where she is, what she's doing, and how she's reacting to her new environment.

Maintaining control is an easy thing to suggest, but it can seem difficult to achieve. For example, you might occasionally hear your hawk (through her bells) flying off in completely the 'wrong' direction and out of sight. Then it is your turn to follow, probably in a blind panic. When you catch up with her, she is perching on a branch with no apparent reason for her sudden disappearance. However, it is highly likely that she was chasing something, which managed to find cover. Before you call her back or try to persuade her to follow on again, check the area and beat any undergrowth around her position.

It has to be said that, without a dog's nose, flushing game is not at all easy and falls far short of a science. Mainly it involves blundering around undergrowth in the hope that any quarry will be sufficiently alarmed to show itself. However, your 'blundering' should at least be systematic and comprehensive. It can be slow, hard, and tedious work, and it is very tempting to rely more on your hawk's superior vision and other senses by letting her do her own thing. If at all possible, *don't* relinquish this element of control on a long-term basis for the sake of acquiring flights. The more quarry she finds for herself, the less inclined she will be to take your lead in terms of where to go and when to follow. Ultimately, if you fail to strike the right balance, you will risk losing control permanently. It is much better to fly her somewhere where you can be more certain of serving her.

Flushing is actually possible without a dog if you work the ground well. But it is totally unnecessary to thrash hedgerows or other cover violently with the stick – a few well-directed taps and pokes are sufficient. When you poke the stick in undergrowth, wiggle it from side to side to disturb it as much as possible. The technique is simply to keep moving forwards disturbing ground cover as you go. Indeed, just *walking* through a clump of nettles or ferns should achieve a flush if there is any game in there.

Even when you manage a flush, a catch is by no means certain. Pheasants in particular will sit tight until you virtually step on them, then they explode from the ground and make for the nearest alternative cover at high speed – certainly much faster than the average broadwing. Similarly, fit, healthy and wise rabbits rarely stray far from a burrow in daylight and they usually manage to get underground or at least in dense cover such as bramble or gorse, before the hawk catches up with them. Don't despair. Often a hawk, after an unsuccessful flight, will perch above (mark) the spot where she saw the quarry disappear. Whatever else you do, *don't* be tempted to call her back and move on. Instead, go to that spot and attempt to re-flush the quarry. Re-flushing quarry can account for a significant proportion of successful flights because the hawk is already in a good position to intercept and is totally 'tuned in'. More importantly where an eyass is concerned:

- it will improve her *commitment* to chasing quarry because she will learn that, even if she can't secure it on the first attempt, she might get a second chance through your efforts. Consequently,
- it will reinforce your role in the partnership.

It pays, therefore, to grasp any re-flushing opportunity with open arms — not least because you know there is something in there. However, if it's a rabbit which has found refuge in a warren it will be irretrievable without a good ferret.

Off-the-Fist Flights

These days flights straight from the fist with broadwings are used in very open country with few or no significant trees for the hawk to work from. Alternatively, the method is useful when it would be unwise to fly the hawk free – for instance, in the spring when there is a plethora of nesting birds (rooks, crows, doves and the like). If she gets into a nest harbouring several chicks, she will eat the lot and totally ignore any attempts to retrieve her. Off-the-fist flights are also used in ferreting (see the section on *Hunting Aids*) if the hawk is prone to catch the ferret as it ambles between rabbit holes.

Rough ground with vegetation such as nettles, fern or bracken; clumps of gorse and bramble; tussocks of long grass, and so on, is ideal country for this method of flying. But the technique can also be used in large featureless fields provided there are hedgerows likely to harbour quarry. The hawk is carried on the fist as normal (controlled by flying jesses), and game is flushed in the same way as for follow-on flights – by walking through such cover or beating it as you go.

Once game is flushed, the hawk is released and uses the fist as a launching platform. Some hawks are faster than others off the fist, but to an extent lack of initial speed can be compensated for by the relative openness of the terrain, which gives the hawk more time to catch up and the quarry less chance of reaching effective cover. Off-the-fist flights can be very exciting, therefore, because:

- you get to see the whole flight instead of at least part of it being obscured by woodland
- the flight itself is usually longer and more testing for the hawk
- on rough ground in particular, you get more opportunities for a successful re-flush.

However, the technique can also involve difficult judgements, especially when they conflict with the hawk's. For example: quarry is sighted in the distance and you consider it to be too far away. You hold her back and she bates. You might be right to restrain her, but – even if she can't catch up with it on this flight – she will probably put it into cover from which it can be re-flushed. In addition, it is quite amazing how fast and persistent a fit broadwing can be when she feels she has a chance of securing prey. The best advice I can give is this: back her judgement, and let her go – you won't lose anything, and she might learn a great deal.

Another kind of problem is presented by quarry, such as a rabbit, which has 'frozen' in full view in the middle of a field. You can see it plainly, but the hawk doesn't seem to notice it. Superior to our own it might be, but a hawk's vision is attuned to movement and as long as the rabbit remains absolutely still it is unlikely that she will recognise it as potential quarry. The rabbit 'knows' this which is why it has frozen. Even if you throw (cast) her off the fist in an attempt to get her to chase it, she will simply fly around looking for somewhere to land. Of course, once the rabbit moves she will see it, and the trick is to provoke this movement – preferably manoeuvring between the quarry and close cover before you do.

The main drawback to using off-the-fist flights exclusively is that the hawk won't become fully fit because she won't spend enough time in the air. But they can be extremely valuable in helping a fit bird to develop stamina and persistence. If you want to try the technique, it is best to combine it with follow-on flights as long as you use those as the primary means of exercise, especially if you're only able to take the hawk out at weekends. Otherwise, you will have to rely on artificial fitness programmes (see the section headed *Maintaining Fitness*).

Retrieving Quarry

When your hawk catches her first head of game, get to her as soon as you can. Take hold of the quarry, then throw a generous portion of food to one side so that she jumps off to feed (exactly as you did when training her with the quarry-lure). Dispatch the quarry as quickly and humanely as possible (see opposite). Cut off the head, then put the rest in your game pouch out of sight – hopefully before the hawk has finished eating. Call her back to the fist with the head of the quarry, secure the jesses, and let her eat her fill. Then take her straight home. Repeat this procedure for *at least* the next half-dozen 'kills'.

Unfortunately, retrieval is not always easy or straightforward. Good hawks – those with real persistence and commitment – will often pursue and catch quarry in very difficult cover such as the middle of a bramble bush. Indeed, you may stand and wonder how she managed to find *any* opening to fly in there. But the fact is that she has, and you will have to extricate her together with her catch. She won't be able to fly out with it, and she certainly won't release it. The longer you take to get them both out, therefore, the more you will prolong the quarry's suffering (assuming it isn't already dead). In short, you will have to get *in there* yourself as quickly as possible, being especially careful not to collapse all the foliage on top of the hawk. The best way is to lift or tread the obtrusive vegetation down carefully until you've created a feasible escape route for both of you.

When you reach your hawk, *don't* attempt to grab her and pull her out. Instead, take hold of the quarry, and manoeuvre it out as best you can. The hawk will follow, still gripping it with her feet. You can be assured that – whatever else happens – she won't let go of it, so concentrate on extricating the quarry, making sure at the same time that your hawk has a clear exit.

Once your hawk has caught her first head of game her self-confidence will increase noticeably. To build on this, develop her fitness and stamina, and ultimately her full potential, you will need to take her out as often as you possibly can. If you do, she will improve as the season progresses. Then next season she will be even better.

Dispatching Quarry

For many people, in particular those new to country sports – this aspect of falconry is the most distasteful and the most unfamiliar. These days, for the vast majority of us, killing animals for food – or for any other reason – is not a skill we grow up with. Indeed, it is one we assiduously avoid acquiring if we can, and one which we are happy to leave to professionals. However, if you want to persist with falconry, it is essential that you learn how to dispatch quarry quickly and humanely. This is because

- no broadwinged hawk will kill quarry instantaneously. She will eventually if you let her – by penetrating its vital organs with her talons; *or* by tearing it apart and eating it alive until it dies from shock or loss of blood
- a good hawk will always target the *head* of the quarry. Somehow she knows that this is the most effective way of subduing it. Consequently some quarry will suffer head wounds – in particular penetration of the eyes.

As a civilised human being, you can't allow a slow death or a serious injury to prolong suffering. It is your responsibility to make sure that the quarry is dispatched as soon as possible in these circumstances.

The quickest and most humane method is to sever the neck vertebrae. With mammals (such as rabbits and hares) this is done by gripping the animal by the hips with one hand, and at the point where the head meets the neck with the other. A sharp pull outwards (which requires a fair amount of force) will then separate the skull from the spinal column killing it instantly. With birds, the quickest method is to twist the head and neck sharply in opposite directions. If the task is performed properly, both kinds of quarry will display involuntary muscular reactions at the point of death – mammals by kicking their legs, birds by flapping their wings. Neither should be taken as a sign that they are still alive, and still suffering.

Of course, if the quarry is completely uninjured or its injuries are minor you can let it go if she's already in the habit of hunting and you don't need the quarry to reinforce the message. However, this will have to be done out of sight. Releasing it where the hawk can see it will only result in a swift re-capture. This is because it will be suffering from shock – a physical state which will render it incapable of evasive action for some time. If it is caught a second time, you might then have to dispatch it because it has acquired a serious injury. The best place to release uninjured quarry is in dense undergrowth which it can sidle into, rest up, and recover from the shock without being seen from overhead. Otherwise, if you happen to be in the middle of a field, a suitably-sized empty pocket of your falconry bag or hawking vest will perform the same function until you can release it safely.

Carrion

For any falconer flying broadwings, carrion can be a real nuisance. Whatever age it is, it seems to be just as palatable as live quarry (but much easier for the bird to secure). In addition, the attraction is not limited to animals they normally catch –the remains could be fox, badger, buzzard, sheep, any other kind of animal, or something totally unidentifiable. Even though they have difficulty recognising live but immobile quarry in the field, they seem to home in on carrion with unerring accuracy and I know of no rational explanation for this discrepancy.

However, from the hawk's point of view, she has 'caught' the carrion and, if you want to get her off it, you will have to treat it in much the same way as live quarry, in other words, offer her a generous portion of regular food in exchange. If you are unfortunate enough for your hawk to come across three or four such pieces of carrion in a day's flying it can affect the whole session, simply because you will use up much of her food ration just by retrieving her.

In addition, once you've recovered your hawk, it is short-sighted to leave the carrion where it is. Unless she finds something else to occupy her interest very quickly (such as live quarry), she will probably fly straight back to it and 'catch' it again. There are only two practical solutions to this problem:

1. You get rid of the carrion while she is eating the food you've offered her – either by hiding the remains somewhere in the undergrowth, or putting it in your game pouch for disposal later; *or*
2. Once she's finished the food-offering, you collect her up on the fist and carry her well away from the scene.

In practice, the option you choose will most likely depend on the carrion itself. For instance, if it is the best part of a whole sheep it will be difficult to take with you (always assuming you would be willing to do so). Similarly, such a large specimen would be very difficult to hide effectively in the limited time you have.

Missing Hawks

Disconcerting though it might sound, there will be occasions when your hawk goes absent without leave in the field, in particular, if you attempt to fly her in too high a condition. If you do, she is likely to display a degree of independence not conducive to discipline and go her own way. In this case, the penalty might be a permanently lost hawk. Any attempt to recover her will probably prove futile because there is very little you can do to persuade her to return. Indeed, by flying off she has already decided to reject what she knows you have to offer.

This aside, even if your hawk is at flying weight, there might still be times when she goes missing, usually in pursuit of quarry. You could be fortunate enough to have a broadwing which is both fit and determined, and will chase game such as pheasant over a long distance. Depending on terrain, you might lose sight of her very quickly – over the brow of a hill, along a line of trees, or through a wooded area.

One problem is that, out of sight, she could change direction any number of times, depending on the evasion tactics of the quarry. Indeed, she may even see another type of game during her pursuit which looks easier to catch, and chase that instead. A missing hawk easily becomes permanently lost, and you will need to take positive action to avoid this outcome.

The first rule is: *never panic*. This is easy to say, but controlling panic is actually the most difficult part of the operation, especially when you view the vastness of the terrain in front of you and realise that your missing hawk could be anywhere.

A second thing to bear in mind is that the hawk will know where she left you. If she's in the habit of returning automatically after abortive flights, assume she failed to secure the quarry and give her a chance to return. If the flight was long and energetic, she might want to regain her breath before starting back, and she will probably do the return in easy stages. For the moment, therefore, stay in the vicinity and listen out for her bells. Once you hear them, or catch sight of her, make your way towards her calling her in for food using a whistle (if she is familiar with one) and the swing lure.

If she's not in the habit of returning automatically, or there's no sign of her after a reasonable length of time, you will have no option but to move. Make your way in the direction she was flying when you lost sight of her, but get onto open ground if possible such as the middle of a field (or better still, the brow of a hill) to give yourself the best chance of seeing her, and the hawk the best chance of seeing you. Study any visible fields to see if you can spot her on the ground. If she has caught the quarry she will spread her wings (mantle) over it to hide it from other predators. A large, mantling hawk out in the open can usually be seen from quite a distance. Alternatively, scrutinise trees and hedgerows for large perching birds. If both these draw a blank, look for other clues such as a mob of rooks or crows which might be trying to drive the hawk away (but don't rely on this; they could be harassing a wild hawk, or simply squabbling amongst themselves).

Use the whistle and swing the lure frequently as you move, but stop occasionally to listen for her bells. The whistle will give her an audible clue to your position, and she should be able to see the swinging lure from a long way away if you are in the open. You might even catch sight of her before you hear any bells – large hawks in flight are not difficult to see in an open landscape – but either way, once you have located her, make into her as quickly as you can.

The worst possible scenario is that the hawk has caught her quarry in cover and is waiting for you to show up. In this situation she will not respond to either the whistle or the swing lure because she won't let go of her kill. Even worse is that for several minutes at least (perhaps longer) she will stand absolutely still on top of the quarry. This is an instinctive reaction to avoid the attention of other predators in the area which might attempt to rob her. But because she is not moving, you will hear no bells. Depending on how thick the cover is, you could be two yards away and be unable to see or hear her.

In this situation one consolation will be the knowledge that she will move eventually. Another is that she is much more likely to have flown at most a few hundred yards – certainly not several miles. When she is satisfied that there are no other predators around, she will start to feed and, as she tugs at the meal, her tail bell will ring. It will take her a long time to eat her fill off a rabbit or a pheasant, and even then she may be reluctant to leave it.

You will, therefore, have some time to locate her, but you will have to rely on hearing her bells. By all means search any cover around, but listen out constantly for the tell-tale ring. If you do disturb cover, be careful that you don't trample it on top of her or stab her with your stick. Lift the cover, and look underneath. Obviously if you have been flying the hawk with a dog, give him free rein – his nose could save you a great deal of time.

A hawk whose rations are regularly restricted to maintain flying weight will continue gorging herself until well after dark if she feels safe enough, so don't despair if night is pressing in. Stay with it as long as you can. Keep searching, even if this means covering the same ground several times and, above all, keep listening. It is important that every attempt is made to find her *while she is still on the kill*. This is because she will be easy to retrieve by picking her up with what is left of the quarry, then taking control of her jesses. If she has already gorged herself and flown off into a tree, she is unlikely to come to the fist or a lure for more food – at least, not for several hours.

If she's in a tree and refuses to come down to you, or you fail to locate her, you will have no option but to return to the area before dawn the next day. If you can find it, leave the remains of the quarry where it is before you go – she is less likely to fly off hunting elsewhere with a large parcel of food at her feet – and pray that it isn't stolen by a fox or something else overnight. Prior to your return, collect up every piece of food and equipment likely to be useful for retrieving her – the swing-lure, quarry-lure and, above all, lots of her favourite meals (rats, quail, or whatever else she is particularly fond of). Even a creance line is useful.

Assuming that you can find her the next day, the strategy is simply to tempt her as much as possible back to the fist by giving her every opportunity to indulge her inherent greed. Probably the best place to start is with the remains of the quarry if it's still there. Pick it up and call her to it. If she's unimpressed, try throwing it in the air and letting it land on the ground. Use other types of food if she's still reluctant, as well as both types of lure. Even if she's not very responsive, such activity should at least keep her attentive and less inclined to move on.

Greed and conditioning should eventually overcome her reluctance, but if she persistently refuses the fist or the lures, she *might* be willing to come for food if you are well away from it. Attach a large piece (preferably one that she can't easily carry) to the creance line and unwind thirty or forty yards, then drag it slowly along the ground in full view. If and when she lands on it, you can then wind the line around her feet by walking round her in large circles.

Obviously if you are unable to locate her when you arrive on the scene, the previous day's search technique – using the whistle and lures and listening for bells – will have to be repeated. And on following days if necessary, until you either give up the search or you locate and retrieve her. Of course, the longer she is free, the further she is likely to range and after a few days she may be impossible to find except through a stroke of luck.

Never discount luck – many hawks are retrieved through its auspices. In fact it would be wise to give it a helping hand by making it widely known that the bird has gone missing. Tell landowners and their staff in the area, advertise in local newspapers and shops, or even further afield if you can stand the cost. Make sure that everyone has a full description of the hawk as well as her ring number, and who to contact if she is found. Many reports of sightings will turn out to be false, but if you want to recover her, you will have to follow-up every one of them however unlikely they might seem. If you do manage to locate her, make use of every possible inducement to persuade her to return.

Hunting Aids: *Dogs*

Introduction

Although never essential for flying broadwings, a well-trained dog can enhance a day's hunting to such an extent that you might wonder how you ever managed without one. Indeed, it is difficult to see how the combination of a dog's nose and a hawk's eyes, brought to bear on a good choice of ground, can be improved upon. With a reliable dog as a team member, you will probably get dozens more flights every season, and even areas you thought were scarce in quarry might suddenly come to life.

You will probably read elsewhere that Harris' Hawks abhor dogs. This is said to be because, in the wild, coyotes steal their food and are their only natural enemies. This might be true, but don't let it put you off buying a Harris' Hawk or a dog. In fact *all* broadwings dislike having a dog around at first and will scream or bate at the sight of it. But all species, including Harris' Hawks, can be persuaded to put up with them. The secret is to introduce dog and bird to each other as soon as you acquire the hawk, then have the dog present during her manning and training sessions.

One necessary requirement is that the dog is fully-trained before you acquire the hawk. It takes many months to train a working dog properly – certainly a lot longer than it takes to train a hawk – and a boisterous and disobedient puppy could put your hawk off dogs for life. Trying to train them both together is likely therefore to end in disaster. Whichever kind of hawk you have, she will only tolerate a dog that behaves well towards her and, when she's entered, finds game for her to chase. Indeed, the latter will be the only motive she has for maintaining her tolerance once she's free to claim her independence.

Choice of Dog

Unfortunately no dog breed has yet been developed specifically for falconry, but falconers usually make use of varieties bred for working with guns (gundogs). Of these, there are four basic types
1. Hunters
2. Retrievers
3. Pointers
4. Versatiles.

These categories describe the dog's *expertise* – the purpose of its breeding. Any kind of dog will use its nose to find quarry, but breeds like the English Springer Spaniel excel in this respect. For example, if there is a rabbit or a pheasant anywhere on a large piece of ground, a well-trained Springer will find it every time, no matter how rough the ground is or how much cover it provides. Indeed, another of their virtues is that they will work through difficult cover, such as bramble, like a miniature tank. Most dogs can be trained to retrieve, but retrievers (including Labradors) excel in this particular skill, especially in water. Such breeds also have what is known as a 'soft mouth', which ensures that game is returned to their handler in good condition rather than as a mess of mangled remains. Pointing breeds also use their noses to find game, but instead of flushing it as soon as it is located, they will stand 'on point' until told to flush. This gives the sportsman time to prepare himself, increasing his chances of a 'pot'. It is no accident, therefore, that organised shoots usually include at least two types of gundog, each contributing its own expertise to the success of the event.

Versatile breeds, such as the German Shorthaired and Wirehaired Pointers or the Hungarian Viszla, were developed in mainland Europe primarily to remove the need to take several dogs on a shoot. They are sometimes known as HRPs (an acronym for Hunter-Retriever-Pointer) and, as their classification suggests, they possess all three field skills. As 'jacks-of-all-trades' it is generally acknowledged that their level of skill in each case falls slightly short of their specially-bred cousins but, if they come from good working stock, and if they're trained properly, they make excellent sporting dogs in all field conditions.

Retrieving is not a canine talent that falconers require. The reason is simple: the hawk catches the quarry and the falconer retrieves it – from the hawk. What falconers do need is, first and foremost, a dog which will find any game in the vicinity. Springers might be superb in this respect but, even if the dog is trained to stop (which means to stand still, sit or lie down) as soon as he flushes game, the hawk might be lagging someway behind and her chances of catching the quarry are therefore reduced.

For this reason many falconers use pointers. With goshawks and broadwings HRPs are usually preferred. When trained properly they will hunt much like a spaniel and, once game is located, stand 'on point' until given another command. If the dog is reliable, the next command will be to flush the game, otherwise the falconer performs this function himself. This temporary stand-off enables him to bring his hawk into a good position before the quarry is flushed.

English Pointers are also used in falconry, but normally only with game hawks (particularly peregrines). Their point is very reliable and precise, but they tend to range too far afield for broadwings. More importantly, they don't instinctively point ground game (such as rabbits) which is the basis of broadwing falconry.

If you can't afford a good pedigree working dog, any cross-breed or mongrel will find and flush game, even though he might miss several chances which would never get past a specialist. Whichever kind you use, if the dog doesn't point, it will be imperative to have the hawk working closely with him by getting her (through experience) to recognise that he is a potential source of quarry. She will then follow him rather than you. Out in the field all *entered* hawks learn to watch a successful dog's activity intensely once they have experienced two or three flushes, and they will stick close by in anticipation. This is one of several reasons why good dog control is of vital importance. In effect, the dog will take over from you as the hawk's motivation for following-on. If he is ranging two hundred yards ahead, the hawk will probably stay with him and you might as well go home for all the use you are as a team leader.

Any dog's behaviour – pedigree or otherwise – is, therefore, of paramount importance in the field. A disobedient one will *always* spoil a flight or a flight opportunity. In fact, such dogs are a real nuisance. They will either flush and drive all potential quarry into deep cover before you or your hawk arrive anywhere near the scene or, if the hawk is working well with him, you will never get to see a flight because the two of them will go off on their own. You might then have trouble locating the hawk and, if you do, she will probably have gorged herself on a kill and be very difficult to retrieve.

Controlling your dog – especially in these circumstances – means you will also stay in touch with the hawk and her activity. *Remember*: loveable as he might be, he is only a flushing tool, not the manager of the day's sport. If he's going to be useful, you must decide in which direction the team goes and when – meaning which ground you want to cover, which route you want to take, and at what pace.

Training Requirements

Although all pedigree working dogs have been bred to perform certain tasks, their inherited characteristics are present only as a potential which has to be realised and developed through proper training. No dog, however good its pedigree, will retrieve or point automatically.

There are people who sell dogs ready-trained if you don't feel confident enough to do that for yourself, but you will have to pay a high price for one. Even then, whilst the dog might behave impeccably for his trainer (whom he is accustomed to treating as 'top-dog'), you might find that his response to you in the first weeks is less than satisfactory. This is hardly surprising. He has formed no bond with you and, although part of his training will involve socialisation with other people, as far as he's concerned, you're just another member of the pack. As such he will do everything he can to assert his dominance and, in the process, he could give you all sorts of trouble depending on the strength of his personality.

There is a mass of literature on training any dog for field work, and it is inappropriate to cover the same ground here. But for work with broadwings, obedience to the following commands must be instant and consistent:

1. Walk to heel – on your right-hand side if you carry the hawk with your left hand, or vice versa – with and without a lead
2. Stop (which means stand still, sit, or lie down) for as long as you want him to, whether you are in sight or not, and however far away you are
3. Quarter (which means zig-zagging over the ground across the wind), or change direction on your call
4. Search cover at your direction
5. Return to you, in or out of sight, from any distance, and in all circumstances.

All these disciplines will be needed at one time or another in the field. For example, walking to heel will be necessary when you are carrying your hawk to circumvent an area the landowner has asked you to avoid – such as one containing pheasant pens. A dog causing havoc amongst them, and a hawk bating furiously to get at them, is hardly likely to enhance the day's sport or your temper. Equally, a dog which ignores all attempts to make him stop and which persists in chasing game he's just flushed will ruin the hawk's flight. Even if she's willing to make the attempt, she will always have one eye at least on the dog, and if he gets anywhere near the quarry she will back off.

As an *absolute minimum*, therefore, you must be able to make the dog stop what he's doing instantly, and return to you instantly, whatever temptation he's exposed to. If he can do that, you can keep him out of trouble and you might have a chance of training him to be even more useful. It doesn't matter whether you use hand signals, your voice, a whistle, or a combination of all three to control him, but if you use a whistle, make sure it is different to any the hawk responds to. Similarly, if you make use of hand signals, don't use the gloved hand, which might provoke the hawk to return to you unnecessarily.

Out in the field, your dog must be capable of full control whether he's actually working with the hawk or not, especially when there are sheep, chickens or any other farm animals around. Nothing will get you banned from a hunting ground more readily than a delinquent hound harassing a landowner's pets or livestock. If he's caught worrying sheep, especially at lambing time, he could be shot in front of your eyes and you will have no cause for complaint in law. Should he prove to be a menace, the guilt is entirely yours – for allowing him a degree of freedom that he was insufficiently disciplined to appreciate. Lack of proper training, or persistent irresponsibility on your part, might inflict on him the ultimate penalty – judicial execution.

It is much the better policy, therefore, to steer well clear of fields containing livestock, at least until you can be completely confident of his behaviour and response to discipline in such circumstances. Even if you are confident, you might have to convince a landowner that your confidence is justified, otherwise he will rightly insist that you avoid any fields harbouring livestock. For the dog's sake, and for the cause of falconry in general, you must respect such a stricture – even if you think it's unfair.

Hunting Aids: *Ferrets*

For the purposes of falconry, ferrets are only employed to flush rabbits out of their burries (warrens) or hedgerows for the hawk to chase. They are not used to hunt rabbits *per se* – with purse nets, or any alternative device. Also, they tend to be utilised as a last resort when flushing rabbits becomes difficult by any other means. This can happen, for example, where there are large populations of predators – which have the effect of keeping rabbits underground in the daytime – or where the number of rabbits has been drastically reduced by guns, other ferreters, myxomatosis, farming practices, or bad weather.

It has to be said that there are several disadvantages to using ferrets to serve a hawk:
- few hawks can be trusted not to catch a ferret wandering from one rabbit hole to another, which usually means keeping the hawk under control on the fist until a rabbit bolts well clear
- achieving a flush with a ferret can take time – particularly in a large warren – and the wait can be very boring for the bird as well as you
- even with a successful flush, the rabbit often escapes by going down a different burrow close by
- if you get a flight, it is usually very short – perhaps ten or twenty yards, depending on the speed of the hawk off the fist or the proximity of the nearest alternative cover for the rabbit
- if you have to fly the hawk off the fist, you might need an assistant to handle the ferret which means carrying it to and from the site, collecting it up when you want to transfer it to another warren, and so on
- occasionally the ferret will catch and kill a rabbit underground, especially when there are young in the warren. If she does, she will eat what she wants, then have a nap. Unless you're prepared to dig her out with a spade (which means going back home for one or taking one with you), she will stay underground for at least an hour, and possibly overnight
- keeping ferrets is another animal-management responsibility to take on. Like all others, they have their own feeding regime, housing, equipment, social and exercise requirements

The dilemma for falconers is that, where most broadwings are concerned, rabbits provide 'bread-and-butter' sport. If the hawk finds nothing else to chase in a hunting session, a few flights at rabbit can usually be guaranteed and make it all worthwhile. If these are also scarce, then flying a broadwing can be very disheartening as much for the hawk as for the falconer. Ferrets, therefore, might be the only way you can get regular flights at rabbit in the daytime. If this is the case, they are well-worth considering. Also, on the positive side:
- they are very cheap to buy – even free if you know someone who has a surplus
- they are easy to feed. Being meat eaters, they do very well on the same kind of food you would give to any hawk (including day-old chicks)
- although the degree of individual enthusiasm varies, they need no formal training to go down rabbit holes
- using them as a flushing tool is very straightforward: you put them down any entrance to a warren and they find their own way through it. If there are rabbits there they will usually bolt as soon as they scent, see, or hear the ferret

Another positive aspect and nothing to do with hawking, is that ferrets are delightful creatures which make wonderful pets. With a harness and lead, they can be taken for walks and, if you let them, they will explore your whole house. They will 'play' for hours ferreting every crevice, cupboard, bookshelf, settee, nook or cranny they can find, and they will devour any food you leave lying around – including any meant for other pets. Usually they get on famously with dogs (to which they are distantly related) but not so well with cats.

They are also totally fearless, and completely undaunted by the size and bulk of any potential adversary. Unfortunately, when they *really* feel threatened (which takes some doing) they will – like a skunk – give out a very unpleasant odour which can hang around for days. Worse, if it ends up on your clothing or the soft furnishings in your home, you might never entirely get rid of it. They also have a reputation for being vicious but this is totally unfounded. If they are handled frequently, especially at an early age, they are as tame and as comfortable with human beings as any other kind of pet.

Ferrets come in a variety of colours depending on their ancestry. Some are similar to their wild progenitor, the European polecat, which gives them a predominantly grey and black colouring, usually with a burglar-type mask around the eyes. Others can be ginger, or sandy, or anything up to pure white (albinos). These colourations are derived from recessive mutations in wild populations. But in terms of temperament or flushing ability, what they look like makes no difference. However, albino or sandy ferrets are much easier to see in hedgerows and other cover, and 'polecat' ferrets are easier to see in snowy landscapes. In addition, some hawks mistake polecat ferrets for grey squirrels (which are potential quarry in the field), and albinos or sandies for large white rats – especially if the hawk has been fed rats at any time as part of her diet. Consequently you should give careful consideration to the circumstances in which you intend to use them, but in the end what they look like is very much a matter of personal preference.

All ferrets are extremely sociable animals and they don't do well on their own unless you are prepared to spend a couple of hours every day handling and entertaining them. It is best, therefore, to acquire at least a pair. Males are known as *hobs* and females as *jills*. For falconry at least, jills are a better option. They are smaller and less aggressive than hobs, and much less likely to kill a full-grown rabbit underground as opposed to bolting it. From the social point of view, there is no problem with keeping a pair of jills, but they will both come into season in the spring and their oestrus will continue unabated until the autumn. The only natural event which will 'switch this off' is mating, whether it produces any result or not. Constant oestrus can lead to health problems and in extreme cases, death from anaemia.

Obviously the problem can be solved by acquiring a hob and a jill, but unfortunately this usually leads to breeding success whether you intended it or not. You might want to raise eight or nine young every year, but if you don't, at least one of the ferrets will have to be neutered. It is better if this treatment is given to the jill because any problems with oestrus are then avoided, but you can choose the treatment for either one of a mating pair. In the end, it comes down to cost. Alternatively, if you decide to have two jills, they will both need neutering.

Whichever way you go, make sure that any operation is carried out by a vet who is familiar with ferrets – many will never have dealt with them before. If you experience any difficulty, the RSPCA (who are regularly involved with rescuing feral ferrets, and neutering them) might be able to point you in the right direction.

Notes On Quarry

Introduction

For falconers, the word *quarry* simply means 'the object of pursuit of any falconry bird'. Where generalist hawks like broadwings are concerned, the term can encompass many kinds of mammals and birds from squirrels to the more readily-accepted 'game' species such as hares and pheasants.

Most falconers discount smaller creatures such as mice, voles, frogs, worms, dragonflies, grasshoppers and the like, which tend to be an irritation (because they affect the hawk's weight and response) rather than the object of any 'pursuit'. A hawk's flights – the only means by which her qualities can be tested – are the essence of the sport, and just dropping from a fence-post onto a vole or a grasshopper immediately below can't be regarded as 'legitimate' in this respect. Of course, from the hawk's point of view, food is food and she has no scruples about how she should acquire it.

All the animals described in this section are commonly pursued and caught, and they can all be regarded as suitable quarry. However, no list can ever be complete. Eventually your hawk might succeed in catching any one of many other species not included, but it is much more likely that she will catch two or three regularly with the occasional successful flight at something else.

All recognised quarry species present particular types of problem for a hawk, and obviously the more kinds she pursues, the greater the variety of flights you will get. But what any hawk succeeds in catching depends a great deal on her fitness, her individual propensities, the terrain over which you choose to fly her, the diversity and abundance of wildlife the area supports, how successful you are at serving her with an assortment of quarry, and so on. It follows that the more you know about the lifestyle of any potential quarry, the better chance you will have of hunting it successfully (see the section headed *Vital Homework*).

As a general rule, feathered game tests a hawk's flying skills more than ground game (especially when she achieves mid-air contact), but ground game can sorely try her courage and commitment, especially when it finds hostile cover like bramble, thorn or gorse. Indeed, flights which result in her catching ground game in such cover can be just as admirable as those requiring full mastery of, and good footing ability in, the air.

Eventually, when you have a seasoned hawk fit and working well, it will be the type of flight you enjoy most which will tend to dictate (perhaps even subconsciously) where you go and what kind of game you hunt. Ideally, of course, any good flying session will incorporate both furred and feathered quarry, and I would recommend that you always try for both to develop your bird's full potential.

One other general statement needs to be made. The size or gastronomic value of any catch has nothing to do with the quality of a hawk or her flights. You might dream about bringing home a brace of hares after an afternoon's flying, and in comparison a single crow might seem very unimpressive. But, if she caught the crow after a fair and skilful flight, any experienced falconer would be impressed by her prowess.

This doesn't mean that hares are easy prey – they're certainly not. In fact, no fit and healthy quarry is. But the Corvid family of birds (which includes jays, jackdaws, magpies, rooks and crows) are scientifically-rated as the most advanced in evolutionary terms. In other words, they are intellectually superior to hawks (most of which are in the bottom 10 to 20 per cent on the same scale). Any broadwing which can out-smart, out-fly and catch Corvids on a regular basis is, therefore, the equivalent of a cross between Einstein and Lindford Christie. She would certainly be well worth boasting about.

My list of potentially-attainable quarry on a regular basis for a good broadwing is as follows:

Aerial Game (Birds)	Ground Game (Mammals)
Wood pigeons Feral pigeons Stock doves Collared doves Magpies Rooks Crows Moorhen Coot Mallard Pheasant	Rabbits Grey squirrels Hares

Pigeons and Doves

Perhaps the first thing to say about this group of birds is that it is best to avoid entering your hawk with one of them if you can. They all seem to carry diseases such as frounce (see the section headed *Falconry Terminology*), which are invariably passed onto the hawk if she kills and eats part of one. Not only is any illness expensive to treat, but there is always the risk of fatality and such risks are best avoided. Having said that, once your hawk is in the air and in pursuit, there is nothing you can do to stop her. If she catches such quarry, *get to her as quickly as possible* – preferably before she has time to break into it. Retrieve the quarry, and on no account feed any of it to the hawk. It will be useful later once it has been frozen, but at this point it is a high-risk meal. If it happens to be one of her first half-dozen kills, feed her up with lots of her regular rations as a substitute and hope that she isn't too miffed.

All pigeons and doves are fast and wily birds capable of producing exciting flights, whether these are 'accidental' or not. Any kind can outstrip a broadwing in level flight, so attacks tend to be purely opportunistic – for example, when one unwittingly flies past a perching hawk. But, if the hawk then feels she has a chance, she will switch on her turbo-charger and produce a sprint worthy of any Olympic athlete.

There isn't much you can do to initiate flights at this kind of quarry by finding and flushing them. If you want to catch them, options are usually limited to locating places where they are abundant, then giving the hawk the freedom to deal with them in her own way.

Corvids (Rooks, Crows and Magpies)

As a family of species, these are all very clever and crafty birds – qualities which make them extremely difficult to catch on a regular basis. The most common in standard broadwing flying-grounds are rooks, followed closely by crows. These days magpies tend to be more 'suburban' – living much closer to human habitations – but you can still find them in open country, albeit in fewer numbers.

All corvids are sociable birds, but the strength and extent of their social behaviour varies between species. For example, it is common to see a dozen or more rooks together compared to two or three crows. However, crows are bigger and more aggressive than rooks. If your hawk succeeds in catching one and brings it to ground, she is in danger of being assaulted not only by the quarry itself, but also by any of its clan in the vicinity. Crows are capable of inflicting terrible injuries on a hawk (their main weapon is a long and powerful beak, which they use like a pick-axe), and one of the first anatomical features they will attack is her eyes. It will, however, take time for any one of them (apart from the victim) to generate enough courage to mount an attack, especially if there is a human being close by. Fortunately most broadwings – because of their overall size and the length of their legs – can avoid a serious injury from a captured crow, but it is important, nevertheless, to make in to the hawk as quickly as possible to minimise the risk.

Rooks display similar behaviour, but they seem less inclined to press home their attack relying more on vocalisations and general harassment, in the form of close encounters, as a strategy for driving the hawk away. Magpies will also congregate to some extent if one of their number is caught, but they confine their protest to noise rather than active assistance, being much more wary of exposing themselves to a similar fate.

One advantage of hunting rooks and crows is that you don't need to flush them. On the contrary, they will usually find your bird. Rooks especially will collect to 'mob' any hawk in their vicinity. At first you might see only one or two, but within a few seconds a dozen more seem to appear from nowhere. Neither species can be regarded as elegant flyers, but both can be surprisingly agile even though they generally prefer to use their wits to keep out of trouble. For example, when harassing a passing hawk they will usually stay *above* and *behind* her. Such tactics deny her any opportunity to gain the advantage of speed – by stooping, or using downwind flight. If the hawk is perching in a tree, they will often congregate in the same tree but in higher branches, knowing that extra height gives them a good edge if she attempts a direct attack.

An inexperienced eyass can easily be driven off and led astray downwind by a mob of rooks or a family of crows, particularly if the wind is strong. In a short space of time she could be a long way away and out of sight, and you could then have difficulty finding and retrieving her. She could also attempt to secure one simply by trying to outfly it, but this is usually a lost cause. After a few abortive flights, she might decide that both species are beyond her and stop chasing them altogether.

But, bright though they are, even rooks and crows make mistakes and occasionally present a hawk with a golden opportunity. In the excitement of the mob, any individual may move unwittingly into a position below her, passing the advantage of height to the hawk. You could then witness a rapid but short-lived stoop ending with a dramatic mid-air strike. If such a thing happens early on in the hawk's attempts at either species, it will convince her that she can catch them, and she will continue to chase them. Later on, when she's gained more experience, you might be lucky enough to see her develop a more reliable strategy and that is to flip over onto her back in mid-flight and take the quarry from below. A confident and experienced hawk might also attack a rook or a crow which has taken station above her in a tree. Her technique is usually to ladder up the branches towards the quarry, eventually driving it to the outer edge of the canopy. Then, when it takes off to escape, she puts in a quick sprint and catches it in mid-air.

In the breeding season, rooks congregate in colonies which can contain dozens of mating pairs in close proximity. Their nests are built in the uppermost branches of tall trees – often several in each – and eggs are laid in March. Young hatch after about eighteen days, and there could be as many as six in each nest.

If you are still flying your hawk towards the end of April, and she gets anywhere near a large rookery, you are presenting her with a seemingly endless banquet from which you will probably never recover her. All she has to do is to land in a nest, eat all the chicks, then, if she's still hungry, move down a couple of branches to the next. With such a feast in front of her, she will totally ignore the colony's attempts to drive her away, as well as frantic efforts on your part to get her back. Any sizeable rookery will maintain her attention until young rooks still uneaten have fledged and flown, which won't be until mid-May. The message is therefore clear. Don't take your hawk *anywhere near* rookeries during the breeding season.

Compared to rooks and crows, magpies as quarry are an entirely different proposition. For a start, they will not attempt any kind of physical harassment. On the contrary they will make for the deepest cover they can find if they feel threatened in any way. Once there, they are difficult to dislodge, especially if they know that there is a hawk waiting for them outside. Flights at magpie, therefore, generally have to be 'engineered', which means that you as the falconer have to find a way of serving your hawk if you want to catch this kind of quarry regularly.

Magpies are comparatively slow flyers, but they compensate for their lack of speed by using cunning which they employ to a much greater degree than any other Corvid. In addition, they have two other 'survival' qualities: they never lose their heads through excitement or panic and they never admit defeat. Even when they have been caught fair and square by the hawk – and retrieved by you – they will still actively seek an escape route until they succeed or life is finally extinguished.

For hawks and humans alike, hunting magpie can be a very testing and exhausting pastime and you really need to be young and fit to achieve success consistently. You will also need at least two assistants to help you to flush them once they are located. Considering their conspicuous plumage, they are actually not easy to find. This is because they spend a great deal of time on or close to the ground – in ditches, hollows, long grass and the like, or moving along hedgerows. In fact they are often heard before they are seen, and when a group of them is in the vicinity their raucous chatter is unmistakable.

If a magpie is located in a hedgerow (which is usually its safest refuge from a hawk), it will use all its guile to avoid flying over open ground. Even if it does break cover, it will simply keep moving along the hedgerow – flying out, then flying back in a few yards further down. With a single beater, therefore, it can move up or down at will without exposing itself long enough to give the hawk any real chance. However, once the quarry is sighted, the hawk should be brought up to a nearby position. If there is any wind, the beater should position himself to flush the magpie *into* it if this is possible – because of their lack of speed in flight, magpies have even less chance against the wind.

Bear in mind that when it is flushed the quarry will fly away from the beater – in other words, from the opposite side of the hedgerow. The falconer and his remaining assistant should, therefore, position themselves on that side, and on either side of the quarry's location. Their job is to prevent the magpie from flying along the hedgerow when it breaks cover. Obviously the falconer himself needs to be where the action is so that he can retrieve his hawk and the quarry quickly if the flight is successful.

The following diagram illustrates the basic technique:

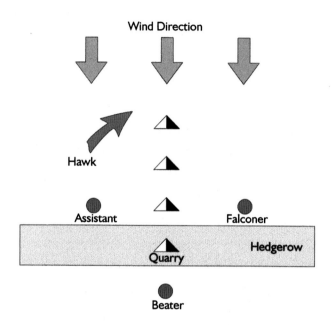

When everyone is in position, the falconer and his assistant should remain still until the beater succeeds in flushing the quarry. Then, when the magpie breaks cover, they can prevent it from flying along the hedgerow by waving their arms and shouting.

If the magpie succeeds in evading the hawk and finding alternative cover (which is highly likely for the first two or three flights), the process begins all over again from the new position. It might take several re-flushes before the hawk is successful (assuming that she eventually is). In the meantime the falconer and his helpers will have to run from one clump of cover to the other to reach the magpie before it is able to slink away unobserved – along the ground, or a deep ditch, or yet another hedgerow.

An experienced hawk, in particular one which has caught magpie before, might be prepared to fly into the hedgerow itself after the quarry. There she will either catch it, or flush it out. And if she is really determined, she will pursue it into its next piece of cover and attack it directly, or flush it again. If she is also fit enough, she will continue these tactics until she catches the magpie which, after a few short flights, will begin to tire increasing her advantage. Obviously if you have such a bird, you can leave her to it without the need to resort to the labour-intensive flushing technique described above.

Water Birds (Moorhen, Coot and Mallard)

Quarry on ponds or lakes will introduce you and your hawk to another set of strategic and tactical problems. For example, all water birds will dive if they are threatened on the surface, and an inexperienced eyass trying to snatch one off the water invariably ends up having to 'row' herself ashore (using her wings) with nothing to show for her efforts. Once she is soaking wet, she will find it difficult to get any lift when she reaches the bank, and you might then have to wade in to rescue her – even if the water comes over the top of your boots. She won't be able to fly again that day, and with wet feet you won't feel much like carrying on either.

If you intend to hunt water quarry, it is best to work out a strategy beforehand. Coots prefer large expanses of water such as lakes, reservoirs, even river estuaries, but moorhens can often be found on small ponds and rivers. Where either species is concerned, your hawk will have a much better chance of catching them if they are off the water – preferably in an adjoining field. Both periodically forage for food away from water; but of course, if they see you coming, they will make a dash for the water immediately because it is, in the end, their safest refuge. You will need, therefore, to be as stealthy as possible using all available cover to mask your approach. With an experienced hawk it is best to let her work out her own tactics, but with an inexperienced one you may have to carry her on the fist until you get within range. Ideally the hawk should be positioned in any tree at the edge of the water which will put her between it and the quarry. Once she is in position, give her a minute or two to size up the situation.

An experienced hawk will choose her own moment to strike, but again you might have to help a novice by flushing the quarry when she is in position. You can do this simply by showing yourself, or at worst by walking up to the quarry. It should then take off towards the water giving your hawk a chance of mid-air contact.

If the quarry makes it back to water, you will need to flush it off again if you can. A dog which will swim on command is ideal for this purpose, otherwise you might have to resort to sticks and stones. Even then the quarry may take cover under foliage overhanging the bank, in which case you will have to get in there to drive it back out and into the open.

The main problem with wild duck (mallard) is that they are very easily spooked, and stealth has to be at least SAS standards if you want to avoid flushing them before you are within range. Whether they are on the ground or on water, they will take off as soon as they see the *slightest* sign of danger approaching – perhaps as much as two hundred yards away – and it is highly unlikely that even the fittest of broadwings could catch one already in the air and climbing at full speed.

With duck, therefore, you need to get yourself and your hawk as close as possible before attempting a flush. How you achieve this will obviously depend on what cover you have to work with. Hawks which have flown ducks before are usually very good at picking their own tortuous route to avoid detection, but eyasses usually fly too soon giving themselves no chance of success. Consequently a novice hawk should be restrained on the fist until she is well within striking range, then planted in a tree close by giving her time to ladder up the branches to gain height if she chooses to do so.

Any broadwing's best chance will be when the quarry is just taking off – in other words, before it has had time to generate any real speed and height. Bear in mind that when the duck does take off it will usually fly into the wind to obtain immediate lift, then either keep climbing steeply to get out of trouble or veer off downwind to gain more impetus.

If its initial take-off is towards the hawk (because she is upwind of it), she will have a good chance of securing it – assisted by height and a downwind flight.

Such flights are difficult to engineer even with experienced hawks, but if you want to catch ducks regularly with any broadwing your tactical options will probably be limited to this kind of scenario. However, there is an alternative set-up which is particularly useful for inexperienced hawks, but it is also very much harder to find.

It involves locating ducks on a shallow brook or stream which runs through a wooded area. Shallow water prevents them from diving, and trees either side will deny them a clear space to climb above the hawk out of danger. If the location is right, the ducks' only option will be to fly up or downstream and find cover on the bank from which they can then be re-flushed, or – if the cover is thin enough – attacked directly by the hawk.

Pheasant

Pheasants are not native birds. They were brought here from Asia and were introduced purely for sport. Thousands of them are reared in special outdoor pens every year specifically for shooting. Once fully-fledged, they are released into wooded areas ready for the start of the shooting season.

A small number might survive the shoot as well as the ravages of winter, foxes, wild birds of prey, and death on the roads. They then become truly wild, living and breeding as if they were indigenous species. There are, consequently, some wild populations of pheasants but these are indistinguishable from those reared by organised shoots. They also exist in very much smaller numbers. If you come across any pheasant in the course of a day's flying, it is usually wise to assume that it already belongs to someone who also wants to hunt it.

The only exception to this general rule is when a pheasant is found on the property of a landowner who does not allow shooting on his land, but who has given you permission to fly your hawk there. In this case, it does not matter whether it is truly wild or has strayed from a neighbouring shooting territory. Technically, the bird belongs to the landowner simply because it is on his land. As long as you have his authority, you can hunt them legitimately.

In falconry terms it is suicidal to hunt pheasant on shooting territory *unless the shoot organisers have said you can*. If you do it nevertheless – and they complain – the landowner will quite rightly ban you from his land. After all, it is much better for him to lose your non-paying 'custom' than his revenue from the shoot. Even worse, you could find yourself prosecuted for poaching, and if you are, you might find other landowners withdrawing their favours as well.

However, assuming that you are hunting pheasant legitimately, they are probably the ultimate feathered quarry for any broadwing. They will test to the limit her speed and endurance, her footing ability, her determination and persistence, and her courage if they manage to reach difficult cover.

Although they roost overnight in trees or bushes out of danger from main-stream predators such as foxes, they are essentially ground birds feeding mainly on seeds, fallen fruit, wild plants and insects. They are also much more associated with woodland than open fields, even though fields are where they are most often seen by the public. Hen pheasants in particular never stray far from cover, which is usually ground-based – bramble, gorse, thick bracken or fern, or beneath an equally dense bush or hedgerow.

Pheasants have three qualities which make them very difficult for any hawk to catch:

1. They do not flush easily. They are surprisingly well camouflaged (particularly hens) and they will sit tight until you virtually step on them

2. When they do flush, they

'explode' from the ground

3. Even when found in the open, they are masters at taking off at *exactly* the right moment – in other words, just as the hawk is about to connect

Many flights are provoked by the quarry ambling in cover below a perching hawk. The hawk drops towards it and, just as she extends her talons to secure it, the pheasant takes off. The hawk then ends up standing bewildered on the ground with the pheasant nowhere in sight. Indeed, a foot full of tail-feathers might be the only indication that she came anywhere near catching it.

But, as she gains experience, she might learn to maintain momentum until she connects or drives the quarry towards alternative cover. She might also learn that pheasants don't always fly directly into cover. Instead they sometimes land on the ground a few yards in front and *run* into it. This is the point at which they are most vulnerable and, if she can keep up her momentum, she will have a fair chance of taking it before it reaches safety.

If you have one, pointers are extremely useful simply because they will locate the pheasant without flushing it. This gives the hawk time to get into a good, high position overhead. Otherwise you will need a dog with which the hawk works very closely, and which can be kept under tight control. The problem is that, with a dog which simply flushes, you will never know that the pheasant is there until it actually takes off. Then the hawk's only chance will be if she is positioned high above the quarry's location enabling her to swoop down to it just as it is rising. Similarly, if you don't have a dog, the hawk will need to be close by you when the pheasant takes off.

Apart from landing on the ground in front of cover, pheasants have another weakness. Although their acceleration is impressive, they are not long-distance flyers and as soon as they are in the air they will look for alternative ground cover. One will probably succeed in outstripping your hawk at first, but if the hawk is determined enough she will continue the chase and mark the spot where the quarry disappeared. This will provide you with an opportunity for a re-flush.

Bear in mind, though, that if the pheasant *does* reach cover, it will run yet again to get well clear of danger. In a hedgerow, for example, it could be many yards either side of the hawk's position, depending on how long it took you to arrive on the scene. In other words, the hawk might not be marking the spot where the pheasant actually is – only where she saw it disappear. However, a good dog should be able to find and re-flush it, otherwise you will have to do the best you can with your stick.

Rabbits

It has to be said that, for broadwings at least, this quarry provides the basis of the sport. Your hawk will probably catch more of them than anything else. This doesn't mean that they are easy prey – just more abundant than most other quarry-species. In fact mature, fit, and healthy rabbits can be very difficult for a young broadwing – especially the smaller males – to secure.

Rabbits sleep and breed underground in a network of tunnels called a *warren* (individual tunnels are called *burrows*). These are usually sited on a slope or high ground to keep them clear of flooding, and close to a good food supply – which means any ground-vegetation from grass to cabbage. Warrens can sometimes be found on open land, but more usually in the margins of a wood, copse or spinney; on the banks of a wooded rivulet; or even on the banks of a ditch beneath a hedgerow.

The peak of the rabbit's activity is usually between dusk and dawn to avoid the attention of predators, but they are not exclusively nocturnal animals. Far from it. They can often be seen well before dusk or well after dawn foraging for food on farmland – depending on the local density of predators (including humans). If they don't feel threatened at all on a regular basis, you will find them bold enough to forage for food throughout the day.

In the 1950s myxomatosis (which was introduced deliberately by humans and is carried by fleas) wiped out over 95 per cent of all rabbit populations, but in some areas their numbers are now back to at least half of pre-myxomatosis levels. This means they have developed *some* resistance to the disease, but not total immunity. Indeed, it still decimates their numbers, but usually only in dense populations.

Before it eventually kills them, myxomatosis makes rabbits very slow moving and dull witted. Its more advanced stages render them partially, or even totally, blind, and it is often possible to walk up to one and pick it up without much resistance. Indeed, an easy way of establishing that a rabbit has the disease, even in the early stages, is to look at its eyes which will be bulging and rheumy.

Although any rabbit with myxomatosis can be immensely useful for entering a newly-trained hawk (see the section headed *Entering and Basic Hunting*), once she is in the habit of hunting, such quarry can no longer be considered fair game – it is pathetically easy to catch and will not test her skills in any way. Myxomatosis, by the way, is completely harmless to birds of prey. In other words, if your hawk kills and eats any part of a rabbit suffering from the disease, she will not catch it herself. It is also harmless to human beings.

Healthy rabbits are an entirely different proposition. They are nervous and wary animals with all-round vision, large independently-controlled ears, and a keen sense of smell. These senses make them difficult to catch unawares. In addition, they have powerful hind legs which propel them along the ground at considerable speed and enable them to change direction very quickly. Their first line of defence against attack is to bolt into cover, preferably their warren, but if this is unreachable, a thick hedgerow, bramble bush, or other impenetrable vegetation. If they fail to reach cover in time, they will attempt to outrun or outmanoeuvre a predator. For example, when a hawk is closing in rapidly, it is not uncommon for a rabbit to make a 180° turn, which leaves the hawk flying on in the same direction and the rabbit racing away in the opposite one.

A healthy adult rabbit can weigh 4lb – twice the flying-weight of most broadwings – and it can give a hawk a considerable amount of 'rough and tumble' in the field if she catches up with it. Using powerful hind legs – the last line of defence – any full-grown rabbit is capable of 'bucking' a hawk off its back if she doesn't bind to it properly. A good hawk will target, and land, on a rabbit's head. Training with the quarry lure will have encouraged her to do this, but to a large extent it seems to be an intuitive action which certain individuals demonstrate more quickly than others. Rabbits (and other quadrupeds) remain relatively docile with a hawk grasping their heads, but some hawks only learn this through trial and error after losing several rabbits.

It is a waste of time expecting a hawk to catch a rabbit grazing outside a warren for as soon as it feels threatened by you or the hawk, it will bolt down the nearest burrow before she has any chance of reaching it. Although a broadwing can fly faster than a rabbit is able to run, as a general rule, if she is more than twice as far away as the rabbit is from its warren, she won't catch it. Clearly, therefore, you need to find rabbits well away from home which, fortunately, is not that unusual. Food supplies in the immediate vicinity of any sizeable warren soon become exhausted, and its inhabitants will then forage further and further afield. In such forays they might not stray far from other cover (especially in daylight) but, as long as they are unable to get underground, there is always a chance of re-flushing them.

From the falconer's point of view, flights out in the open are the best simply because you get to see the whole drama, including the rabbit's attempts to evade the hawk and her response. However, longer flights in woodland can also be exciting because often the hawk has to manoeuvre at high speed between thickly-clustered branches, and their ability to do this is quite amazing. The rabbit's evasion tactics can be not only interesting to watch, but also dangerous for the hawk. For example, her quarry might run through a barbed wire or other wire fence hoping to shake her off. In the excitement of the chase she fails to see the fence in time and crashes into it. I have even witnessed one rabbit take refuge under the body of a grazing sheep! What's more, the ploy actually worked. The hawk circled around the sheep two or three times because she had lost sight of her quarry, and each time her circuit widened. When eventually she was well downwind, the rabbit ran out from under the sheep, upwind, and gained the sanctuary of a burrow in a hedgerow about fifty yards away (the sheep, by the way, carried on grazing and either ignored, or didn't even notice, the drama).

If rabbits are abundant, they can usually be flushed fairly easily but if they are scarce, or if they are excessively wary because of the predominance of predators (which amounts to the same thing), you might have to adopt alternative hunting strategies. One way is to take the hawk out much closer to dawn or dusk, when you should find them feeding in greater numbers. If you have a choice, it is much more sensible to hunt them just after dawn. This has nothing to do with catching rabbits *per se*. It's just that, if things go wrong and you have difficulty in retrieving your hawk for whatever reason, you will have several daylight hours left to solve the problem. If she goes missing at dusk, you will have to leave her overnight, then be back at the same place again before dawn in an attempt to retrieve her when it gets light. Even then, there is no guarantee that she won't have moved on somewhere else prior to your arrival (see the section headed *Missing Hawks*).

Another way of dealing with a scarcity is to use ferrets, which are employed to flush them out of their warrens. The best warrens for this method are sited in the open, for example, in the roots of a large oak tree in the middle of a field, so that bolted rabbits have to run over open ground to reach alternative cover. Otherwise, flights at rabbits flushed by ferrets tend to be short, especially if the warren is a large one. The quarry either reaches another burrow and disappears down it, or the hawk catches it before it is able to do so. Her flight, therefore, might be only a matter of a few yards. Small warrens reduce the possibility that the quarry will find another convenient burrow, but they obviously house fewer rabbits – perhaps only a pair, which might not even be at home. You may find, therefore, that you have to visit several small warrens before you get a bolt, but once this is achieved, you should be rewarded with a longer flight.

There is yet another method of dealing with a scarcity. It is done during the hours of darkness using powerful spot lamps to light up the quarry for the hawk. The technique is called *lamping*, and it is by no means exclusive to the sport of falconry. However, apart from the requirement for specialised equipment, hawks (which are not, by nature, nocturnal hunters) need additional training to help them deal with such field conditions. But this method does give falconers who work all week a way of flying their hawks in the long nights of winter. Even so, I recommend that you do not try it with a young, inexperienced hawk – primarily because it will greatly increase your chances of losing her. It is better that you gain some experience of hunting with your bird in normal conditions first. Establishing a partnership in the field will get her in the hunting habit and give you an understanding of her personality and idiosyncrasies, which in turn will help you to determine whether this technique is feasible for her (and you).

Grey Squirrels

Squirrels live in trees, feeding on produce such as acorns, hazelnuts, chestnuts, fir cones and the like. They rest up and breed in holes in the tree trunk, or in shelters made up of bundles of leaves woven between twigs and wedged into branch forks. These homes are formally called *dreys*.

Squirrels are smart and agile animals. They can run up or down a tree trunk, or along a branch, very fast and, if the tree-canopy is dense enough with overlapping foliage, they can run or jump from one tree to another. Although they take much of their food from the tree itself, they can often be seen on the ground amongst the leaf litter foraging for, or storing, fallen nuts. Once there, like rabbits, they will use any available ground cover if they are threatened from the air.

For any hawk, they can be very difficult to catch – in particular on an opportunistic basis. A young hawk might successfully pluck one off a branch or the trunk of a tree, but usually the squirrel sees her coming and darts round to the other side of the trunk just as she is extending her feet to grab it. Then, all she has to show for her efforts is a few slithers of bark in her talons with the squirrel nowhere in sight. If she has the determination to persist, she might even attempt to chase the quarry vertically down the tree, crashing into all its branches on the way. But, when the squirrel reaches the ground, she has totally lost flight-control and the squirrel scoots off into a dense thicket nearby.

Experienced hawks eventually learn to keep above the squirrel and, starting at the top of the tree, gradually ladder down its branches in an attempt to drive the quarry to the ground (a visual sighting of the hawk is sufficient to achieve that). Once it is there and making for alternative cover, the hawk puts in a quick swoop and takes it on the ground. Another strategy I have seen a hawk employ – especially when the squirrel is along a branch well away from the tree trunk – is to use the trunk itself to mask her approach. Then, at the last moment, she flips around the trunk and plucks the quarry off the branch.

Happily flights, even for seasoned hawks, are often unsuccessful. Squirrels regularly find refuge in their drey, or even in ivy growing up the tree trunk if the ivy is dense enough. I say 'happily' because there are two major problems with squirrel-hunting which prompt me to recommend leaving them well alone if you have the option:

1. Squirrels are light enough for a large hawk to carry, and if your hawk catches one on a branch she will see no reason to bring it down to earth. Once she's killed it, she will stay up there until she's gorged herself. You might then end up losing her unless you can climb the tree to retrieve her

2. Whichever way they are caught, squirrels defend themselves with determined aggression. Like all rodents, they have long, sharp front teeth (incisors) which they use to good effect. These are capable of inflicting deep lacerations, and if they manage to sever an artery you will end up with a dead hawk.

Hunting squirrels is, therefore, risky – even more so if your hawk has not yet demonstrated the skill of catching quarry by the head. But, having said all this, the excitement for falconers lies not so much in the quality of the flight itself (which is likely to be very short-lived) but in *the quality of the hawk's brains*, which she will have to use to work out a general strategy, then amend and improvise according to current field conditions.

Hares

Hares are not just big rabbits. The two species might be closely related scientifically, but they are entirely different animals with dissimilar physical appearance, life-style and habitat. To begin with, they are twice the size and weight of rabbits (up to 9lb). Their ears are proportionately longer, and each has a distinctive black tip. Their fur is also unmistakably brown compared to the greyer rabbit. They are tall and leggy in silhouette, and their gait is much more like a deer's. Although the underside of a hare's tail is white like a rabbit's, they run with it folded down so that no white is visible.

Hares do not burrow, which means they don't live or breed underground. In the daytime they rest up in shallow depressions scraped out of the ground called *forms*. Lying still protects them from birds of prey soaring above, and the fact that they are in a depression means that they do not present a profile against the skyline for ground predators (such as foxes) to see. Forms also protect them from the wind and the cold. Like pheasant, to flush a hare from a form you virtually have to step on it.

There are other differences. Compared to rabbits, hares wander much further afield, their home ranges covering anything from 50 to 250 acres depending on what food these provide. They eat a variety of vegetation, and if they are found on cultivated land at all it is arable with different kinds of crop growing in adjacent fields. But they only thrive where one crop or another is available throughout the year – for example, winter wheat, followed by spring barley, followed by summer turnips, then perhaps meadow grass and wild herbs when nothing else is available.

As quarry for a hawk, they are also entirely different, not just because of their greater size, weight and power. Like rabbits they are basically nocturnal, but because they rest up in forms in the daytime, they can be found and flushed, especially with a good dog. Also, the form is likely to be in the middle of a field well away from cover but, unlike a rabbit, cover is not a hare's first priority. It relies on speed. It will attempt to outrun any predator, and a fit hare is capable of reaching 40mph over short distances (about 100 yards). They also have a high level of stamina, and can maintain a marginally lesser pace for several minutes. In addition, they know every yard of their range intimately. Indeed, some naturalists believe (from field observations) that hares work out a 'race track' – an escape route, every twist, turn and obstacle of which they know well, and over which they practice running at full speed many times.

In the initial stages of a chase hares appear to run fairly slowly, enabling the hawk to close in quickly. But, when she gets near, they change up a gear and will move away from her unless she can increase her own momentum sufficiently to keep up. Unlike rabbits, they can outpace a hawk, and they will use any territorial advantage available in the meantime to shake her off. For instance, they will run uphill, downhill, upwind, across the wind, through fences or hedgerows, or they will make swift changes in direction to frustrate her. It is often, therefore, the hawk which gives up the chase.

One aspect of catching hares, which many people find distasteful, is that they are powerful enough to drag a clinging hawk along with them until they run out of steam, which can be many yards later. Like all mammals they are vocal when caught, and their distress is therefore audible as well as visible. In addition, the hawk's attempts to stop or slow the hare down inevitably means that her fragile plumage makes a great deal of contact with the ground. Even worse, she risks more serious injury if the hare manages to reach thick cover such as a hedgerow, which the hare will push through in an attempt to brush her off.

If speed, stamina and guile don't succeed, the hare's last line of defence is its hind legs. If it can't rid itself of the hawk any other way, it will attempt to kick her and, if it succeeds, it is capable of killing her by shattering her rib cage. You might have a hawk which catches several hares, but if the next kicks her and she survives, she will never chase a hare again.

An Analysis Of Flights By A Female Harris' Hawk Hunting On Average Four Times A Week In Her Second Season		
Quarry Species	**Number Caught**	**Escapes**
Rabbit	27	7
Pheasant	8	11
Grey Squirrel	3	5
Moorhen	2	0
Duck	0	4
Wood Pigeon	1	0
Collared Dove	1	0
Rook	0	6
Crow	1	3
Magpie	2	0
Jackdaw	1	0
Stoat	1	0
Non-Quarry Species	**Number Caught**	**Escapes**
Sparrowhawks	0	2
Kestrels	0	3
Roe Deer	3*	0
Domestic cats	3*	0
Working Ferrets	2*	0

Two of the three deer she actually brought down, but she was eventually brushed off all three because they crashed through dense hedgerows. The cats and ferrets were rescued more or less unharmed apart from minor wounds, shock, and (for the cats) loss of dignity.

Firstly, this table illustrates that there is always an element of opportunism in the flights of broadwings. For example, the wood pigeon and collared dove were caught simply because they presented this particular hawk with an unusual chance of success. In other words, neither I nor the hawk was deliberately hunting them. Secondly – but in a more obscure way – it illustrates that all hawks learn to hunt through experience. An example is the grey squirrel. Of the eight she flew, the first four were dismal failures. Then she caught three in a row, and the last only survived because it was within inches of its drey when she launched her attack. Thirdly, it shows that broadwings are 'blunt instruments' which don't just catch the quarry you want them to catch. They are *indiscriminate*, working solely on the basis that if it runs or flies it is potential food. If your hawk is physically fit, confident, and at flying weight, she will probably have a go at anything, especially during her early years in the field.

Obviously this puts an obligation on you to maintain as much control over your young hawk as possible, at least in terms of where you fly her. The very last thing you want is that she catches a neighbour's cat, or one of the landowner's chickens – or infinitely worse, a spring lamb. *All hawks are potentially dangerous.* If yours catches something you don't want her to catch, it isn't her fault and you can't legitimately blame or punish her. She is simply acting in accordance with a pattern of behaviour genetically transmitted by her ancestors, which the training you have given her has switched on. This makes *you*, and you alone, fully responsible for any of her 'misdemeanours'.

Lanner falcon (*Falco biarmicus*)

PART 4

Maintenance

Maintaining Fitness

Training a hawk up to free-flight, and beyond to the point of entering, should in itself develop the fitness levels required for a broadwing. From then on, the best way to maintain fitness is to have her chasing and catching quarry every day. Unfortunately this is rarely possible. For example, the weather might be so extreme that you can only fly her for three or four days in a particular month. Even if the weather isn't a problem, work, social commitments, ill-health, or other unavoidable disruptions could, in total, cancel out several weeks of the season.

Lack of fitness is a serious problem for falconry birds. If yours has been languishing in her aviary for three or four weeks for whatever reason, you will find that, when you call her from a perch a hundred yards away, she probably won't even reach you. Instead she will end up panting on the ground well short of her target. In this condition she is unlikely to catch anything, however good she previously was.

Thankfully, it *is* possible to maintain a trained hawk's fitness in disruptive circumstances through the kind of physical workout practised by humans (though much less sophisticated). In addition, hawks starting a new season after the moult can be brought back to fitness in a matter of days rather than weeks. The method is known as *high jumps*.

Jumps have been used for centuries in the East, but much less so in the West – until recently. The Americans have developed a way of prolonging jumping sessions, through a process of variable reward for the hawk, which produces a significant impact on fitness development over a relatively short period. Full credit must be given to Doctor Nick Fox for introducing this method into British falconry in his book *Understanding Birds of Prey* (see *Helpful Literature* page 241).

The basic technique is to get the hawk to fly almost vertically off the ground onto your gloved hand held as high as you can manage. The hawk starts off close to your feet, and ends up on the glove above your head. Flying high and steep like this is hard work for hawks, and it develops the muscles and stamina necessary for fitness in all kinds of flight. Even a fat and unfit broadwing can manage a dozen or so of these 'jumps', but to be fit enough to fly after quarry she needs to be able to do a hundred or so in each session.

The problem is that she has to have a motive for doing it and, as always with hawks, the motive is food. Normal rations might only amount to twelve or thirteen tidbits to offer her, and this number of jumps will achieve very little. Which is why variable reward is so important. Eventually you might ask her to do twenty jumps in a row without getting any food, then give her a piece every time for the next three or four jumps. With the glove held high above her, she can't see whether you are offering food or not, and because your offerings are entirely at random, she can't predict the outcome. But if she doesn't jump, she doesn't get the chance of food, which means she might have to go hungry. This technique exploits the fact that all hawks are not only greedy, but also programmed to accept disappointment. It makes it possible to keep them trying until they are physically worn out.

First, you need to get the hawk in the habit of flying from the ground to the fist, which isn't too difficult. If you intend to exercise her indoors because of the weather or because it is dark outside, you will need a room with a ceiling high enough to enable her to land on the fist comfortably when it is held two feet or so above your head. In addition, you will need an old piece of carpet on the floor for her to land on comfortably. If you're able to exercise her outside, a lawn is the best surface.

Carry her to the training ground on the fist, then throw a morsel of food onto the ground (or carpet). Let her eat, then call her back to the fist (which, at this stage, should be held in the normal carrying position) for another piece. Let her see the food held in the glove, particularly if she shows any reluctance to fly. Repeat this routine until she will fly down to the ground without the need to throw food onto it. If she's reluctant to leave the fist after she's been given several tidbits on the ground, drop your hand to encourage her to fly down for no reward.

When she's flying to the ground consistently without reward, continue calling her to the fist feeding her a visible piece of food every time. Then, when she's flying from ground to fist without hesitation, start hiding the food in the glove making sure that she gets her reward as soon as she lands. Once she's flying to the fist for invisible pieces of food consistently, its time to up the exercise a gear or two:

1. Raise the fist in easy stages until she is flying to it as high as you can hold it
2. Gradually vary the reward she receives on landing.

Don't push this variable reward too far too soon. If you do, your hawk might become bored and give up altogether. It is best to begin with one disappointment, say, in every ten jumps but varying its position on the scale. For example, she might get nothing in the first jump of the series, and in the next disappointment is at number five, or at number three, and so on. Then gradually increase the number of disappointments, but still placing them randomly throughout the jump-series. If you can get her to jump ten times in a row without reward, increase the series to twenty and use a similar random-reward sequence. When she starts to struggle to reach the fist, or she lands on it panting, it's time to stop the session.

At first, training a hawk to do high jumps can take a couple of weeks to the point where the work she has to do starts to pay dividends. But once she's learned the basic technique, it can be used at any time. In addition, the routine enables you to measure the amount of work she is doing, and the progress she is making, simply by counting the jumps she achieves. A longer-term advantage is that she learns to come to the fist whether she can see a food-offering or not, and this can be very useful in the field. Even then, it is essential to give her food on occasions to maintain her motivation for returning to you.

Illness And Injury

Birds of prey seldom show any sign of illness until their condition becomes acute. This is a natural survival strategy – hawks showing signs of weakness attract other predators. Like all wild animals, they are exposed to a wide range of health risks – particularly when they are in the field chasing and catching game. For falconry birds, the most common causes of ill-health are:
- nutritional deficiency
- cuts and abrasions
- bone fractures or breaks
- infestation by parasites
- bacterial, viral, or fungal infections.

Most of these could be attributed to their natural life-style as hunters, but some at least can be avoided by good management. For instance, it is *possible* for a hawk to infect herself by eating food or drinking water contaminated by her own mutes. A hawk will grip food with her feet and tear it apart with her beak. If she's been standing in mutes – on a perch, the floor, or a feeding table – she could, potentially, foul the food she eats.

The following guidelines will help to eliminate unnecessary risks:
- her quarters – including any manner of perch – should be cleaned every week and disinfected thoroughly every month. 'Vircon' (a disinfectant used by vets and available from them in powder form) is a good substance to use
- similarly, gloves, jesses, leashes and lures should be kept clean, especially if you decide not to de-yolk day-old chicks (see the section headed *Hawk Food*)
- *all* food should be served 'fresh' and consumed within twenty-four hours. Bin any left over after that time
- throw out any food that looks suspect, for instance dirty or discoloured chicks
- food cut up by yourself – for example beef or rabbit – should be prepared on a clean surface with clean equipment
- drinking water should be replaced daily and her bath cleaned and sterilised once a week. Milton, which is used for sterilising baby bottles and other equipment, does the job well.

This is the best possible husbandry practice for any kind of hawk, and it is a standard that you should strive to achieve. But there is no need to go overboard or become obsessive about hygiene. Indeed, if your hawk is housed in a totally sterile environment, she will never develop any real resistance to bacteria, so there is even a point where cleanliness starts to become counter-productive. There is no need to panic, therefore, because you have missed cleaning her accommodation for a couple of days because of other more pressing commitments. She will, no doubt, survive a short lapse. But the point is, the longer you leave it, the greater the risk to her health.

The most important hygiene elements have to be the hawk's food and water. If you do nothing else, make sure that these are as clean and fresh as possible. For example, de-frost only the supply of food you need for that day using the method described in the section headed *Hawk Food*. On warm balmy days, if you use a hosepipe to replenish her bath, make sure that the water runs through the pipe for several minutes before filling the container. Bacteria will breed in the warm water already in the pipe, and if you pour it straight into her bath you will be taking an unnecessary risk.

Despite the best precautions, problems can still arise. Day-old chicks themselves can pass on potentially fatal infections which have nothing to do with how you handle them. Over the course of a few years, you might feed thousands to a hawk without any ill-effects. Then, in the next batch, there is one infected chick which kills her. This is just bad luck, and there is nothing you can do about it. On the other hand, you might never experience a problem, either because all your chicks are safe, or because the hawk's immune system deals with whatever she picks up from them. But the risk is always present, however small it might be. And there is a similar risk with any other captive-bred poultry, such as turkey chicks or quail.

In general, infections are passed from one animal to another more easily if they are the same animal type – for example, birds to birds and mammals to mammals. Cross-infection – from a mammal to a bird or *vice versa* – is possible but much less likely. This is also true of parasites, such as mites and intestinal worms. Feeding a hawk on a kill is therefore riskier where avian prey is concerned.

For falconry birds, hunting itself is also a health risk. Traumatic injuries (such as cuts, fractures or broken bones) can occur when the hawk is crashing through trees, hedgerows, undergrowth, and wire fences. One of the greatest hazards for any hawk in the field – wild or otherwise – is an electricity pylon which, to them, is just a different kind of tree. But if, during take-off or landing, a hawk's wing-tips happen to touch both cable contacts on the pylon, the voltage passing through her body will kill her instantly. The larger female broadwings – because their wing-span is greater – are much more vulnerable to this hazard than the males.

Quarry can also cause death or inflict serious injuries. Squirrels, for example, have a habit of fighting back, and their teeth and claws are capable of causing deep cuts. Even worse, if one succeeds in severing an artery in the hawk's neck or thigh, she will bleed to death very quickly. Rooks and crows also have a reputation for attacking a hawk holding one of their group, and they will peck first at her eyes. Even a humble hare can shatter a hawk's rib cage with a kick from a hind leg. These are normal risks that all predators have to take, and you can't avoid them if you want your hawk to hunt as she would if she were truly wild. All you can do is take out insurance to cover yourself in the event of a disaster, and deal with any retrievable situation in an appropriate way.

Whatever the problem, the earlier you deal with it the better. It is, therefore, good falconry practice to look your hawk over after each flying session to check for obvious signs of cuts, abrasions or parasitic infestation. There is no need to cast her, but look out in particular for bleeding, and insects slipping between her feathers.

Remember, anything beyond first aid is, in law, the province of the veterinary profession (see the section headed *Falconry and the Law*), but there is much you can do to help your bird even within these limits. One or two more enlightened falconry suppliers sell first aid kits which can be taken out into the field for treatment on the spot, and these will normally include:

- crop syringe and tube
- glucose powder for low condition or fits (hypoglaecemia)
- electrolyte or similar solution for the treatment of shock
- exposure blanket for the treatment of shock
- potassium permanganate crystals for the treatment of broken talons etc
- pevidine iodine for the treatment of open wounds and bites
- antibiotic wound powder for minor wounds and scratches
- leg/wing splint for immobilising fractured or broken limbs

Crop tubing is a method of getting food or fluid into a hawk which will not eat, or for the immediate treatment of shock following a traumatic injury. The crop tube assembly comprises a hyperdermic syringe (without a needle) fitted with a flexible plastic tube for insertion into the crop.

Crop tubing is a two-man operation; one person is needed to cast the bird, the other to hold open the bird's beak and administer the oral therapy. The beak should be opened as wide as possible, and the neck stretched slightly to ease the passage of the tube. A light coating of 'KY' Gel, or saliva, on the tube will also assist in insertion. Care must be taken to insert the tube into the hawk's gullet rather than the windpipe, otherwise you will cause death by drowning. Once the beak is open, the windpipe is clearly visible at the *back* of the tongue. The gullet is the second opening at the *side* of the tongue.

Once the tube is passed down the gullet, its position in the crop should be established by feel, or by observing the external effect of tube manipulation on the crop. Depress the plunger slowly. Any excess fluid will well up inside the bird's mouth. If this occurs, release her head and let her swallow.

Electrolyte for the treatment of shock is usually diluted with water first before crop tubing. If it comes as part of the first aid kit, instructions should be given with the kit, otherwise the supplier will tell you the correct proportions. The solution should then be administered at the rate of 10ml per kg of body weight. After tubing, leave the bird alone in a warm dark place for a couple of hours.

The application of wound treatments is fairly straightforward – the medication is dabbed,

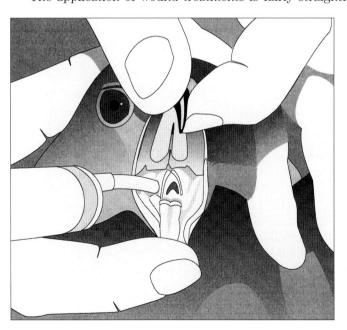

sprinkled or brushed onto the wound. Potassium permanganate, which is used to cauterise pin-point areas of bleeding such as on a broken talon, should be applied by wet cotton bud dipped in the crystals. An alternative treatment is a styptic pencil (obtainable from any chemist). Wound powder for minor wounds and scratches, and pevidine iodine for open wounds should be brushed or sprinkled onto the affected area. The splint in these first aid kits is malleable and can be bent to suit the contour of the leg or wing. The padded side should be rested on the affected limb and the whole thing taped securely with adhesive bandage (also provided in the kit).

Outside these kits, there are other propriety remedies available which could be classed as 'first aid', such as Johnson's Anti-Mite to control external parasites, and worm treatments such as Panacur in liquid or powder form. Anti-mite is simply sprayed onto the bird's plumage – in particular in the armpits and underneath the wings – but care must be taken not to spray it in the hawk's eyes. Panacur is administered as part of the bird's food in dosages and frequencies recommended by a vet.

First aid is fine if you know what's wrong and you're sure about what to do. However, things are not always straigthforward. Because of a hawk's plumage, even open wounds are often difficult to spot unless they're on an exposed area like feet, legs, beak or cere, and a cursory check after flying may not pick them up. Another problem is that a hawk will generally ignore even a serious wound and carry on as normal until infection takes a hold, perhaps two or three days later. Then she will lose weight, and her behaviour will mimic that of low condition (see the section headed *Weight and Condition*). In fact *any persistent change in a hawk's normal behaviour or body language should start alarm bells ringing and prompt careful monitoring.*

Except for obvious ailments like broken bones, a hawk off colour can display similar symptoms whatever the cause, which makes it very difficult to diagnose the specific problem. And the fact that the symptoms themselves might not appear for several days after the 'event' is a further complication. If you have any doubts about your hawk's health, consult a specialist vet immediately. A sick bird can deteriorate rapidly and any undue delay in treatment might be condemning her to death or lifelong disability.

An experienced vet will often be prepared to give you advice over the phone if you can describe the hawk's symptoms accurately enough for him to make a confident diagnosis, and the table which follows might help you to do that. Accurate symptom description will also help him to decide whether he needs to see the bird himself, or whether you can deal with the problem with the benefit of his advice.

SYMPTOMS	POSSIBLE CAUSES
Slitted eyes and puffed-up appearance	If the hawk is not in low condition, these symptoms may indicate dehydration
Playing with food without ingesting it; weight loss, and general weakness	Viral or bacterial infection
Reluctance, or inability, to use one leg	Broken or fractured bone, possibly due to excessive bating
Voracious appetite without weight gain	Often due to parasitic infestation such as worms
Fits	Low blood sugar levels due to starvation; or they may indicate a thyamine deficiency

Reluctance or inability to fly	Traumatic injury
Drooping wing	Broken or fractured wing bone; infected flesh wound, sprain, frostbite or similar injury
Laboured and noisy breathing	Numerous respiratory infections including avian tuberculosis
Lesions inside the mouth	Microbial infection
Swellings on the feet (particularly the balls of the feet)	A condition known as *bumblefoot*, which requires prompt veterinary attention (and probably subsequent perch improvement)
Green or bloodstained mutes	Green mutes may simply mean that the hawk has no more food left in her gut and it is common with hawks at flying weight. Bloodstained mutes indicate parasitic or bacterial infection and these, as well as any other abnormal mutes, should be checked out by an experienced vet
Castings loose, mushy or misshapen	Mushy castings can occur when the hawk's diet does not provide enough roughage (eg day-old chicks). Otherwise any unusual castings should be checked out with an experienced vet
Insects slipping between feathers	Parasitic infestation

A hawk might display one, or a combination, of these symptoms depending on her specific condition. But don't accept this, or any other table, as complete. Like other life forms, hawks can suffer from all sorts of disorders which might have nothing to do with being a falconry bird. These could be genetic or acquired, and include heart disease, ulcers, cancers, bone disease, or nervous disorders.

Whatever the problem, any sick hawk should be kept warm (about 21° C) and be disturbed as little as possible. Temperature is important: if it's too hot or too cold she will burn up whatever energy she has faster. Hawks also use a lot of energy tearing up food, and you can help matters by doing that for her, feeding her (if she will eat) small easily-swallowed pieces. She should be offered good quality meat without any roughage likely to produce a casting – such as shin of beef or quail breast. Once she is eating on her own and putting on weight, she's usually on the mend. If she won't eat enough even under these conditions, *get veterinary help as quickly as possible.*

Much of what has been said so far about illness has concentrated on dealing with problems after they have arisen, but there is action you can take to help prevent some common infections. Apart from general hygiene considerations in the hawk's food, water and accommodation, there are preventative (prophylactic) drugs available known as *probiotics*. A probiotic is, in effect, a collection of beneficial bacteria which reduces the chances of infection arising – in contrast to an *antibiotic*, which is designed to kill harmful bacteria already causing illness.

There is no need to give your hawk a probiotic constantly, but one should be considered when she is most at risk of infection. High risk periods arise most commonly when the hawk's diet is altered for any reason. A change of diet can upset the balance of natural bacteria in the bird's gut causing uncontrolled development of harmful strains. Dietary changes will occur, for example, when her training begins, or when you stop flying the hawk to moult her. In such cases, you will probably make changes to the amount, type, and quality of food she is given over a period.

If you decide to use a probiotic, make sure it is one developed especially for birds rather than mammals or reptiles. Any avian (bird) vet will advise you about suitability and dosage, and he should also be able to supply the drug.

Another kind of prophylactic treatment concerns inoculation but, where hawks are concerned, there are no established vaccination programmes similar to those available for cats and dogs. However, a vaccine has been developed to give all captive birds protection against so-called 'Newcastle's Disease' (NDV) – also known as Fowl Pest – which is the most deadly. Indeed, NDV is so serious, and so easily spread, that it is 'notifiable'. This means that any bird owner is legally obliged to tell the Department for Environment, Food and Rural Affairs (DEFRA) if he has any bird with the disease.

DEFRA's response to a confirmed case will be to set up an 'exclusion zone' incorporating the whole area within a ten kilometre radius of the affected site. *Every* bird keeper in this area (whether he keeps hawks, budgerigars, parrots, chickens or any other kind) will not be permitted to move them off his premises – even if a sick bird needs emergency treatment for an unrelated illness. Neither will he be permitted to bring others onto his premises. Exclusion will remain in force for thirty days starting from the latest confirmed case in that zone. In addition, if an owner has a bird which has contracted the disease, it is likely that DEFRA will carry out the compulsory slaughter of every bird he owns, and if someone else has a collection of birds close by, slaughter might well extend to those.

Newcastle's Disease is prevalent throughout mainland Europe and breaks out in Britain from time to time. The virus is transmitted mainly through contact with infected birds, but is also carried (short distances) by the wind, or on clothing, footwear, and even vehicles if they have been through a restricted area.

The problem for falconers is, therefore, twofold:
1. They could unwittingly travel through, or close to, a restricted area to hunt their hawks
2. A hawk could catch a wild bird (such as a pigeon) which has travelled through a danger zone and picked up the disease.

Vaccination provides good protection in both cases. Much more importantly, it will prevent you and your hawk from spreading the disease, not only to any other hawks you might possess, but also to other people's birds in your area. In short, it will avoid the possibility that you become responsible for introducing NDV into your community, and it will protect your own collection from other people's irresponsibility.

Vaccination itself is a two-course treatment, the second dose being given three weeks after the first. Protection then lasts for six months. In this case, the involvement of a specialist vet is unnecessary – vaccination can be given by any local vet. It is good practice to ensure that your hawks are inoculated regularly, whether or not there are any confirmed outbreaks in Britain. It would be sensible as well to combine these visits to the vet with a routine health check.

Maintaining Beaks And Talons

It might sound strange, but any captive hawk's beak and talons easily become overgrown. Both are composed of a cellular substance called *keratin*, which is the same material human finger nails are made of. One feature of keratin is that it grows constantly. New cells are 'programmed' to replace older ones at a steady rate, irrespective of whether you bite your nails, or let them grow at will.

On the whole, a wild hawk is able to keep this growth under control by hunting, killing and eating natural prey animals. For example, regularly tearing the flesh off the hard bones of mature prey will keep her beak in trim. Similarly, making frequent contact with rocks, branches and other natural perches during the hunting process, will both sharpen her talons and keep growth within acceptable limits. Most falconry birds eat 'soft' food such as day-old chicks and don't have the luxury of eating everything they catch, or hunting at will from different kinds of perch. Consequently their beaks (in particular) and talons can soon become overgrown, and re-shaping them is known as *coping*.

Although keratin grows constantly, it grows very slowly. When you see your hawk every day, it is often difficult to recognise that her beak and talons have, in fact, become overgrown. If you acquired her as an eyass, both should have been in perfect shape when you collected her and it is useful, therefore, to take a photograph of them as soon as you can afterwards. This will give you a permanent guide to their proper dimensions.

It is also difficult to give advice on how often the operation needs to be carried out. This obviously depends on many factors – individual growth rates, the extent to which the hawk's life-style keeps things under control, and so on but in the worst cases coping will be necessary at least three or four times a year. In others, perhaps only once or twice. However, it will be necessary at some point, and proper maintenance is a skill you must acquire.

Like many other keratin products, beaks and talons have a 'quick' which contains nerves and supplies the new cells with essential materials for growth. If the quick is cut, it will cause pain and bleed. This means that there is always a limit to what you can pare off at any one time without causing discomfort. The situation is further complicated by the fact that, as beaks and talons grow, the quick tends to grow to match them. Conversely, if the beak or talons are kept trimmed, the quick stays in proportion.

Unfortunately, because a hawk's beak and talons are opaque if not jet black, you can't see the quick. There is no way of knowing, therefore, where the quick ends – until you pare too much off. Then you will need frequent applications of a styptic pencil to stem the bleeding. The tip of the beak or affected talon will remain tender for several days, and your hawk's feeding will become very tentative to minimise her discomfort. There are only two solutions to this problem:
1. If you've let either get really overgrown, clip off little but often from that point on to give the quick time to recede
2. Identify the problem early and don't let things get too much out of control.

By far the worst problems are presented by overgrown beaks and, as Sod's law has it, these are more difficult to cope than talons. This is partly because metal tools have to be used close to the bird's head, and partly because the operation itself is much more complicated.

A healthy broadwing beak, together with its various components, should look as follows:

Even without previous experience, there are two ways that you can identify whether or not your hawk's beak needs attention:

1. As the tip of the upper mandible grows, it will start to curve underneath the lower mandible

2. As the tip of the lower mandible grows, it will interfere with the operation of the upper mandible: when your hawk closes her beak, you will hear a click as the two parts make contact.

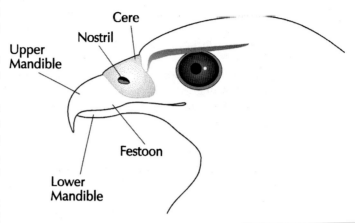

Eventually overgrowth will affect the hawk's feeding, and she will become less able to tear-up and swallow her food. If you let maintenance slide to this extent, you will have more difficult problems trying to put things right and she might need several coping operations to get her beak back to normal.

Coping itself involves clipping off the overgrown tips of beak and talons, then filing the inner edges to bring the new tips back to a point. To do this, there are certain specialised tools you will need:

• a pair of dog's 'toe-nail' clippers, available in any pet shop
• a set of needle files, available in most DIY stores.

'Needle' files are simply small files four to six inches long with differently-shaped abrasive surfaces. The minimum you will need is one with a flat edge, and another with at least a 'half-round' edge for filing the inner curves of the beak and talons. If you buy a set, they will come with more options than this. For example:

Needle File Profiles (in section)

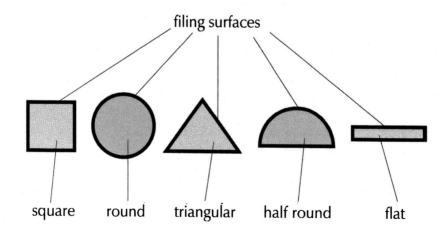

For broadwings, just the 'half round' file illustrated should satisfy all your coping needs. Unfortunately such tools are difficult to find except as part of a set. Of course, the rest can be used as spares. If you can't find a pack of these files in a local DIY store, then falconry equipment suppliers stock them, but again, at a far higher price.

Coping is another job which requires the help of an assistant, who will need to cast and hold the bird firmly during the operation. Coping a beak might take anything up to half an hour, depending on the severity of the problem and your own experience and dexterity. This is a long time to hold a bird, keeping her still at the same time, and it will certainly test the patience of your assistant as well as the hawk. It helps, therefore, to organise things so that you can all be as comfortable as possible.

The ideal set-up is a narrow table where both of you can sit opposite each other. The table should be narrow enough to avoid either of you having to over-stretch. If you haven't got a narrow table, use the corner of a normal one. The hawk should be cast, then lowered onto a cushion placed between you so that she has something padded to grip with her feet. To help keep her calm and still, a handkerchief or a small scarf should be placed over the hawk's head to obscure her vision or, better still, a hood. The procedure is as follows:

1. Clip off the tip of the upper mandible with the nail clippers, then file the cut with a flat file to prevent the tip from splitting
2. Bring the new tip back to a point with a round file, keeping the inner curve smooth and in proportion
3. If necessary, file the leading edge of the festoon to bring it back to shape
4. Check the lower mandible. If the forward end is too long, file that back sufficiently to eliminate any obstruction to the upper mandible
5. Check the whole beak (in particular the festoon) for scaling, and remove any scale with a flat file
6. 'burnish' the whole beak with a moistened finger and thumb, which will help to show up any remaining deficiencies
7. Check that both mandibles close properly without any abrasive contact.

Filing the inside edges of both mandibles and festoons will obviously have to be done with the beak open. Applying gentle pressure behind the festoon and beneath the cere where upper and lower mandibles meet, should persuade the hawk to open her mouth. You will then have to keep it open with the forefinger and thumb of your free hand. Alternatively, since she will want to 'bite', you can get her to bite on a gloved finger. The problem with this is that the finger tends to get in the way when you're trying to deal with the festoon. If you use the first method, make sure you don't close off her nostrils with your thumb and forefinger.

Never work a file from the front to the

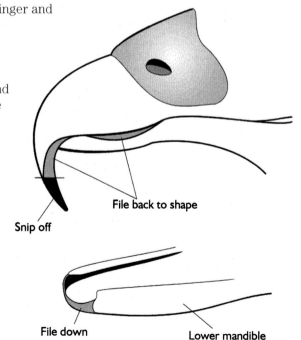

File back to shape

Snip off

File down

Lower mandible

back of the beak. One slip and you could do a lot of damage to your bird – to her cere, or even one of her eyes. When you're filing the inner surfaces of the upper mandible, it is best to work *across* the beak which has the added advantage of dealing with both sides at once. If the tip of the lower mandible is too long, simply file it back until it is able to close well clear of the upper mandible.

There's no doubt that beak-coping is a difficult and delicate task requiring confidence, patience and manual dexterity. If you're really worried about having to do it yourself, particularly the first time, there are falconers (usually equipment suppliers) who provide such a service. If you're unsure of what you're doing, it is often helpful to see a professional perform the operation first, then try it for yourself the next time it's required.

Coping talons is a much easier task, and tends to be needed less frequently. For instance, if the floor of the bird's aviary is covered with gravel, and there is a rock or two beside her bath, both will help to keep her talons at a reasonable level of growth. In addition, the more frequently she catches mature game, the more the need for artificial control will subside. It is, however, harder to recognise when the coping of talons is necessary. Basically, a hawk should be able to stand on a flat surface (such as a table) without the talons lifting the ball of her foot off it. In a sense, this is an arbitrary kind of measurement, but it's the only reliable one I know.

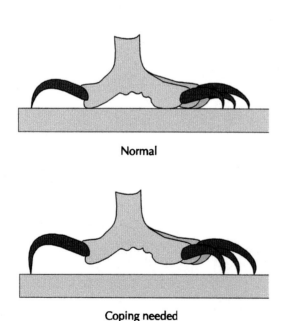

Normal

Coping needed

The real importance of controlling overgrown talons is that a bird can actually puncture her own feet, particularly on a perch that's too small – for instance when she lands on a twig during a hunting foray – or even when she folds her toes up to stand on one leg in her weathering. If a foot-puncture occurs, for whatever reason, infection can take a hold very quickly. This is because each talon is grooved at the back, and each can harbour particles of old and rotten food.

In fact it is good practice to check these grooves occasionally and, even if coping itself is unnecessary, scrape out any food residues with the point of a small file. Hawks attempt to do this for themselves each time they feed. They will 'pick' their front talons with their beak to devour any surplus food sticking to them, but unfortunately they are not always precise enough.

Coping talons is very straightforward. Simply clip off the end of each one with the clippers, then file them back to a point. File from the underside, and clean out the back grooves at the same time.

Obviously coping should be done whenever it is necessary, but one of the most convenient times is at the end of the hunting season when the hawk starts her annual moult. During the moult she will usually be grounded. Feeding her as much as she wants to bring her back to top weight so that her feathers grow well might also cause a mini-explosion in the growth of beak and talons. The problem is that the stress imposed by casting a bird to cope her half way through a moult could affect the healthy growth of new feathers, and such a risk is best avoided.

Casting her to undertake coping operations at the start of the moult will also provide an opportunity to get rid of worn or redundant equipment – in particular tail-bell fixings. She will shed the tail-bell anyway when she drops her deck feathers, and you might as well reclaim the bell before she does. Similarly, it is good practice to check the condition of her beak and talons before you take her up again, at the end of the moult, ready for the next season. If she needs coping, do it, then fit whatever new furniture she requires – all in the same cast.

Repairing Feathers

Certain elements of a hawk's plumage are essential for efficiency in flight. These are, in order of their importance,

- primary wing feathers – the pointed, finger-like feathers at the tip of each wing
- tail feathers
- secondary wing feathers – the large rounded feathers between the primaries and the hawk's elbow joint

All three groups are known as *flight* feathers – they have a profound affect on speed and manoeuvrability through the air. Put simply, primaries provide power in flight and are equivalent to the propeller of an aeroplane; secondaries provide lift; and tail feathers act as rudder and brake as well as giving additional lift.

Other wing and tail plumage plays a part in flight but its role is generally a passive one. 'Coverts', for example, cover the bare quills of flight feathers and prevent air passing through them, thereby supporting their aerofoil qualities. The rest of a hawk's feathers constitute what naturalists call 'contour' plumage, which is primarily designed to reduce drag, provide insulation, and maintain body temperature.

On any hawk which is flown regularly, flight feathers are subjected to a great deal of hard wear and tear. This is not just because of contact with the elements, but also flying through trees and undergrowth, and the rough-and-tumble of catching quarry, especially on the ground or in close cover. By the end of the season, therefore, many hawks acquire a distinctly ragged and tattered appearance. This is particularly true of juvenile plumage, which seems to be neither as waterproof nor as resilient as adult plumage. Also, because they are kept as captive birds, contact with the ground or wire mesh of their weathering can cause additional damage.

Hawks deal with feather degradation naturally by shedding and re-growing all their plumage every year, usually during the breeding season. Falconers call this period *the moult*, and even under ideal conditions it takes five or six months to complete. Nevertheless, severe damage to important feathers can seriously impair a hawk's efficiency, and if it happens early in the flying season her ability to catch quarry will be reduced. In addition, if part of a flight feather has broken off, flying will put much more strain on those adjacent to it and they are also liable to break. Falconers, therefore, don't often wait for the moult to solve the problem. Instead they have devised ways of fixing bent, broken or fractured feathers artificially.

It is only possible to repair a damaged feather – you can't replace one which has dropped out of its socket (follicle) or been pulled out by whatever means. All you can do is let nature take its course, and the hawk will eventually grow a new one. Otherwise, the nature of the repair will depend on the extent of the problem, but the worst situation is that the quill is completely severed leaving only the lower portion of the feather in its follicle. In this case repair is achieved through a very old technique known as *imping*.

To imp a feather successfully the first requirement is to have a matching feather to replace the missing part of the old one. However, it should be noted that *every flight feather is a different shape and size*, depending on its exact location. For example, a hawk's tail is made up of twelve feathers – six on one side, and six on the other. The two middle ('deck') feathers have their quills roughly (though not precisely) in the centre, but moving outwards from these, each quill is positioned progressively further towards the left or right edge of the feather as shown below.

No. 6 (left)   Deck feather   No. 6 (right)

Similarly, wing feathers are sized and shaped slightly differently depending on their placing, and those on one wing are mirror images of those on the other. Because of this the only feathers that *can* be matched successfully are ones which have come from the same place (but not necessarily the same hawk).

Not surprisingly, falconers obtain their supplies of matching feathers from their hawk's annual moult, discarding those which are too badly damaged and sorting the remainder into type and location. After two or three years it is possible to acquire a complete set of 'spares' from healthy hawks, especially if you have more than one of the same species and sex. However, for a beginner with a first bird in her first year, finding replacement feathers can be a real problem – if not impossible. Unless you know another falconer with a few seasons behind him, who flies a similar bird, and who is willing to let you have a matching feather, you might have to live with the damage until it is superceded by the moult.

If you *do* manage to acquire matching feathers, and you're prepared to give imping a try, the operation is (in principle) fairly straightforward. Repair is achieved by joining the two quills with a piece of re-inforcement called an imp (the word comes from the Latin *imponere*, which means to 'put in'). One of the virtues of quills is that they are (more or less) hollow, but one of their disadvantages – in terms of mending them – is that they taper from base to tip almost to the size of a human hair. Also, the nearer the tip the less hollow they are. A break close to the tip, therefore, is not as feasible to imp than one nearer to the base. Consequently imping often requires cutting the quill at a place where it *is* possible to implant a suitable re-inforcement.

The imp itself is, in effect, a 'needle' secured in both the quill of the damaged feather and the quill of the new feather at a point where they actually match – meaning that the feather's proper dimensions, appearance, and efficiency are maintained.

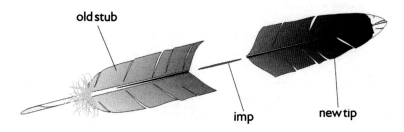

old stub   imp   new tip

These days imps are made either from slivers of green bamboo or carbon fibre. Garden canes or chopsticks are a source of bamboo, and carbon fibre can usually be obtained from angling shops where it is sold for repairing broken rod-tips.

197

Imps work best if they are triangular in section – or at least oval. If they are cylindrical, the new portion of feather will most likely rotate around them in flight rendering the whole repair more or less useless. But, for additional security, or to make up for slight deficiencies in the imp, you can use a powerful quick-setting glue such as 'Superglue' or 'Araldite Rapid'.

It is both feasible and advisable, once you have obtained a matching feather, to do most of the preparation before you take up the bird to cast her. Your main problem will be establishing where you need to cut the new feather to match the old one. However, once the actual imping process begins, you can cut back the old feather a little if necessary, so it is better to *slightly* over-estimate the length of the repair. The initial procedure is as follows:

1. Cut the new feather at an appropriate place
2. Whittle the imp to fit *both* parts of the new feather (there should be some friction between the imp and the two quill halves, but be careful not to split either of them)
3. Once you are satisfied that the imp fits both portions of the feather satisfactorily and the joint is sound, glue the imp into the replacement tip.

In other words, you are using both parts of the new feather as templates to perfect the imp before you attempt to fit it to the hawk. If the feather is a proper match, the lower portion of the imp should be a reasonable fit for the quill still attached to the hawk, although it might need slight refinement.

Imping is another operation which requires the hawk to be cast for some time, and the set-up recommended for managing a bird to cope her should also be used for imping. In addition, you will probably need a bowl of cold water for wetting neighbouring feathers to keep them out of the way, and a small but sharp pair of scissors for clipping off the damaged quill at the right place.

Repairing a tail feather is the easier task because your assistant can hold the bird more comfortably, keeping both wings and legs fully under control. However, control is much more difficult where a wing feather has to be repaired since the wing itself must be spread out to expose the damaged feather. The fact that it is spread rather than pinioned gives the hawk more scope for interfering with the operation. In this case, the hawk should be cast as normal, then laid on her back on a cushion. Once she is in that position, your helper should take hold of her legs to keep her feet under control, and hold the unaffected wing against her body to discourage her from trying to flap.

Once the hawk is under control, test the intended repair against the broken feather using adjacent plumage as a guide to its proper length. Then, if necessary, mark the damaged quill where it needs to be cut with a felt-tipped pen. (At this stage it is perhaps useful to know that cutting a feather still attached to the hawk is not at all painful – indeed, it is roughly equivalent to cutting a human hair.)

Cut the quill (but not the barbs) with the scissors and check the imp for fit. Don't be tempted to force it. If you do there is every chance that you will split the damaged quill and the imp will not hold. If necessary, refine the imp with sandpaper, or by scraping it with a sharp knife, until you have a stressless friction-fit. In other words, the imp should make contact with the sides of the quill without stretching or otherwise misshaping it. Although a good glue will compensate for minor imperfections, the neater the fit, the less stress the glue will be put under and the less chance that the imp will fail on a long-term basis.

Once you are satisfied with the joint, apply a small amount of glue to the imp and put it in place. If you use too much glue, you might have difficulty getting rid of the surplus, and you could end up gluing the barbs together as well as the adjacent feathers. Once you've cleared away any surplus glue, make sure that the whole feather is aligned properly with its neighbours –

meaning that it is capable of being folded in neatly. Don't release her from your assistant's cast until you are satisfied that the glue is properly set otherwise, if she starts to preen, she might dislodge the imp and you will have to start all over again.

Another way of repairing damaged feathers is with a *splice*. This method is appropriate where the quill is fractured but not severed. If the fracture is not repaired quickly, it will eventually break off altogether and will then require an imp. The splice is also a piece of reinforcement, but an *external* one. It is glued to the two sound parts of the quill either side of the fracture, so bridging it.

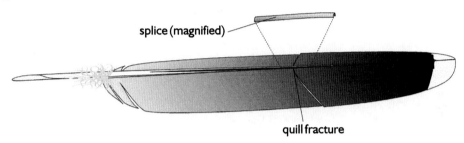

splice (magnified)

quill fracture

Splices should be concave to fit as neatly as possible over the affected part of the quill, but they are extremely difficult and tedious to make from bamboo or carbon fibre. There are two other options

1. Using part of the quill from another (discarded) feather
2. Using a sliver cut from a plastic drinking straw.

It doesn't matter which kind of bird's feather the splice is made from (it could be anything from a crow to a chicken), but a quill which has roughly the same dimensions as the affected feather will give you the best result. Obviously a moulted matching feather from the same bird, but which is no good for imping, would be the ideal choice.

To provide an adequate bridge the splice needs to extend half an inch or so either side of the fracture. If you are using a section of another quill to fashion the splice, clean out the underside if necessary so that it is as smooth as possible (the glue will give the splice additional strength, but only if it has good contact with both parts). The splice itself should be fixed to the upper side of the damaged quill. This is simply because the underside of most feathers has a central 'gully' running down its whole length which makes a good fit virtually impossible.

In this case the hawk will have to be cast so that you have access to the upper surface of her feathers, which means with her feet (rather than her back) resting on the cushion. Once she is secure, test the splice for fit. It doesn't have to be perfect by any means, but make it as close-fitting as possible. In particular, when the splice is pressed down into position on your 'dry' run, pare off any edges overlapping onto the barbs of the feather. Once you're satisfied, apply the glue and get on with it as quickly as you can. Again use only the amount of glue necessary for a good bond, and don't release the hawk until it is properly set.

Feathers that are simply bent out of shape and other minor damage can usually be repaired with hot water, and this method takes very little time once the bird is cast. Simply pour the hot water over the affected feather and straighten it out. But be very careful to keep the water off any fleshy parts of the bird's body, otherwise you will scald her. Unfortunately there are two problems with using this method.

1. Using hot water too frequently will make the quills brittle and more prone to snapping

2. Hot water will wash off any preening oil on the feather and it will no longer be waterproof. It may take the hawk several weeks to replace the missing oil, but feathers can be made more weatherproof in the meantime by wiping them over lightly with a very small amount of baby oil once they have dried out again. However, this is never worth doing unless the hawk has a number of damaged feathers, for example on her tail.

As an alternative to hot water, some equipment makers supply heated tongs specifically designed for straightening bent feathers, and these work in a similar way to hair curlers (but with the opposite outcome). Unfortunately overuse of these, too, tends to make feathers brittle. But on a long term basis, and if you have several hawks, it might be worth exploring this option. Otherwise the cost may not make it worthwhile, especially if you only need to use it once or twice. If you want to try this, buy a decent one – some tongs cool down much too quickly to be of much use.

PART 5

Supplementary Information

Notes On Anatomy: *External*

This illustration gives the external features of a bird of prey with particular reference to falconry nomenclature, but also incorporates the ornithological versions of the parts described.

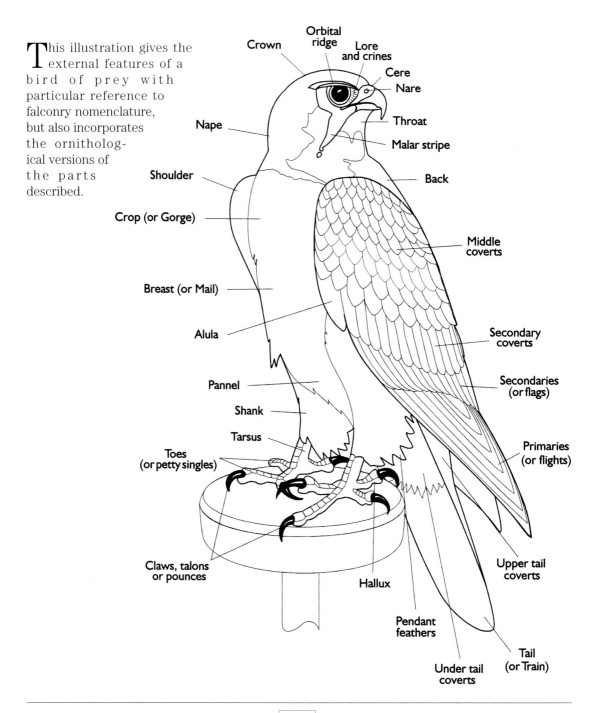

Crown
Orbital ridge
Lore and crines
Cere
Nare
Throat
Malar stripe
Nape
Shoulder
Back
Crop (or Gorge)
Middle coverts
Breast (or Mail)
Alula
Secondary coverts
Secondaries (or flags)
Pannel
Shank
Tarsus
Primaries (or flights)
Toes (or petty singles)
Claws, talons or pounces
Hallux
Upper tail coverts
Pendant feathers
Under tail coverts
Tail (or Train)

Plumage

Although feathers evolved from reptilian scales, they are unique to birds. There are many different kinds of feather, but in birds of prey at least they are all, in one way or another, designed either to maintain body temperature or to aid flight directly or indirectly. They are, therefore, of paramount importance to both bird and falconer. The diagram below illustrates the plumage of a Common Buzzard, but feather groups are more or less the same in all birds using powered flight, differing only in points of detail.

PLUMAGE
Buteo buteo (Common or European Buzzard)

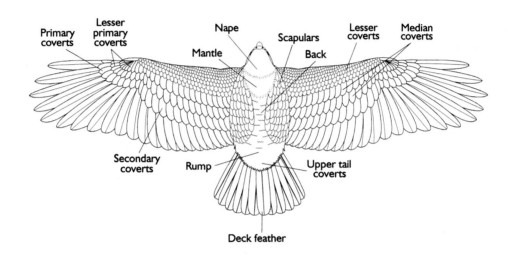

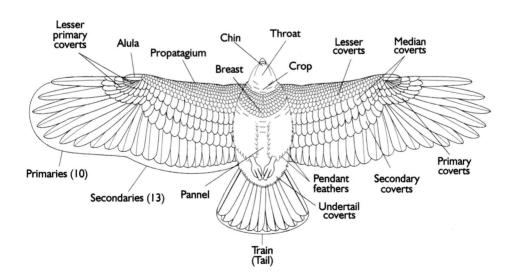

'Flight' feathers are arranged in three major groupings:
1. **Primaries** – the long finger-like feathers at the tip of each wing and attached to the hand area
2. **Secondaries** – the large rounded feathers between the carpal (wrist) and elbow joints
3. **Tail feathers**.

Put simply, primary feathers provide the power in flight and are equivalent to the propeller of an aeroplane, secondaries provide lift, and tail feathers act as rudder and brake as well as giving additional lift and balance. Like reptilian scales, flight feathers overlap each other, for two main reasons: firstly so that they can be folded in and out like a fan and secondly to prevent air passing through them in flight. Overlapping also means that flight feathers are layered when folded in. In the tail, for example, looking from above, the deck feather is uppermost with the outer feathers at the bottom.

All flight feathers have bare quills and the job of the *coverts* on wing and tail is to cover these quills – again preventing air passing through. Coverts, therefore, play an indirect role in flight by maintaining the aerofoil qualities of the wings and tail. Body feathers – known as *contour* plumage – play no part in flight except by reducing drag. Their main function is to provide insulation and help to maintain body temperature.

The alula feathers (which number from two to seven depending on species) are attached to the alular (the 'thumb'). This area is also known as the *bastard wing*, and has a very specific function in flight – to prevent stalling at slow speeds by modifying the turbulence over the upper surface of the wing. The alular digit is the only one capable of independent movement in the upper limb, and other wing adjustments are achieved entirely by muscles attached to the wing bones.

The *propatagium* (or patagium for short), which carries most of the lesser coverts, is simply a flap of skin extending from the shoulder to the wrist. Its primary function is to provide a clean leading edge to the wing between the two joints, thus improving the wing's aerofoil properties.

The finger-like primaries, evident when many birds' wings are extended, are characteristic of slower fliers and soaring birds such as buzzards, vultures and eagles. Air passes through them on both the upstroke and the downstroke, and they use each primary to push themselves forward on the downstroke. Where faster fliers are concerned – such as swifts, swallows and most falcons – there is little passage of air through the primaries in powered flight. Instead they use this whole group of feathers almost as one unit to power them through the air. This is achieved by folding the wing in and out from the carpal (wrist) joint to the tip of the primaries, and it requires a lot more energy. In effect, 'upstrokes' and 'downstrokes' are replaced by 'instrokes' and 'outstrokes'.

Notes On Anatomy: *Internal*

Introduction

All birds are characteristically vertebrate, but within this broad classification they have evolved several physical features which make them totally unique. Apart from obvious adaptations like feathers, which no other animals possess, this uniqueness permeates most of their internal and external structures. When compared with the general pattern of vertebrate development some of these structures have undergone radical changes, largely to accommodate, or facilitate, the high-energy demands of powered flight. In the process sacrifices have had to be made. In particular birds have lost the forelimbs of their bipedal reptile ancestors which were capable of grasping and manipulating objects, though they have developed other structures to compensate for their loss. Both these evolutionary forces – adaptation to flight and compensation for loss – have operated on bird anatomy to make them what they are today.

They are so characteristically different compared to other vertebrates that these differences have a profound impact on their husbandry, management, and use as falconry birds and in this respect alone it useful to know something about their anatomy. The sections below briefly describe the main differences, and explain the impact they have on birds' lives.

The Skeleton

Any vertebrate's body contains a high proportion of soft tissues (epithelia), but if it was composed entirely of these it would be a flabby, formless, unfunctioning mass. The skeleton reinforces epithelia, welds them together, gives them strength and support, and protects the vital organs from external forces. In addition it is an anchor for the vast majority of body muscles and it is, therefore, the agent through which all bodily form and functions are accomplished.

The illustration on page 206 is a diagram of the skeleton of a bird – in this case a rock dove (*Columba livia*) – which shows the main structural elements.

The main skeletal framework has had to evolve to meet the dual demands of aerial and terrestrial locomotion, both of which impose different stresses and strains on bone structures. On the ground a bird's whole weight has to be supported by its hind limbs, and in the air by its wings. This duality of function has been achieved through three basic modifications to the general vertebrate model. The first is a radical shift in centre of gravity which aids the switch from aerial to terrestrial locomotion. The second is the development of a more rigid skeletal framework to provide greater muscle support and the ability to absorb the shocks of landing. The third involves a reduction in weight of major bone formations to minimise the energy needed for take-off and sustained flight.

Compared to reptiles and mammals, whose weight can be distributed between all four limbs, a bird's body is considerably foreshortened. This reduces the distance from hip to shoulder, beneath and between which the main body mass is arranged. On land the hip joint acts rather like a fulcrum, balance being assisted by the adoption of a predominantly upright posture, but in flight the shoulder joint takes over and a horizontal alignment, with head and legs outstretched, helps to maintain balance as well as reducing drag.

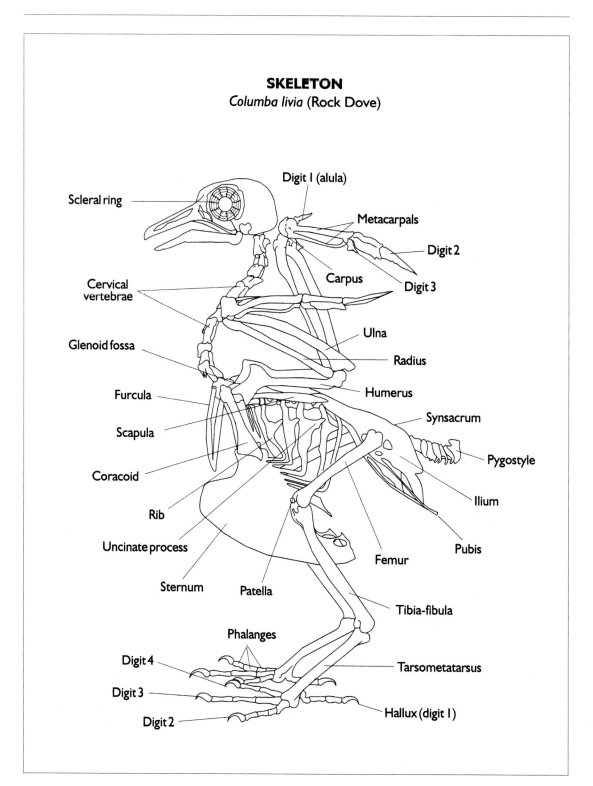

SKELETON
Columba livia (Rock Dove)

Scleral ring

Digit I (alula)

Metacarpals

Digit 2

Carpus

Digit 3

Cervical
vertebrae

Ulna

Radius

Glenoid fossa

Humerus

Furcula

Synsacrum

Scapula

Pygostyle

Coracoid

Ilium

Rib

Pubis

Uncinate process

Femur

Sternum

Patella

Tibia-fibula

Phalanges

Digit 4

Tarsometatarsus

Digit 3

Digit 2

Hallux (digit I)

Many bones, which are quite separate in other animals, are fused together. In the central framework of the body these fusions have assisted foreshortening, but for the most part evolved to increase rigidity. In other vertebrates the backbone acts as the principal longitudinal girder from which, ultimately, the body's whole weight is suspended, but in birds fusion of some vertebrae has made the spinal column into (almost) a solid rod from shoulder to tail. But this rod is only one part of a total assemblage which is more akin to a structurally rigid box. Other parts making up the box include the coracoids, ribs, pelvic girdle, and sternum (breastbone).

Fusion takes place in the chest (*thoracic*), middle back (*lumbar*), hip (*sacral*) and tail (*caudal*) vertebrae eliminating all flexibility in these regions. Thoracic fusion helps to brace the wings in flight, and the lumbar and sacral elements have evolved into an elongated plate (called the *synsacrum*) which supports the pelvic girdle and the thigh bones. The caudal area is foreshortened and capped by the so-called ploughshare bone (*pygostyle*) – also formed from fused vertebrae – which supports the tail segment and acts as a point of attachment for its muscles.

Ribs in the neck (*cervical*) area are fused to the vertebral column and the only free-standing ribs – which are confined to the thoracic region – carry reptilian strap-like expansions (known as *uncinate processes*) to one side. These are for the attachment of muscles supporting the shoulder blade (*scapula*) but, by overlapping the rearward rib, form an additional brace giving immense strength to the rib cage.

Three pairs of bones – the furcula, coracoids and scapulae – between them form sockets to hold the wings in place, bracing them against the sternum. The furcula (or wishbone) is really composed of two separate bones (the *clavicle* and *interclavicle*) fused together at their lower end for additional strength. The coracoids are sturdy struts meeting at an angle at the *glenoid fossa*, important for the attachment of flight muscles. The sternum is a large ossified structure providing anchorage for the ribs and the mass of chest muscles vital in flight. Except in the case of flightless birds, it also incorporates a massive keel at its lower edge for the attachment of additional flight muscles. So long and strong is this structure that it forms a bony sheath over the ventral surface of the body fully capable of protecting the abdominal area – which holds the mass of vital organs – from fights, accidents, and heavy falls. During flight it bears a large proportion of the bird's total weight, and by doing so keeps the centre of gravity well below the centre of air pressure on the wings.

The pelvic girdle provides an intermediary through which the weight of the body is transferred from wings to hind limbs. It has to be robust enough to withstand the considerable stresses imposed by landing. It is a firm plate fused to the synsacrum and incorporates the *acetabulum* – a large rounded socket which receives the head of the thigh bone – and the *ilium* which forms the dorsal part of the girdle and assists with weight transfer. The broad surface of the plate also offers an area of origin for the powerful leg muscles. On land the foreshortening of the thoracic-caudal areas of the spine places the centre of gravity low down and far back towards the pelvic girdle. This puts it directly over the bird's feet providing greater stability.

In contrast to the rigid thoracic-caudal area of the backbone, the cervical region has high motility and a variable number of vertebrae depending on the species concerned. In mammals the number remains consistently at seven – even in giraffes and 'neckless' whales – but in birds it varies between eleven and twenty five. Different parts of the neck also have different flexing capabilities. In addition to sideways and twisting motions, the front (head) section can bend downwards, the middle section upwards, and the back section both ways. This adaptation evolved largely to compensate for the loss of manipulatory forelimbs and enables the beak to reach all parts of the body, particularly for preening which is of vital importance in the maintenance of flight efficiency.

Compared to reptiles the avian brain is much expanded and the cranium is a swollen structure almost completely surrounded by extremely thin bone. In all vertebrates the skull is made up of several bony plates knitted together with zigzag seams called *sutures*, but in birds it has such a close fusion of elements that sutures are in general obliterated. The extra strength resulting from this arrangement has enabled the development of a thinner – and therefore a very much lighter – skull. Large sockets (*orbits*) house the eyes which are held in place by rings of equally thin bone called *scleral rings*. These are stiff ossified structures which help preserve the shape of the eyeball and resist pressures which might otherwise produce distortions affecting vision. Fossil evidence shows that scleral rings were present in all ancestral vertebrate groups but have since been lost in most. They persist only in certain fishes, some reptiles, and all birds.

The beak is not composed of skeletal material but is a protein-based tissue called *keratin* which is more closely related to skin than to bone. In other vertebrates keratin has developed into an enormous variety of special structures – for example, horns in cattle, fingernails in primates, shells in turtles, and warts in toads. Beaks as such are not confined to birds – they occur, for instance in turtles and octopuses – but uniquely in birds they have evolved into an extremely light and strong tool with a remarkable variety of functions associated with the diet of particular species. The outer-surface cells of keratin tend to be lost through injury or normal wear-and-tear, and they are constantly being renewed from the cells below.

The hind limbs of birds are designed along the same general lines as those in other vertebrates but they differ markedly in points of detail. These differences reflect the development of bipedalism, and later specialisations associated with flight and diet. In all land vertebrates they are composed of three major segments – the thigh, the shank (or shin), and the foot (pes).

The thigh is constructed of a single bone (the *femur*) which is basically a cylindrical structure with expanded ends forming the hip and knee joints. The spherical hip expansion, offset from the main shaft, fits into the acetabulum, the round socket in the pelvic girdle. It projects the femur sideways from the body enabling a fore-and-aft swing of the limb in a horizontal plane. The femur is a major weight-bearing bone and in addition acts as a point of origin for the tendons, powerful thigh muscles, and other muscles serving the tail. In most birds this section of the leg is covered with plumage and is rarely visible.

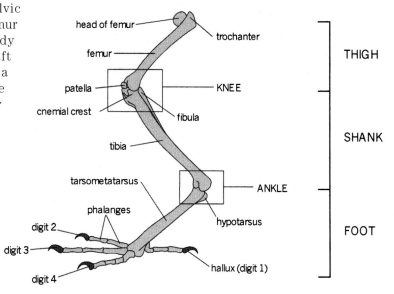

The lower expansion of the femur connects with the second segment at the knee. This section is composed of two bones, the *tibia* and *fibula*. In ancestral vertebrates these two bones were quite separate, the tibia acting as the main supporting strut of the lower leg and the fibula as anchorage for tendons and muscles. In birds the fibula, unnecessary for support, has undergone extensive weight saving reduction. It is a slender structure separate at its upper end but fused to the tibia at its lower end. In contrast the tibia is a stoutly-built bone which articulates rearwards at the knee joint. A separate nubbin of bone, the patella or knee cap, carries the main tendon of the thigh and facilitates its smooth passage over the joint on its way to the lower leg.

The third segment – the foot or *pes* – is the site of major deviations in birds compared to other groups of vertebrates. The tibia terminates at the ankle joint which in birds looks like a reversed knee. The joint itself is greatly simplified and forms a strong single-action articulation ideal for withstanding the stresses of take-off and landing. In most reptiles and mammals the area between the toes and the tibia is made up of a series of small bones, known as *tarsals* and *metatarsals* (the functional equivalent of the wrist and palm), which are collectively called the *tarsus*. In birds these bones have been fused into a single limb element which, though known anatomically as the *tarsometatarsus*, is also called the tarsus for short.

In the reptilian ancestors of birds the fifth toe disappeared early in their development and the first toe (or *hallux*) was turned backwards as an additional prop for the foot. The second, third and fourth toes remained forwardly-pointing and were symmetrically arranged, the centre one (digit 3) being the longest. Each of these was composed of a number of elements, called *phalanges* – the second and fourth toes had 3 and 5 respectively, and the middle toe had 4. The foot structure of modern birds is indistinguishable from these to the extent that the footprints of ancestral dinosaurs, when first discovered, were thought to be those of gigantic birds.

As one might expect, the construction of forelimbs in the majority of terrestrial vertebrates is similar to that of the hind limbs since the design evolved in four-legged animals. They are also divided into three anatomical segments – the upper arm, the forearm, and the hand (or *manus*).

The first segment consists of a single bone, the *humerus*, which is similar in form to the femur. It is basically cylindrical, elongated (except in flightless birds), and slenderly built. It, too, has expansions at both ends, one being housed in the socket made by the conjunction of the furcula, coracoid and scapula, and the other forming the upper half of the elbow joint. Unlike the femur the humerus is not a weight-bearing bone because birds are bipedal animals, but it is important for the attachment of major flight and wing muscles. The functional switch from load-bearing to muscle anchorage has enabled the development in birds of 'honeycombed' or tubular bone, and the humerus is an example. In

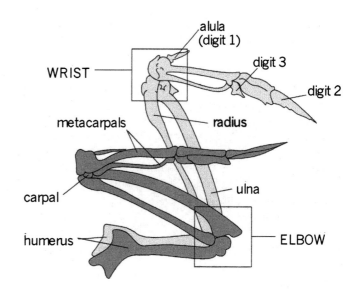

these the bone is hollow but supported internally by a framework of bony bars or struts just sufficient to preserve the shape and rigidity of the structure. The development of this type of bone has helped to lighten the skeleton so reducing the energy needed for sustained flight. The feature is most pronounced in large gliding and soaring birds such as vultures and buzzards and in many of these leg and other bones are hollowed out in the same way.

The second segment, the forearm, is made up of two separate bones called the *radius* and *ulna*. The ulna is a stout columnar bone which acts as the wing's main supporting strut and as the point of origin for the secondary flight feathers. It articulates with the humerus at the elbow joint which moves only in a horizontal plane parallel to the long axis of the body. This increases the limb's rigidity during flight. The radius lies lateral to the ulna, seldom bearing any stress, but it is important for the origin of muscles concerned with wing adjustments.

The third segment, the *manus*, includes the wrist (*carpus*), the palm region (*metacarpus*), and the finger bones (*phalanges*). As in the hind limb this is an area of major adaptation in birds. The carpal bones have reduced in number through fusion to two providing more rigidity of the joint in flight but sufficient movement for wing adjustments. Similarly, the metacarpals have fused into two elongated bones to provide anchorage for most of the primary feathers which propel the bird through the air. Birds have evolved from reptile forebears which possessed only three fingers, and these are preserved in a greatly reduced and modified fashion. Phalange joints have been lost through fusion, and the first digit (the thumb) – the only one capable of independent movement – carries the alula feather (or bastard wing) which helps to prevent stalling at slow speeds. The remaining primary feathers are carried by the second and third digits which are fused together into (almost) a single bone.

Musculature

In all vertebrates muscle tissue makes up between a half and a third of their bulk, and activity of the nervous system – in particular the brain – has little means of expression other than through the contraction of muscle fibres. It is this ability to contract which distinguishes muscle tissue from other epithelia, and these contractions can be involuntary, as in the beating of the heart, or voluntary, as in the deliberate movement of a hand or a limb.

Muscle tissue is categorised into three different types according to its location in the body and the embryonic material from which it is derived. Two of these are similar in that they possess a highly-organised structure capable of rapid (but relatively short-lived) contractions, and they constitute *striated* muscle – so-called because of its striped appearance under the microscope. The first of these is associated with the skeleton and is sometimes called *skeletal muscle*, and the second is peculiar to the myocardium of the heart which is known as *cardiac* muscle. The third type has a poorly organised contractile structure in comparison, but it is capable of low-energy contractions of considerable extent. Because of its appearance it is known as *smooth muscle*, and its particular type of contraction makes it especially suitable for regulating the body's internal environment. It is found in many regions of the body such as the lining of the digestive tract; the ducts of glands associated with the gut, bladder, trachea and bronchi of the lungs; and the circulatory vessels, genital organs, and connective tissues of the skin. In birds smooth muscle is also associated with the movement of individual feathers. But it is with skeletal muscle that major variations between vertebrate groups occur.

There are basically two types of skeletal muscle fibre, red and white. Red fibre contains relatively large amounts of a substance called *myoglobin* (a variety of haemoglobin) which stores oxygen, and they use fat rather than carbohydrate as a source of energy. Weight-for-weight fat releases larger amounts of energy than carbohydrate and red fibres are, therefore, more efficient. It is believed that they evolved to enable longer periods of sustained effort.

No animal appears to have exclusively red or white fibres, and it is likely that they are two extremes of a continuum containing various mixtures of both. Certainly bird muscles contain both, the proportion of red to white depending on how prolonged the activity of the muscle needs to be. In the chest muscles of strong fliers, such as pigeons and swifts, red fibres predominate but in birds like fowl, for whom flight is usually short-lived, they are predominantly white.

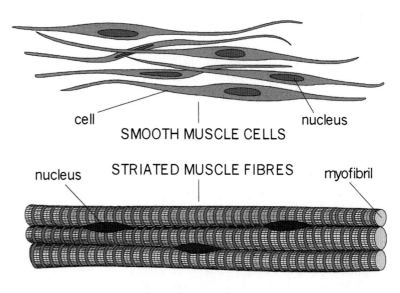

cell   SMOOTH MUSCLE CELLS   nucleus

In general skeletal muscles make up the flesh of the body and they are arranged as units which attach to and move skeletal structures. Attachment is via connective tissue (tendons) at both ends of the muscle, one of which is more stable and is called the area of *origin*, the other the area of *insertion*. The force of the muscle is exerted through shortening of its fibres which results in a pull on the bone to which the insertion is attached.

In all land vertebrates trunk muscles are greatly reduced in relative volume compared to sea vertebrates due to the fact that limbs have taken over as the means of propulsion. The bipedalism of birds, and in particular the foreshortening and rigidity of their thoracic-caudal vertebrae, have enabled them to further abandon the complicated system of muscles to support and move the weight of the trunk.

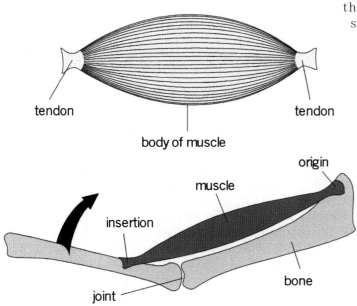

Trunk muscles can be divided into two major groups – *epaxial* (back) muscle which controls sideways movement of the trunk as well as bending of the spinal column, and *hypaxial* (abdominal) muscle which supports and sheathes the abdominal cavity. In birds epaxial muscle on the back itself is limited to several small rhomboid muscles, which attach the shoulder blade to the vertebral column, and a series of short slips attached to the ribs, which are involved in expanding and contracting the rib cage. But epaxial muscle is best-developed in the neck and tail regions. Those in the neck are comparatively large, and cervical vertebrae have developed special projections (called *hypapophyses*) for their attachment. Muscles in this area are characteristically sub-divided and overlapping which, combined with the motility of the vertebrae, enable the neck to perform an enormous range of subtle movements. The tail muscles are another complex group arising from the pelvic girdle, synsacrum, and caudal vertebrae. They also enable a wide range of movements mainly concerned with tail adjustments in different flying conditions and, in certain species, sexual display.

Hypaxial muscles sheathe the viscera and surround the abdominal cavity, and on land, therefore, they support the bird's weight. The chest (pectoral) muscles which, though sited on the trunk, are neither epaxial nor hypaxial in nature, are concerned primarily with movement of the wings. These muscles are massive and powerfully built, accounting for (on average) 15 to 20 per cent of total body weight. The *pectoralis major* depresses the wing by giving a strong downward and backward pull on the humerus. It runs from its origin on the keel of the sternum to its insertion on the underside of the humerus and the great depth of the sternum serves to increase the length, and therefore the contractile ability, of its fibres. Elevation of the wing is produced by the *supracoracoideus* which is a deep-set muscle also originating on the sternum. It acts rather like a pulley passing between the furcula, scapula and coracoid to its insertion on the upper side of the humerus (see illustration opposite).

The *supracoracoideus* is best-developed in birds which specialise in hovering, most notably the hummingbird for whom it provides an additional power stroke. Normally only the downstroke provides lift, the upstroke being one of recovery in preparation for the next beat.

In the wing there is considerably less development of those muscles used by other vertebrate groups for locomotion, standing and balance. Such a system of braces is not necessary. In the air birds balance on their wings through the great strength of the pectoralis major with the coracoid bones acting as compression members. The majority of arm muscles are therefore concerned with folding and unfolding the wings, adjusting major flight feathers, and changing the wing surface in many other ways to respond to different flight requirements.

In most land vertebrates leg muscles are relatively bulky and birds are no exception. In fact leg muscles are second only in volume to those of the chest. As the pectorals serve for flight, so the leg muscles are the means of propulsion on land. In addition they must be powerful and robust enough to provide sufficient thrust for take-off and act as shock absorbers during landing. They are used for balance and walking (or hopping) in ways that appear to show interesting similarities to those of man, although the actions of many of them have not yet been conclusively established.

One interesting difference concerns the muscle actions of the hip joint, which humans use to maintain balance when only one leg is on the ground. This is achieved by a series of 'abductor' and 'adductor' muscles which are virtually non-existent at this site in birds. They compensate by a sideways rotation of the femur which brings the body's centre of gravity over the supporting foot. This results in the characteristically waddling gait which is most pronounced in birds with short legs such as ducks and geese.

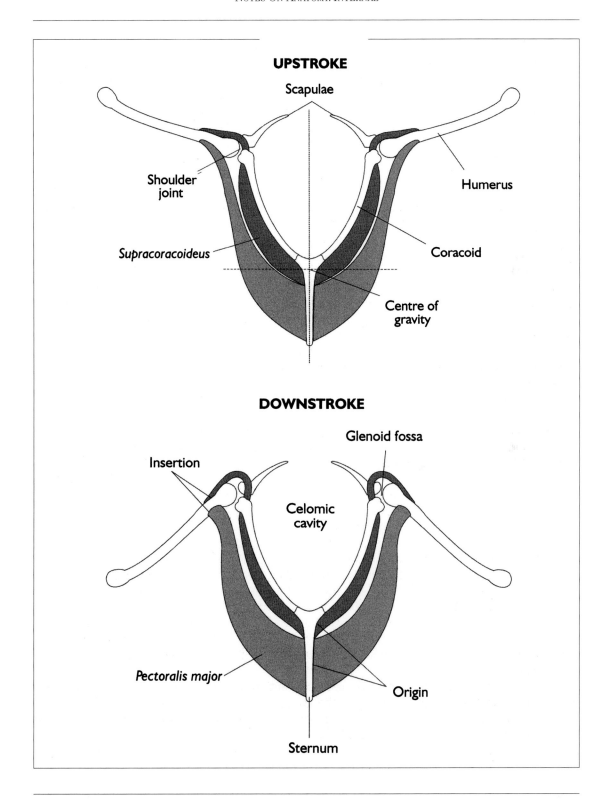

UPSTROKE

Scapulae

Shoulder joint

Humerus

Supracoracoideus

Coracoid

Centre of gravity

DOWNSTROKE

Glenoid fossa

Insertion

Celomic cavity

Pectoralis major

Origin

Sternum

Metabolism and Respiration

In all animal life muscles work through the complex process by which food is converted into fuel then burned with the assistance of oxygen carried by the bloodstream. The production of fuel is part of a wider process known as *metabolism* – the continuous series of chemical changes by which life itself is maintained. In this process food and tissues are broken down, new substances are created for growth and cell regeneration, and energy is released. Apart from its use in visible muscle movements energy is vital for the maintenance of respiration, blood circulation, peristalsis (the waves of contraction and relaxation by which food is moved through the intestines), normal muscle tension, body temperature, and many other functions.

By any system of measurement the metabolic rate of birds is faster than that of any other vertebrate, and in this sense at least they live life more fully. The cost in energy of powered flight, as well as the common problems of avoiding predators, obtaining food, and reproducing, is about 75 per cent higher than that of mammals. In normal flight birds increase their consumption of oxygen by a factor of thirteen above their base metabolic rate and they can sustain this level over many hours. During take-off and flights in turbulent air this factor can increase to thirty for short periods. In contrast a human athlete might achieve fifteen times his normal consumption, but only for a few minutes.

More notable is the energetic performance of birds at high altitudes. Although they spend most of their lives below 500 feet, during migration many fly much higher. Experiments have shown that the house sparrow (*Passer domesticus*) is able to maintain level flight at 25,000 feet, and radar echoes have detected other small birds migrating across Europe at 23,000 feet. In contrast a mammal of similar body weight (a mouse for example) becomes comatose at the equivalent of 20,000 feet through lack of oxygen. Performance like this is not confined to smaller birds. Each year geese (*Anser indicus*) rise from sea-level to fly across Himalayan peaks in excess of 29,500 feet, and a vulture has been reported killed colliding with an aircraft at 36,000 feet.

The problems of altitude do not only concern oxygen intake. Air temperature falls by about 1.7°C for every 1,000 feet of ascent – although this is not an entirely linear scale (if it was temperatures would eventually fall below absolute zero). If the temperature at sea-level is 10°C, at 36,000 feet it would be -50°C and at 25,000 feet it would be -33°C. Yet the energy production of birds, even in such a low oxygen environment, enables them to maintain sufficient body heat for flight in these temperatures.

Birds live their lives at what – for humans at least – would be fever pitch and to a time scale of their own. At rest the healthy human heart beats at 65 to 70 times per minute and body temperature is maintained at 36.9°C. By way of comparison, a crow's heart beats at a rate of 342 per minute, a sparrow's at 460, a robin's at 570, and a hummingbird's at 1,000. For all of them normal temperature is around 41°C rising to 43.5°C during flight. One reason for the disparity in heart rates amongst different species is that heat is lost through the body's surface area, and larger birds have less area in relation to total body mass than smaller ones. In fact doubling the size of a bird roughly halves the rate at which it loses heat. Small birds, therefore, need to burn energy at a faster rate to maintain body temperature, and consequently they eat more food – about one third of total body weight per day compared to one seventh in large birds.

All of this indicates a high-performance circulatory system which excels in the transport of oxygen and points to a fundamentally different method of supply. Indeed, the avian lung is unique amongst vertebrates and its gas-exchange functions are generally recognised as the most efficient of all animals.

In vertebrates – and in the more highly-organised invertebrates – most of the body's internal organs (the viscera) are situated in a fluid-filled space known as the *celomic cavity* or *celom*. This enables the relatively free movement of viscera during normal functional activity, and facilitates changes in their size and shape during the process of growth. As an additional element the celom of birds is divided in a rather complicated way to enable the development of several paired pockets called *air sacs*. These sacs – and to some extent the division of the celom itself – promote the efficiency of the breathing apparatus.

RESPIRATORY SYSTEM

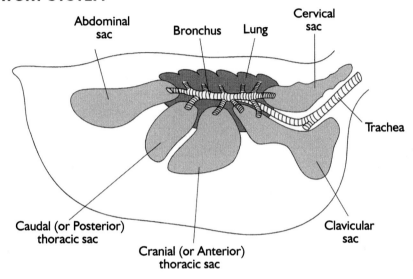

LUNGS, SHOWING
AIR SAC CONNECTIONS

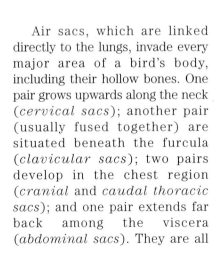

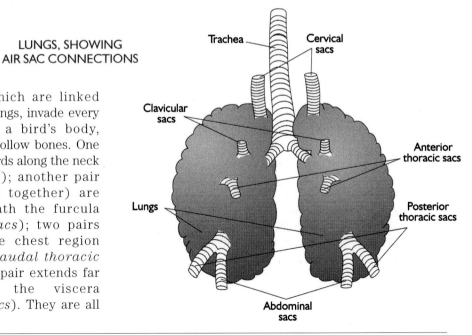

Air sacs, which are linked directly to the lungs, invade every major area of a bird's body, including their hollow bones. One pair grows upwards along the neck (*cervical sacs*); another pair (usually fused together) are situated beneath the furcula (*clavicular sacs*); two pairs develop in the chest region (*cranial* and *caudal thoracic sacs*); and one pair extends far back among the viscera (*abdominal sacs*). They are all made of thin membranous material and their lining is smooth. Consequently they play no part in the process of gas-exchange but act as bellows keeping a constant supply of air passing through the lungs. They may also assist in the regulation of body temperature.

In the case of mammals the whole lung expands and contracts through use of the diaphragm in each breathing cycle. The diaphragm draws air into the lungs where gas-exchange takes place, then it contracts to expel carbon dioxide, and the cycle is repeated. Birds have no diaphragm, and their small compact lungs do little in the way of expansion and contraction. Although their breathing mechanism is still that of a suction-pump, air is drawn through the lungs into the air sacs by a forward and upward movement of the ribs and sternum which expands the trunk capacity. This results in a drop in atmospheric pressure in the sacs causing air to rush in to equalise pressure, and little or no gas-exchange takes place on the way. Muscular contraction of the ribs and sternum then forces air out of the sacs back into the lungs, and it is in this part of the cycle that gas-exchange occurs. During flight this mechanism may be supplemented – or even replaced – by the action of the wing muscles.

The Digestive System

All living beings need oxygen, water, a variety of inorganic salts, glucose, fats, amino acids, and vitamins for the cells which make up their bodies to grow and function. Oxygen is processed via the respiratory system: the rest – harvested through 'food' – are processed by the digestive system. Here, the simple and ancient Anglo-Saxon term 'gut' (by which I mean the digestive system coming into play after swallowing) is both relevant and convenient.

Put simply, food is taken into the mouth, swallowed, disassembled, then put to use by the body or ejected as waste. The gut relies on chemical activity to break food down into useable and non-useable elements but, for these chemicals to work, solid material has to be reduced to a soft pulp first. Once this breakdown has been achieved, useful substances are absorbed by the intestinal wall for circulation to body cells and storage areas via the blood stream and specialised organs.

Although food might be taken into the mouth as small particles, or brought down to size by chewing, where birds (and many other vertebrates) are concerned, it is frequently passed into the gut *en masse*. In these, therefore, pulping is mainly accomplished by muscular action in food-holding areas. To assist in this, the system includes – throughout its length – mucous cells and mucous-generating glands which not only help its passage but also produce the pasty consistency required for effective chemical breakdown. The (involuntary) musculature involved in this reduction, and in the passage of materials through the system (*peristalsis*), is 'smooth' muscle arranged in sheets both longitudinally and laterally along the gut.

The first part of the gut is the *oesophagus*. In mammals, food is torn apart, chewed, then swallowed as a partly broken-down bolus coated with saliva. Their oesophagus, therefore, is fairly narrow and smooth. But in birds – especially birds of prey – food is often covered with feathers, fur, scales or spines and swallowed whole or in large lumps with no prior mastication. In these, the oesophagus is much tougher, has a considerably greater diameter, and is more muscular. But in all vertebrates the oesophagus has no function other than that of the transportation of food from the mouth to the important structures of digestion.

The *crop* – which is common to most birds but not all – is an expansion of the oesophagus at its lower end. It varies in size and shape between species, but it is particularly well developed in game birds such as pigeons, and in diurnal birds of prey. In these, it facilitates the consumption of

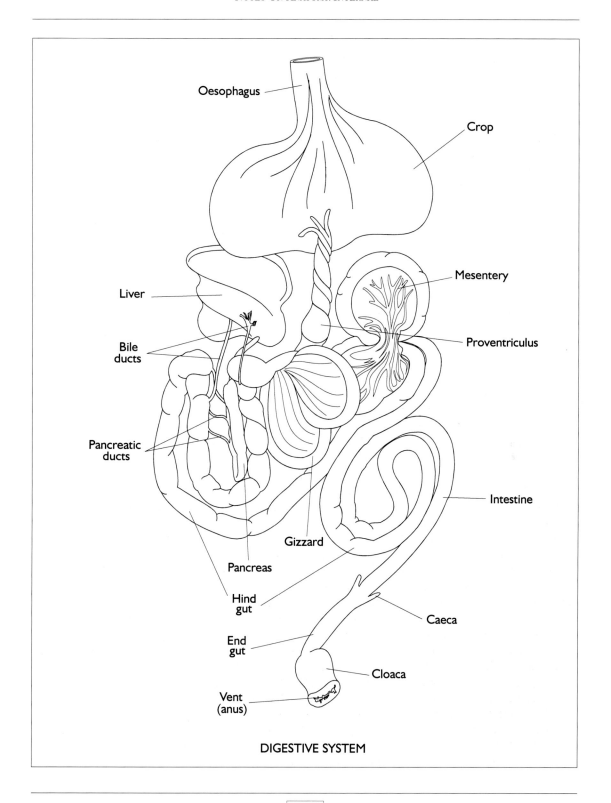

Oesophagus

Crop

Mesentery

Liver

Proventriculus

Bile
ducts

Pancreatic
ducts

Intestine

Gizzard

Pancreas

Caeca

Hind
gut

End
gut

Cloaca

Vent
(anus)

DIGESTIVE SYSTEM

large volumes of food in a short space of time, which can be digested later in the safety of a convenient roost (although raptors gulp food down quickly to avoid being robbed by other predators rather than through fear of predation). The crop is, therefore, primarily a storage area playing no real part in the process of digestion, except by softening its contents and covering them with mucous.

The crop leads to the 'stomach', and it is in this area that the digestive energies of all vertebrates are channelled. The avian stomach, though, is composed of two separate parts – the *proventriculus* and the *gizzard*.

The internal environment of the proventriculus is extremely chemical through glandular activity, although the potency of this activity depends on individual diets. In all cases, its main function is the chemical breakdown of food, and it is here that ingested material becomes thoroughly mixed with digestive substances – in particular the enzyme *pepsin* and a fat-splitting lipase. Pepsin accomplishes the breakdown of proteins with the help of hydrochloric acid, which is also produced in the proventriculus.

In contrast, the gizzard in its most highly-developed form is a muscle-bound grinding tool and is the bird's substitute for teeth. The strong, circular, asymmetric muscles of the gizzard wall are toughened by a special membranous lining made of a substance called *koilin* (similar to *keratin*, the cellular material that beaks are made of), against which food is crushed and pulped by muscle contractions. Birds which feed on digestively-resistant foods – such as nuts and grain – have the best developed gizzards, and many of these also swallow sharp stones and grit to assist with the grinding process.

In less well-developed gizzards – such as those in birds of prey – a minimal amount of grinding takes place and the organ simply allows the digestion begun in the proventriculus to continue for an extra period of time. In these, therefore, koilin is not significantly present. However, in birds of prey especially, the gizzard has another extremely important function. It blocks the passage of indigestible materials, such as teeth and claws, into the delicate intestinal tract so preventing them from causing permanent, perhaps even fatal, damage. These components are rolled into a pellet (*casting*) in the gizzard, then forcibly expelled through the mouth.

Digestible material, after sufficient time has elapsed to ensure its primary breakdown, passes into the next part of the gut – the *intestine*. A sphincter muscle at the bottom end of the gizzard relaxes, and the mushy package is squeezed into the intestine by waves of peristaltic contractions.

The intestine is the business end of the gut. It is the place where all the useful elements of food are absorbed into the body. It has two basic functions – to complete the chemical process begun in the proventriculus, and to provide a large surface area for the optimum absorption of food materials into the blood stream. The chemicals needed come from three different sources – the liver, the pancreas, and the inner wall of the intestine itself.

The liver is a complex organ which is only marginally concerned with aiding digestion. Its major function is the treatment and storage of food materials *after* absorption into the body. Nevertheless, it has a place in the digestive process. Elements of the liver gather cell secretions, the *bile*, which are discharged into the intestine via *bile ducts*. Many of these secretions, which originate from dead body cells, are not useful at all in digestion but bile salts in particular aid a pancreatic enzyme (*lipase*) in the breakdown and absorption of fats.

The sole function of the pancreas, on the other hand, is the manufacture of the remaining enzymes needed to complete the digestive process which, as with the liver, are introduced into the intestine via special ducts (*pancreatic ducts*). It produces a number of enzymes important for the breakdown of all three major types of organic food materials – fats, carbohydrates, and protein.

Most intestinal enzyme production takes place in glandular outgrowths in the intestinal wall, some of which also, when necessary, produce hormones sent via the blood stream to stimulate the pancreas into greater efforts. This final chemical assault results in the breakdown of food into its molecular structure.

To bring about efficient absorption, food elements need to be in contact with a large surface area. In general, this area needs to be roughly equivalent to the volume of material to be absorbed. A short, smooth tube, therefore, will not suffice. Increases in surface area are achieved in two ways – through small foldings inside the intestine, and by elongation of the intestine.

This part of the gut (known as the *hindgut*) in birds is often in excess of eight times the length of the entire body and highly convoluted. In a six foot man, this would be the equivalent of about seventeen yards. The great length of the intestine in birds is related to their hyper-activity and high metabolic rate, which results in an increased food demand compared to other vertebrates, and therefore the consequent requirement of additional absorptive surface in the intestine. Also, because of the rigours imposed by flight, birds cannot allow unrestricted movement of the intestine inside the abdominal cavity so a high proportion of its coils are attached to the abdominal wall by a membranous tissue called the *mesentery*. Following final chemical breakdown, food molecules are absorbed into the bloodstream through a very rich and extensive network of blood vessels in the intestinal wall.

The end gut is relatively short in birds and consists of two elements – the paired caeca, and the cloaca. Not all birds have functioning caeca, in birds of prey, for example, they are virtually non-existent, but they are very important for species which eat herbivorous foods containing cellulose. No vertebrate can digest cellulose by means of its own enzyme activity, but the caeca contain vast numbers of bacteria which can break it down and feed on it themselves. These bacteria can't survive inside the intestine proper, or outside it, so they give up a share of the products of their labours to the host body in exchange for shelter (a relationship known as *symbiosis*).

The function of the cloaca is to collect the waste products of the digestive system ready for expulsion via the *vent* (or *anus*). Unlike mammals, birds do not have a separate urinary bladder so urine and faeces are collected together in the cloaca and expelled as a slushy mass.

Vision

What we know as 'space' is crowded with many different kinds of radiation which constantly bombards the earth and all living things upon it. But we are insensitive to most of it, and we only know it exists through mechanisms (such as radio) which translate its effects into a form identifiable by our own limited senses. Not surprisingly, the majority of radiation reaching earth originates from the sun, and the range of sensitivity any earth-bound animal has corresponds in great measure to the kind of radiation emitted by this body as opposed to the millions of others. Our sun's slower, longer radiation waves are received as heat; its faster, shorter waves are perceived as light. Sensitivity to sunlight, known as *photoreception*, is widespread (but not universal) throughout the animal kingdom and the organ which provides it is the eye.

On a purely mechanical level, eyes work in a similar way to a camera. In both, there is a dark chamber – the camera body and the *eyeball*; in both there is a lens, which focuses light onto a sensitive surface at the back of the chamber – the film and the *retina*; in both there is a means of regulating the amount of light received – the diaphragm and the *iris* – which open or close to produce a variable aperture and *pupil*.

But here the similarity ends. The camera itself is not *responsive* to light. In particular, different kinds of film have to be used for varying conditions (such as daylight or artificial light), and other aids (such as flash or special 'colour correction' filters) are sometimes needed to ensure an acceptable photograph. Even the lens has to be changed on occasions to produce the desired image, for instance in close-up (macro) photography. And at the end of all this, the result depends entirely on how the film is processed.

Even the healthy human eye, which is not (by a long way) the most advanced photoreceptor in the animal kingdom, is very much more efficient and versatile than any camera. With the help of the brain – its processing laboratory – it produces instant and perfectly appropriate images constantly wherever there is light to receive within the range of its receptors.

Vertebrate 'eyeballs' consist of three layers: the outer casing comprising the *cornea* and *sclera*; a middle vascular layer, the *choroid*; and the nerve-based receptors themselves, the *retina*. The sclera is cartilageous tissue whose function is to resist pressure on the eyeball and preserve its shape in all normal operating conditions. In birds (as well as in certain fishes and some reptiles) resistance to pressure is further assisted by the *scleral ring* – a flat ring of thin bone which holds the eye in place. The cornea is also made of scleral tissue, but it is translucent and is the means by which light enters the eye. The refractive index of the cornea (which means its ability to 'bend' light waves) is almost the same as water, so in land vertebrates (including birds) its curvature does much of the work of focusing, leaving the lens to perform the final (but most crucial) adjustment.

In contrast to the sclera, the choroid is a soft material rich in blood vessels which feed the retina and other tissues of the eyeball. However, it has two subsidiary functions which seem to be, on the face of it, highly contradictory. The choroid is heavily-pigmented enabling it to *absorb* light rays penetrating the retina, but in most vertebrates it also has the mirror-like capability of *reflecting* light *back onto* the retina. Its light-reflecting capability is most often seen at night when a powerful light-source is shone directly into the eyes of, for example, a prowling cat or fox. An excess of light can be 'harmful' if it confuses the details of the image, so in certain circumstances absorption of excess light is useful. But in other circumstances – such as hunting at night – the ability to reflect light back onto the retina is also useful enabling the animal concerned to take advantage of any stray illumination available.

All parts of the eye are subordinate in importance to the retina – without one which works, there is no vision. The eye's whole design is, therefore, directed at servicing this third layer. But before we look in any detail at the retina itself, we need some understanding of how the rest of the eye relates to it.

As the illustration opposite shows, most of the eyeball is blank space, but it has to be filled with *something* to help maintain the eyeball's shape under pressure and still enable free movement of other functioning parts. This 'packing' also needs to be 'neutral' – in other words, incapable of blocking or distorting light passing through it. So the fore and aft chambers of the eyeball are filled with clear liquid-based substances – the *aqueous humour* and the *vitreous humour* respectively. As their names suggest, the vitreous humour is a thick, jelly-like material which aids in the resistance of pressure; the aqueous humour is more watery, allowing easy movement of the iris and lens under varying operating conditions.

The *iris* is mainly a combination of choroid and retinal tissues, although here these have lost the functions of vascular supply and photoreception characteristic elsewhere. The iris's job is

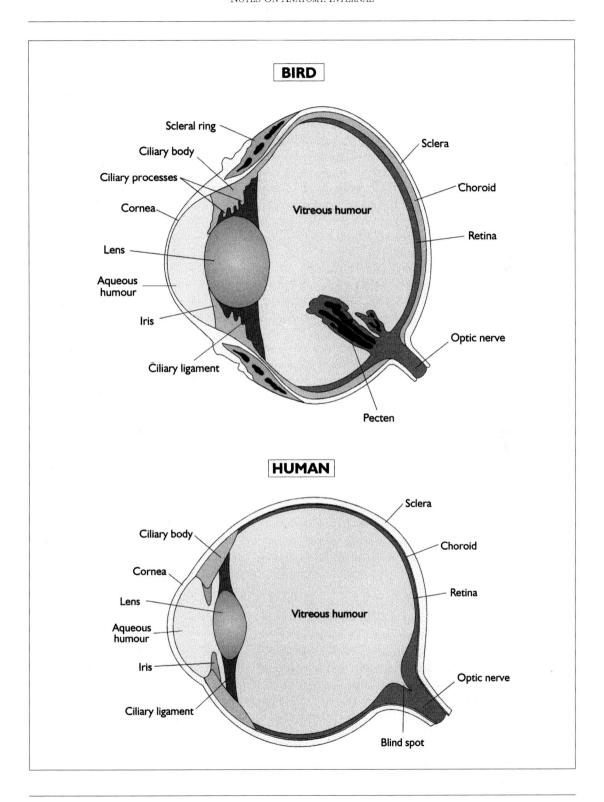

BIRD

Scleral ring
Ciliary body
Ciliary processes
Cornea
Lens
Aqueous humour
Iris
Ciliary ligament

Sclera
Choroid
Retina

Vitreous humour

Optic nerve

Pecten

HUMAN

Ciliary body
Cornea
Lens
Aqueous humour
Iris
Ciliary ligament

Sclera
Choroid
Retina

Vitreous humour

Optic nerve

Blind spot

simply to outline the *pupil* which, by means of reduction or enlargement, controls the volume of light entering the eye. Irises are universally pigmented to block out light, and muscle fibres are also present (smooth in amphibians and mammals, striated in reptiles and birds) to enable expansion and contraction of the pupil. Expansion is necessary in dim light for maximum illumination, and contraction in strong light to protect the retina from damage and for more precise definition.

The *lens* is formed of a protein based gelatin-like material (collagen) which is completely transparent and arranged in concentric layers similar to an onion. In certain groups of vertebrates it also has some elasticity, which permits modification of shape where appropriate. The convex shape of the lens 'bends' (refracts) light rays passing through it enabling image focus at a particular point, and this focusing ability is known as *accommodation*. In all vertebrates accommodation is achieved in one of two ways depending on the animal concerned: (1) the lens moves fore or aft within the eyeball; (2) the shape of the lens itself is changed. In birds and mammals, accommodation is achieved through muscular action on the lens which modifies its shape.

In mammals, the lens is suspended by smooth muscle fibres which originate at the back of the *ciliary body* and insert on the long axis of the lens surrounding it like a doughnut. A pull on the lens results in the uniform flattening of shape necessary for far vision, and relaxation of the fibres enables the lens to revert to its more 'natural' rounded shape appropriate for near vision. However, birds (and reptiles) achieve the same result in the opposite way. In them, the ciliary body is better developed and includes a ring of pad-like *ciliary* processes which, through muscular action, *push* in on the lens forcing it to adopt the rounded form appropriate for close-up focus. Relaxation of the muscle allows it to revert to its 'natural' less-rounded shape enabling long-sighted vision.

The *retina* incorporates the photo-receptors themselves – cells known as *rods* and *cones* because of their shape – and their connections to the brain via the *optic nerve*. 'Photoreception' is actually a chemical process, and both types of cell use different chemicals to stimulate retinal nerves. Most cone cells have an individual pathway to the optic nerve and brain whereas several rod cells converge onto a single pathway. This means that the brain receives no information on which one of a group of rod cells has been stimulated, and this results in lack of precision in rod vision compared to that of cone vision. Also, only cone cells are capable of colour discrimination; rod-cell vision is grey and colourless.

Concentrations of each receptor are situated in different parts of the retina. Cones need good light for efficient stimulation and in human eyes they are packed around the very centre of the field of vision; rods on the other hand are extremely effective in dim light and concentrated around the periphery. As an example of the functional difference between the two, imagine a cloudless night. In such an environment, it is often possible to detect a faint star with 'peripheral' vision but, when you look straight at it, it somehow 'disappears'.

So, as you might expect, the distribution of rods and cones in the retina varies widely from animal to animal. In nocturnal species, rods predominate; in diurnal species, cones predominate.

What has been said so far gives a general picture of the function of the vertebrate eye, but there are some important differences between the eyes of birds compared to our eyes. For example, in both humans and birds the cornea assists in focusing light onto the retina, but birds have a special muscle (*Crampton's muscle*) situated between the scleral ring and ciliary body which pulls on the cornea shortening the radius and helping with near vision. This dual method of accommodation is most fully-developed in diurnal raptors such as accipiters, and it enables an enormous range of focus from 'infinity' to 'macro'. But the most striking differences are in shape and relative size. Indeed, size is a measure of the importance of vision to birds, and the eyes of hawks and owls can be – in total volume – larger than a human's. They take up an enormous amount of space in the avian skull, and much of the brain itself is devoted to servicing them.

This means that birds can't move their eyes to any great extent – there just isn't enough room in their cranium. Human eyes have powerful muscles attached to the sclera enabling them to carry out a large variety of movements so that the image focuses on the centre of the field of vision on the retina. Birds compensate for this lack of eye musculature by having very flexible neck vertebrae and powerful cervical muscles which enable them to perform an enormous range of movements and position their heads in such a way that it achieves a similar result. Indeed, in some cases, the results are markedly better. It is well-reported that owls, for example, can turn their heads through at least 180° and this is no exaggeration.

Human eyes are more-or-less ball-shaped with the cornea providing only a relatively small blister on the surface of this sphere. In contrast, the avian cornea is a semi-circular bulge held in shape by the scleral ring, and the lens itself is bulkier and more spherical. The retinal area in birds is also flattened, which means that most of it lies within the visual angle of the image entering the eye. In diurnal birds, the retina is composed almost entirely of cone-cells, the density of which are about three times that of a human eye. So the cornea-lens-retina relationship in such birds gives them far higher powers of resolution at any distance. In nocturnal birds such as owls, the vast majority of retinal receptors are rod cells. Their colour vision is, therefore, effectively non-existent but they can detect prey movements clearly in what to other animals appears to be an impenetrable blackness.

Perhaps the most obvious difference between the human and avian eye is the existence of the *pecten* in birds. Although we know for certain one or two of its functions, its overall purpose is largely a mystery and the subject of much speculation.

The pecten is a highly vascular organ with numerous pleats or folds, and it is situated in the south-western quarter of the eye looking through the lens. In this area it invades the vitreous humour to a considerable extent, and longitudinally its centre orientates from the south to the north-west. Reptiles have a similar but less well-developed structure (known as the *papillary cone*) whose function is to aid in the supply of nutrition to the retina by diffusion of nutritional substances through the vitreous humour. Like its reptilian counterpart, it has been established that the pecten is a source of supply for the retina but its characteristic shape, with pronounced parallel ridges, leads to the belief that it is also, in some way, a visual aid.

If so, we don't know how it works, although various theories have been proposed. The most persistent suggestion is that the shadows cast on the retina by these ridges aid in the detection of movement. In effect, (so the theory goes) the shadows falling on the retina act as a 'grille' so that small or very distant moving objects are more readily observed as their 'images' pass from one part of the grille to the next. The resulting stroboscopic action produces a number of 'on-off' effects increasing contrast and enhancing detection of movement. Even if this particular theory is wrong, there is no doubt that raptors especially have superb visual acuity when it comes to detecting movement, and it seems highly likely that the pecten is at least partly responsible for this.

Another difference in the visual equipment of birds and humans is the presence of a *nictitating membrane* in birds. This is a transparent fold of skin which is drawn across the front of the eye by a special muscle from the nasal side to the temporal side, and its action is very similar to the shutter blind on a single lens reflex camera. Although like us, birds have eyelids, they close them only during sleep and what we call 'blinking' is performed by this membrane. The function of the membrane – and in us, the eyelids – is to keep the cornea clean and moist which otherwise would dry out and become opaque thus impairing vision. There appears to be no particular advantage in possessing a nictitating membrane as opposed to a more functional eyelid, and it seems to be just a different evolutionary answer to the same problem.

Falconry Terminology

Through the many centuries of its existence, falconry has generated its own unique terminology, much of which persists today. It is a curious mixture of English, French and Latin words, interwoven with the occasional Dutch and Arabic term, most of which cannot be found in any standard dictionary.

There have been falconers in Europe since at least Saxon times, and in Britain it has maintained continuity since that period. For example, historical documents record that in AD 821 a petition was made to the then King of Mercia by the monks of Abingdon. They pleaded with him to stop over-enthusiastic falconers trampling over their crops at harvest time. There are also records dated before 821 of hawks and falcons being presented as gifts to an earlier Mercian king. The Bayeaux Tapestry pictures King Harold and the Comte Guy de Ponthieu with hawks on their fists, and the Normans continued the sport after their conquest.

In mediaeval times, falconry was an essential part of a man's education and most mediaeval kings and nobles took an active interest. It declined in popularity when Oliver Cromwell established his commonwealth, but it revived again when the monarchy was restored under Charles II in the 1660s. The development of accurate guns, the trend towards enclosing land, and the eventual loss of interest by reigning monarchs, brought about a further decline in the eighteenth and nineteenth centuries, but it managed to survive in small pockets, primarily as a sport for the landed gentry.

Falconry's long association with Norman and English nobility, especially in its early history here, has left a residue of French or Latin words. This is not only because the Normans themselves were French, but also because the languages of the court and of education were predominantly French and Latin for a considerable period extending well beyond Norman times. Of course, other terms have been added since to reflect new developments, and contacts with falconers from other countries – in particular Holland, Arabia and the Indian sub-continent – have all had an impact on current usage.

Despite their antiquity, or perhaps because of it, many words have lost their relevance, in particular those concerned with hawk ailments and remedies. Recent advances in veterinary diagnostics have replaced them with scientific terminology and newer treatments. Others have become less well-used because training and management techniques, as well as materials and equipment design, have evolved beyond their modern relevance.

Nevertheless, even the more antique terms still crop up occasionally in books, magazines, or conversation and if you want to read older texts – such as Bert's *Treatise on Hawks and Hawking* published in 1619 (and still available) – an explanation of these terms is essential. The following compendium is, therefore, as complete as I can make it. Where a term is rarely used these days I have said so in the body of the definition.

A

Arms — paradoxically the legs of a raptor (usually a hawk) measured from the thigh to the foot. The term is meant in the sense of 'weaponry'

Austringer — a person who trains and hunts with hawks (accipiters) – in particular the goshawk – as opposed to buzzards and falcons. It originates from the Latin *astur* which means 'goshawk'

Aylmeri   leather anklets or bracelets fitted to the bird's legs by eyelets through which button jesses can be threaded and removed. The device was invented by Guy Aylmer to prevent jesses tangling in branches, fences or undergrowth when birds are flying loose

B

Bate — to fly off the fist or a perch when tethered in an attempt to get away. The term literally means 'to beat the air' and originates from the French *battre*, to beat

Beam feathers — the small number of primary feathers attached to the phalangeal (finger) area of each wing

Bechins — morsels or tidbits of food given to a bird as a reward, especially during training and free flight. It is derived from the French *becquée* meaning 'a beakful'

Bewit — a short, thin strip of leather used to tie a bell to a bird's leg

Bind (to) — to strike quarry and hold onto it

Bird of the fist — a bird trained to return exclusively to the fist as opposed to the lure, or fist and lure

Blain — bursitis in the wrist joint (carpus) of the wing manifested by a watery blister on the joint which could, potentially, develop into arthritis

Block — the word has two meanings: (1) a truncated cone or cylindrical piece of wood with a cambered upper surface and a metal spike underneath for securing in the ground. It also incorporates a closed metal ring for the attachment of the bird's leash, and is used mainly as a weathering perch for falcons; (2) a small block of wood carved in the shape of a falcon's head and neck and used to fashion hoods

Blood feathers — new feathers only partly grown. So-called because the opaque quill-like sheaths protecting the feathers still contain blood

Blue hawk — a falcon, in particular the female peregrine, in full adult plumage

Bob — the repetitive up, down, and sideways motion of a bird's head when she is especially interested in something in her immediate environment

Bolt — a hawk's take-off from the fist straight at quarry (see also *Slip*)

Bowiser — a young hawk able to follow the falconer from bough to bough in the search for quarry. The term is now very rarely used

Bow-perch — a curved piece of wood or metal bent into the shape of a bow and fixed into the ground with spikes, or anchored on the ground by heavy metal feet. It includes a large closed metal ring, capable of travelling from one ond of the bow to the other which is used for attaching the bird's tethering gear. Metal, or other synthetic bows, also have a padded apex covered with leather, cord or Astroturf.

Bowse — also spelt *bouse, boose, bouze,* or *booze.* The word means 'to drink' and is most likely to have originated from the Dutch *buisen* which has the same meaning

Box cadge — a weighted lidless box with padded upper edges used as a perch for the transportation of hooded falcons by road or rail

Brail — a narrow thong of thin soft leather with a long slit cut into it. Used to tie one wing of a restless hawk to prevent it from bating. The device is very rarely used these days and usually only on sick hawks

Brancher — a young bird which has recently left the nest but is still being fed by its parents. The term is also used as a more modern one for *bowiser*

Break into — the act of a bird breaking into the skin of her kill with her beak and starting to feed on the flesh

Broadwing — a bird of the buzzard (*Buteo*) family, so-called because of its broad wing configuration designed for soaring and gliding flight

Bumblefoot — a term used to cover a variety of lesions on the foot caused through constant pressure on a particular area and invasion by pathogenic bacteria

C

Cadge — a square padded wooden frame fitted with straps and worn over a person's shoulders. Used as a portable perch for carrying a number of hooded falcons to and from the field.

Cadger — the person carrying a cadge. Cadgers were not themselves falconers but used to receive tips or gratuities for their work. Hence the term has come to mean 'sponger' in common usage, and the abbreviated form cad means a person fit for no other occupation

Call off — to call a bird from an assistant some distance away to exercise it, or to call it from a perch to a lure or the fist to retrieve it

Carry — the word has two meanings: (1) to tame a bird by carrying it around in a variety of environments; (2) flying away with the quarry or lure after binding to it. Hence carrier, a bird which habitually carries quarry

Cast — there are four separate meanings: (1) a pair (not necessarily the same species) of birds flown together against the same quarry; (2) holding and immobilising the bird in the hands for fitting equipment or some other operation; (3) to disgorge a pellet of indigestible material, such as feathers and bones, some time after feeding; (4) to propel a bird gently forwards from the fist or the hand to get it airborne and give it impetus

Cast-gorge — to throw up the undigested contents of the crop or stomach

Casting — the pellet of feathers, fur, or bones disgorged after completion of the process of digestion

Cawking time — the mating season

Cere — the bare wax-like appendage to the beak which contains the bird's nostrils. Derived from the French *cire* which means 'wax'

Chanceleer — to turn sharply two or three times while stooping. From the French *chanceler* which means to 'totter' or 'stagger'

Check — to abandon the pursuit of one quarry in favour of another (usually easier) during flight

Clutch — to seize the quarry with the feet

Condition — the state of a trained bird in relation to its responsiveness and inclination to hunt. Said to be in 'high' condition when it is overweight, and in 'low' condition when it is underweight

Cope —to trim and pare an overgrown beak or talons with clippers and files

Cower — to quiver or shake the wings. Usually seen in a young bird when begging for food from its parents

Crab — the act of one bird seizing another on the quarry by mistake, or two birds fighting or squabbling with each other

Cramp — one of a group of bone diseases (osteodystrophy) which includes rickets. Manifested by stiffness, especially in the bird's legs

Cray — (also spelt *craye*). A disease in birds which causes stoppage of the lower bowel. A severe form of constipation or impaction of the intestine

Creance — a long light line attached to the bird's jesses and used to train it to come to the falconer before it can be trusted to fly free. From the French *créance*, which means 'credit'

Crines — the short bristle-like feathers between the bird's cere and eyes

Croaks — (also known as *kecks*). An infection in the air passages of birds analogous to a cough, and so-called because of the sound made by the bird during exertion. Difficult and noisy respiration

Crop — the dilation of the gullet which serves as the first receptacle for the food eaten by a bird before it is passed down to the main digestive system

Crossing flight — the act of another bird flying between the hawk and her quarry

D

Deck feathers — the central pair of feathers in a bird's tail

Disclosed — newly-hatched birds (now very rarely used)

Draw — the word has two meanings: (1) to pull the leather braces which open or close a hood (*draw the hood*); (2) to remove a bird from the mews after it has moulted out

E

Endew — to transfer food from the crop into the main digestive system. Derived from the French *enduire*, to lay over

Enew — also *inew*. To drive game into cover or (said of the quarry) to take refuge in cover

Enseam — to rid a bird of superfluous fat, especially after the moult, to bring it back to flying condition. From the French *essimer*, to purge

Enter — two meanings: (1) to initiate a bird into hunting through her first kill on wild quarry; (2) to train a hawk to the hood. Possibly derived from the French *introduire*, to introduce

Eyass — also spelt *eyess*, *eyas* or *nyas*. A young bird taken from the nest for training in falconry. From the French *niais* meaning 'silly', 'foolish' or 'simple'

Eyrie — the nest or nesting place of a bird of prey, most commonly eagles. From the French *aire* meaning 'threshing floor'

F

Falcon — the classical, and correct, name for the female peregrine

Falconer — strictly, a person who keeps, trains and hunts with peregrines. In modern times it has come to mean a person who trains and hunts with any bird of prey

Falcon gentle — an alternative name for the female peregrine. The term 'gentle' here means 'noble', as in 'gentility'

Fall at mark — to land on the ground and wait for the falconer, usually after putting the quarry into cover

Feake — also spelt *feak*. To wipe the beak on the perch after feeding to remove fragments of food. Derived from the French *effacer*, to wipe

Feed up — to give a bird the remainder of her rations, or extra rations to increase weight, eg when putting her into the mews to moult

Fetch — the act of a falcon reaching and turning its quarry in pursuit

Filanders — a term now rarely used. The modern term is *capillariasis* which is caused by intestinal infestation by worms

Flags — the secondary feathers of the wing (attached to the bird's forearm)

Flight — a bird's pursuit of quarry

Flights — the finger-like primary feathers, attached to the bird's 'hand', which propel the bird through the air

Fly on head — to miss the target quarry and pursue another

Foot — there are two separate meanings: (1) literally, a bird's foot; (2) to strike out at quarry, the falconer, or some other object with the foot

Fret marks — lines across the webbing of feathers caused by severe hunger during feather-growth, or some other trauma. They have the effect of weakening the feather making it easily-breakable

Frounce — an infection by a blood parasite (*Trichomonas gallinae*) in the mouth, especially the palate and tongue, which is manifested as debris or a yellowish coating

Full-summed — also known as *fully down*. The condition of a bird when all its new feathers have fully grown after the moult

G

Galbanum — a resinous substance derived from a wild plant (*Ferula galbanifera*) which was used, before modern veterinary science, as an internal remedy for chronic mucous catarrh and rheumatism, or externally as a poultice to relieve tumours and chronic pulmonary symptoms

Get in — also *go in*. To reach the bird as soon as possible after it has caught the quarry or the lure

Gleam — a slimy mucous substance which coats the inside of a bird's crop and which is thrown up by the bird with her casting

Gorge — there are two meanings: (1) an alternative name for the bird's crop; (2) to give a bird as much food as it can eat in one feed

Gurgit — to choke on too large a mouthful of food. From the French *gorger*, to glut or cram

Gyrkin — the male Gyrfalcon (*Falco rusticolus*)

H

Hack — there are two meanings: (1) the state of liberty in which eyass falcons are kept for a few weeks, until they are able to kill for themselves, before being trained for falconry; (2) to come in daily to feed on the meat left out for them during this liberty

Hack back — using the hack method to release a bird of prey back into the wild

Hack bells — heavy bells put onto hack falcons, which will ultimately be trained, to hinder them in catching prey for themselves and make them semi-dependent on the falconer for food

Hack board — the board or platform on which meat is cut up and left for birds at hack

Haggard — a bird of prey caught after completing at least one moult in a wild state (ie one which is two or more years old)

Halsband — a neckband of silk or soft leather placed like a collar around the bird's neck with each end held in the hand. Used to cast a small hawk (eg a Sparrowhawk or Shikra) from the hand to give it extra impetus. Now used mainly in India and Pakistan where it is known as a *jangaoli*. Derived from the Dutch *halsband*, meaning 'neckband'

Hard down / hard penned — the condition of a bird when all its feathers are fully-grown and the shafts have hardened off to a quill. Derived from the Latin *penna*, meaning 'feathers'

Havoc — the traditional cry raised by falconers during the hunt (now rarely used)

Hawk — there are two meanings: (1) the traditional falconry term for every bird of prey; (2) strictly, a true hawk (of the genus *Accipiter*) such as a Sparrowhawk or a Goshawk

Hawker — someone who hunts with birds other than falcons (falconer) or Goshawks (austringer). A generalist

Hey — also spelt *heye*. The Old English form of 'high' when referring to a bird's condition

Hood — close-fitting leather headgear used to blindfold a bird to keep it calm and quiet

Hood shy — describes a bird which dislikes or refuses the hood, usually because it has been spoilt by clumsy handling

Hunger traces — see *fret marks*

I

Imp (to) — a method of repairing broken feathers by splicing on part of a matching feather from a previous moult or another bird to maintain flight efficiency. From the Latin *imponere*, to place in

Imping needle — the splice used in imping, traditionally made of bamboo and oval or trangular in section, which is placed inside the hollow interior of the two matching quills

Imprint — a bird which identifies a human being as its natural parent or partner, in the most extreme case because of hand rearing from hatching

Inke — an Old English term meaning the neck of the quarry, now rarely used

Intermewed — moulted out. The term literally means 'between moults' from the Latin *inter* (between) and the French *muer* (to moult)

J

Jack — the male Merlin (*Falco columbarius*)

Jangaoli — see *Halsband*

Jerkin — see *Gyrkin*

Jesses — narrow straps of leather fastened to the birds legs as a means of control. There are two basic types: (1) *mews jesses* which are slit at the trailing end to accept a metal swivel to which, in turn, a leash is attached; and (2) *field jesses*, without a slit, used when flying the bird free to minimise the risk of entanglement in branches. From the French *jeter*, to throw

Jokin — an Old English term which means (referring to a bird) 'sleeping'. Now rarely used

K

Kecks — see *Croaks*

Keen — a bird willing and anxious to catch game

L

Leash — a length of leather thong or, these days, braided nylon used to tether a bird to a perch or the glove

Lines — also spelt *loynes*, *lewnes* or *lunes*. An obsolete term whose meaning is unclear. There is reference to it in literature from the early and late seventeenth century in which it is used to mean (1) the bird's leash; (2) a creance

Longwing — a bird of the Falcon family. So-called because their wing-tips (primary feathers) are long and pointed. Other distinguishing features include black eyes and a notch on their beaks for separating the neck vertebrae of their prey

Lore — the area between the bird's cere and eye, usually covered with bristle-like feathers (crines) or completely bare

Lure — an imitation bird or animal made up to resemble the quarry to be hunted. Used to train a bird to catch the quarry concerned, lure it back to the falconer or, with longwings, exercise it

M

Mail — there are two meanings: (1) the breast or breast feathers of a bird of prey. Derived from the French *maille* meaning 'speckled'; (2) to envelop a bird in a cloth to calm it down, eg when carrying out some practical operation such as fitting equipment. The second is a term now rarely used

Make — to train. For example, *make to the hood* means to train a bird to accept the hood and *make to the lure* to train a bird to come to the lure

Make hawk — an experienced bird used in a cast with an unentered one with the object of teaching it to catch quarry

Make in — to move in towards a bird on a lure or the quarry to collect it back onto the fist

Make point — said of a falcon which takes position above the spot where the quarry has taken refuge in cover

Man — to accustom a bird to humans and human environments by carrying it around on the fist. In modern terminology, 'socialisation'

Mantle — there are two meanings: (1) to stand over food or a kill with wings and tail spread to hide it; (2) the act of stretching a leg wing and tail in one movement on one side of the body

Mar hawk — an incompetent falconer who spoils a bird through clumsy handling

Mark — the equivalent of *make point* but used for birds other than falcons, especially the Goshawk. It means to perch over the place where the quarry took refuge in cover

Mews — 'mew' means to moult, derived from the French *muer*, to moult. Strictly speaking, mews are the confined quarters where birds are set down to moult each year, but in recent times the term has come to mean simply 'indoor quarters'

Musket — a male Sparrowhawk (*Accipiter nisus*)

Mutes — the combined urine and excrement of birds of prey. From the French *meutir*, to void faeces

N

Nape — the neck or neck feathers of a bird

Nares — the nostrils of a bird. From the Latin *nares* meaning nostrils

O

Ostringer — see *Austringer*

P

Pannel — the plumage on the external lower bowel area (ie between the bird's legs)

Pantas — see *Croaks*

Passage hawk or **passager** — an immature hawk caught during its first migration (*passage* means the regular migration route of birds of prey to and from breeding grounds)

Pelt — the dead body of any quarry caught and killed by a bird of prey

Pendant feathers — feathers situated behind the shank of a bird

Pennes — a non-specific term for flight feathers (primaries and secondaries). From the Latin *penna* meaning 'feathers'

Petty singles — the toes of a falconry bird

Pick-up piece — A piece of meat held in the glove and used to entice the bird from a perch, the lure, or quarry

Pelf — also known as *pill*. The remains of the quarry after the bird has fed upon it. From the Old French *pelfre* meaning 'spoils'

Pin and web — a disease sometimes found in birds of prey which forms a film over the eye causing dimness of vision

Pitch — there are two basic meanings: (1) the height reached by a falcon waiting on before the stoop; (2) the act of a bird landing on a perch

Plume — the act of a raptor plucking feathers off her quarry

Pounces — originally the claws of a hawk (accipiter), but now used to mean those of hawks and falcons. Possibly derived from the French *puncheon*, meaning a punch

Preen — to clean and redress the feathers with the beak using oil from the preen gland

Primaries — the feathers attached to the wrist and hand area of the wing and used to propel the bird through the air

Principals — the longest primary feathers on each wing

Put in — to drive game into cover or (said of the game) to take refuge in cover. See also *enew*

Put out — to drive or flush game out of the cover in which it has taken refuge

Q

Quarry — the object of pursuit of a bird of prey. The word originates from the French *curée*, meaning entrails and other offal given to hounds when they had killed their prey

R

Rake — this word has three uses: (1) to drag a claw over the back of the quarry during pursuit; (2) to fly close to the ground; (3) *rake away* (said of falcons) to drift away downwind too far from the falconer or the quarry while waiting-on. Occasionally used to mean that the falcon has given up waiting or gone after a different quarry

Ramage-hawk — see *bowiser* and *brancher*

Rangle — small smooth pebbles either given orally to a raptor or left by the perch for it to swallow if needed. Believed to aid the process of digestion and help in cleaning out the crop. Also used in the past after the moult to help put an edge on the bird's appetite and help with enseaming

Reclaim — to man a raptor, usually after the moult or some other prolonged period of idleness

Red-hawk — see *sore-hawk*

Refuse — to abandon pursuit of a quarry after a short time, ie without showing any persistence. Also used to mean that the bird will not pursue the quarry at all

Ring perch — an alternative form of bow perch comprising a large ring of welded metal attached to a stand. The ring stands upright in a vertical plane and incorporates a padded upper surface on which the bird perches. Leather straps in the form of an 'X' close off the inside of the ring prevent the bird from becoming entangled if it bates

Ring up — the act of a falcon rising spirally in the air to gain height for the stoop. Hence *ringing flight*, a hunting situation which requires the falcon to ring up after quarry

Ringer — quarry, such as the skylark, which rings up to get above a falcon to prevent it from stooping

Robin — the male Hobby (*Falco subbuteo*)

Rouse — the act of a perching raptor lifting itself up, raising its feathers slightly, then shaking them back into position. Usually taken as a sign of tameness and well-being

Ruff — the act of a falcon hitting quarry in mid-air with its feet making its feathers fly, but without clutching it

Rufter hood — a plain, unsophisticated leather hood made with no attempt to fit any particular bird. Used to calm an eyass or passager when captured and during the initial days of manning. Used by bird trappers rather than falconers. From the Dutch *ruishuif* meaning 'plain cap'

Rye — an old term for sinusitis, manifested by swelling in the bird's head, usually just above the nostrils

S

Sails — the wings of a bird of prey

Sarcel — the rudimentary primary feather (known scientifically as the *remicle*) attached to the terminal finger of the wing. In this position it forms the outermost primary feather. Present in most birds, but not all

Screen perch — a T-shaped piece of wood on a stand used as an indoor perch. A screen, usually made of canvass or hessian, hangs down from the horizontal T-bar to prevent the bird becoming entangled if it bates, and to enable it to climb back on the perch

Seare or (**sere**) — see *cere*

Secondaries — the flight feathers attached to the ulna bone of a bird's forearm. The number varies according to species

Seel — an ancient method of blindfolding a raptor by closing its eyes with silk thread sown into the eyelids. In the West, this method of calming a bird was superseded by use of the hood about the time of the Crusades, but it is still used in some Eastern countries such as India and Pakistan. One or two North American falconers are also beginning to explore this method again as an alternative to hooding. The word originates from the French *ciller*, to blink or close the eyes

Serve — to flush quarry out of cover for a waiting hawk

Sharp set — used to describe the condition of falcons when they are very hungry and keen to hunt

Shift — the act of a quarry baffling a stooping or pursuing falcon by a sudden change in direction

Shortwing — a term used by falconers to distinguish hawks (*genus accipiter*) from falcons and buzzards. So called because their wing configuration is short with rounded ends. Other features include yellow, orange or red eyes, a thick tongue, a long tail, and a wooded habitat

Slice — the action of a hawk, buzzard or eagle ejecting mutes which, in contrast to falcons, are evacuated with some force from the vent

Slight falcon — an old alternative name for the female Peregrine falcon

Slip — to release a hawk from the fist at sighted or flushed quarry

Snite — an Old English term, now obsolete, meaning 'to sneeze'

Snurt — nasal discharge and sneezing caused by rhinitis

Soar — to sail high in the air without flapping the wings using rising thermals or other air currents to provide uplift. The characteristic flight of buzzards, eagles and vultures

Sore-hawk — a wild-caught Peregrine in its first year of plumage. From the French *sorel* meaning reddish brown in colour

Spar — the female Sparrowhawk (*Accipiter nisus*)

Sparviter — a person who trains and flies Sparrowhawks

Spring — used when hunting with falcons to mean flushing quarry (partridge, pheasant, or some other avian game) from cover

Stalke — an old, and now obsolete, term for the lower leg of a bird of prey

Stavesaker — a plant (*Delphinium staphisagria*) formerly used for the treatment of lice on birds

Stoop — the act of a falcon closing its wings and diving swiftly from a height to gain speed to overtake its quarry. From the Old Dutch *stupen*, to 'swoop'

Strike the hood — to open the braces of a hood in readiness for its removal when quarry is sighted

Summed — see *full-summed*

Swivel — two metal rings connected together by a free-turning rivet enabling both rings to revolve independently. Jesses are attached to the upper ring, and the bird's leash to the lower ring. The device is used to prevent the twisting of these pieces of equipment when a bird is tethered to its perch

T

Tarsus — strictly, the foot from ankle to toes (known anatomically as the *tarsometatarsus*) but used to mean the whole leg of a bird

Tewell — the lower bowel of a bird of prey (now obsolete)

Throw up — the act of a falcon swinging up into the air again after stooping

Tiercel — also spelt *tarcel*, *tarsell*, *tassel*, and *tercel*. This is a confusing and problematic term. Properly it means the male Peregrine falcon, but it is often used for the males of other species and sometimes the male Goshawk. It originates from the French *tierce* meaning 'one third', and there are two possible explanations for this derivation: (1) the male Peregrine is roughly a third smaller than the female; and (2) it used to be believed that male Peregrines were born from the third egg of a clutch

Timber — to build a nest

Tire — the act of a bird of prey pulling at a piece of tough meat on the bone deliberately given to help trim the beak and exercise back and neck muscles without increasing weight unduly. Hence ***tirings*** – pieces of meat given to the bird for this purpose. From the French *tirer*, to pull

Train — all the tail feathers of a bird of prey

Truss — to clutch and hold onto quarry in mid-air instead of knocking it to the ground. From the French *trousser*, to bundle up

Turn (tail) — to abandon pursuit of the quarry

Tyrrit — see *Swivel*

U

Urine — a type of net sometimes used to catch birds of prey. Possibly derived from the French *araignée*, which means 'spider'

V

Varvels — a means of attaching leash to jesses before the invention of modern swivels. They were a pair of flat metal washers sewn onto the jesses and through which the leash was passed

W

Wait on — the act of a falcon taking station above the falconer waiting for quarry to be flushed beneath her

Wake — to tame a bird of prey by keeping it awake on the first day and night until it is submissive. Until recently it was believed that achieving dominance over a bird by this method was the only way to man it successfully

Warble — also spelt *warbel* and *warbile*. The act of a bird of prey stretching both wings up over its back until they are almost touching, and spreading its tail at the same time. Now obsolete. See also *Mantle*

Washed meat — fresh lean beef cut into long strips and soaked for a day in cold water. The meat is then squeezed to remove the juices and dried with a cloth. The technique is used to help birds lose weight and bring them back into flying condition by alleviating their hunger but providing little of nutritional value

Weather — to place a bird in the open air tethered to a perch so that it can accustom itself to outside conditions and get the benefit of sunshine. Hence **weathering** and **weathering ground** — the place hawks are put for this purpose

Y

Yarak — a term used specifically for accipiters to describe the body language they display when they are hungry and keen to hunt. The word is Arabic or Turkish in origin, but the original meaning is unknown

Checklist Of Equipment

Falconry is, by any standards, an expensive sport surrounded by all sorts of paraphernalia, some essential, some desirable. However, the vast majority of the expense is in the initial outlay – items which will give many years' service once acquired. Ongoing maintenance costs, such as food, are relatively inexpensive, especially if the hawk is in the habit of catching her own. The following list will give you some idea of the expenditure you can expect before you finish training your first bird, but you can spread some costs over several months. Accommodation and essential equipment, for instance, can be built and acquired well in advance, but food and 'medical' supplies need to be obtained nearer to 'A' day – the day you collect your hawk.

Initial outlay

All-inclusive weathering
Portable bow-perch
Hawk bath
Two bells
Aylmeri anklets (ready-made)
Two pairs of mews jesses (ready-made)
Two pairs of field jesses (ready-made)
Two swivels
Two leashes
Balance scales and weights
Leather dressing
Re-inforced buckskin glove
Leather for bewits and/or tail bells, plus plectrum
Creance stick and line (50 yards)
Swing lure (with line but no wings)
Quarry lure
Travel box
Fly-fishing/stalking waistcoat or falconry bag
Whistle (dog and/or hawk)
Hood if you intend to use one
Field knife for cutting up dead quarry, or cutting your way through otherwise impenetrable
    cover
Basic food (day-old chicks)
First-aid medical supplies
Nutritional supplement
Probiotics

Supplementary Outlay

This list consists of tools and materials either for making your own equipment to save money, or for carrying out essential maintenance tasks such as imping and coping. Once again you can spread the cost over several months, so long as you have them before they are actually needed.

Jess leather
Anklet leather
Eyelets and washers
Screw-type eyelet closing tool
Leash cord
Craft knife with replacement blades
12 inch steel ruler
Leather punch
Long-nosed pliers
Dog's toe-nail clippers
Needle or coping files

In addition there are several other items, the costs of which are much less predictable. By and large they will depend on personal preference, your own ideas of what is necessary, and what you can get for your money locally. Nevertheless, you will need to consider them all at some stage.

Second-hand freezer for storing food and surplus game
Fly-proof bin for disposing of waste food
Hosepipe – preferably with a jet spray – for cleaning out weatherings, plus other cleaning and sterilising equipment (such as Vircon)
Electricity for heating (if required), lighting, and any alarm system you might want to install, plus the cost of these items
Hair dryer for drying out wet hawks
Full set of weatherproof clothing, including sporting wellingtons
Suitable dog, plus all its equipment, food and accommodation
Couple of ferrets with their food, equipment and housing
Bird insurance
Veterinary care for all your animals
Membership fees for any club you might want to join, plus associated costs (for example, travelling to and from regional meetings, field meetings and other club events)
Books and Videos

Helpful Literature

Although the act of flying a trained bird of prey at quarry might be essentially the same as it was hundreds – perhaps thousands – of years ago, the means of getting to this stage has altered dramatically. Many of these changes have occurred through normal evolutionary processes, but a few have been forced upon us. Either way, there are major differences in every aspect of hawk management – manning, training, equipment design, housing, medical care, food, the acquisition of birds, and restrictions on where, when and what you can hunt.

In particular, since the early 1980s, the sport has been based almost entirely on captive-bred birds – a legal requirement which has changed the nature of falconry in Britain (see the section headed *Falconry and the Law*). Because of this, books written only thirty years ago are out of date in many respects – especially if they cover subjects like trapping wild hawks for training, which is currently illegal. The virtues of 'passagers' and 'haggards' might be of nostalgic interest, but in practical terms they are now irrelevant simply because wild hawks are generally no longer available.

As a beginner, therefore, what you need to know is: how you can train, fly and maintain a captive-bred hawk in modern social conditions. On this basis alone, the following books are recommended. They give different points of view about every aspect of falconry (although differences tend to be superficial rather than fundamental), and they all provide an opportunity to learn something more about what is, by any standards, a noble and fascinating sport.

M H Woodford	A Manual of Falconry
A & C Black, London, 1987	ISBN 0 7136 5614 X

Michael Woodford published his original book in 1960 and this is an updated version which attempts to take account of modern trends. He is, essentially, an 'old school' falconer who learned his trade at a time when wild birds could be legally caught for use in falconry. Even so, the book provides a great deal of useful information about general management, the merits of each kind of hawk, hunting techniques and fieldcraft. In these respects it is useful to have. Indeed, the original version (if you can find it) is rated as a modern classic by some falconers, and it is the basis on which many of them learned the sport.

P Glasier	Falconry and Hawking
B T Batsford Ltd, London, 1978	ISBN 0 7134 0232 6

Phillip Glasier was the first modern falconer to attempt a comprehensive manual aimed specifically at the beginner. Although he too was an 'old school" falconer in the same way as Woodford, he had trained enough beginners to give him an insight into many of the fundamental problems facing them. He also wrote the book at a time when all falconers had to be self-sufficient in terms of providing their own equipment, simply because commercial suppliers were not generally available. Consequently much of the book is concerned with making essential furniture (such as gloves and bags), and if you are in any way craft-minded his guidance could save you a great deal of money.

In addition, the book is a very honest and an accomplished account of falconry which is still treated as a bible by many practitioners. Indeed, his hunting anecdotes alone are worth reading and they will give you lots of encouragement because you will most likely find yourself – even as a novice – in similar situations.

Emma Ford	Falconry, Art and Practice
Blandford, London, 1992	ISBN 0 7137 2248 7

In some ways Emma Ford has taken over where Phillip Glasier left off. Her book is difficult to match in terms of practical information and advice on modern falconry based on captive-bred birds. Her book covers all aspects of the training and management of each main category of hawk (longwings, shortwings and broadwings). Emma, together with her husband Steve, founded The British School of Falconry, now based at the Gleneagles Hotel in Perthshire. They have spent years instructing beginners, and Emma's book reflects the knowledge and experience they have gained in that pursuit.

Nick Fox	Understanding the Bird of Prey
Hancock House, Surrey, 1995	ISBN 0 88839 317 2

Doctor Fox is a raptor biologist as well as a falconer and breeder. Before this book, his main claim to fame in falconry circles was the introduction of the New Zealand falcon to this country, and he was the first person to breed the species in captivity. Unfortunately this hawk hasn't (yet) found any recognisable niche here, although it could be said that it is still at an experimental stage.

The material in his book reflects Doctor Fox's scientific background. It covers the physiology, biology and psychology of birds of prey in general, and discusses the relevance of these subjects to the management, training, and hunting strategies of all kinds. The scientific data he presents does not, on the whole, undermine the way that falconry is currently practised, but rather it explains why much of it works. In addition, it gives a scientist's view on how certain elements could be improved, such as the initial manning of hawks, their general motivation to respond, and how fitness can be developed and maintained.

T H White	The Goshawk
Pan Books Ltd, London, 1988	ISBN 0 330 30410 0

T H White was an author mainly concerned with Arthurian legend. Perhaps his most famous book was the novel *The Once and Future King* which is about Arthur's relationship with the wizard Merlin. But, in his later life, he took up falconry and *The Goshawk* is an account of his experiences in trying to train his first bird – an imported wild eyass goshawk.

T H White died in 1964, and *The Goshawk* was first published in 1951. This book is not, by any standards, a manual on falconry. In fact it is quite the opposite. It is a superbly-written chronicle of disaster, which starts the moment the hawk arrives from Germany in a basket covered with sacking. At the time, all T H White had to guide him was Bert's *Treatise of Hawks and Hawking* printed in 1619. He had never met a falconer, and he had never seen a trained hawk of any kind. Consequently he lost his goshawk before she was even ready to be entered, largely through inappropriate equipment and misguided management. But after this experience, he went on to train and fly several kinds of hawk successfully with the help of practising falconers and more modern management methods.

This book's value to would-be falconers is twofold. Firstly, it as an excellent account of 'how not to do it' – and the author himself emphasises this in his Postscript. Secondly, it is a warning to use the most up-to-date material you can find. Ancient though it might be, falconry is still a living and fast-developing sport, and there is no benefit in using outdated techniques.

References

AA / Reader's Digest: *Book of British Birds* — Collins Publishers, London, 1977

Beebe, Frank L: *A Falconry Manual* — Hancock House Publishers, Canada and the United States, 1992. ISBN 0 88839 978 2

Brown, Leslie and Amadon, Dean: *Eagles, Hawks and Falcons of the World, Volumes I and II* — Wellfleet Press, New Jersey, USA, 1989. ISBN 1 55521 472 X

Burton, Philip: *Birds of Prey of the World* — Dragon's World Ltd, Limpsfield, England, 1989. ISBN 1 85028 085 1

Brooke, Michael and Birkhead, Tim (Editors): *The Cambridge Encyclopedia of Ornithology* — Cambridge University Press, 1991. ISBN 0 521 36205 9

Cooper, J E: *Veterinary Aspects of Captive Birds of Prey* — Standfast Press, Gloucestershire, 1991. ISBN 0 904602 04 4

Cooper, J E and Greenwood, A G (Editors): *Recent Advances in the Study of Raptor Diseases; Proceedings of the International Symposium of Diseases of Birds of Prey 1st-3rd July 1980, London* — Chiron Publications Ltd, West Yorkshire, 1981. ISBN 0 9507716 0 0

Ford, Emma: *Falconry in Mews & Field* — B. T. Batsford Ltd, London, 1982. ISBN 0 7134 4047 3

Ford, Emma: *Falconry – Art and Practice* — Blandford, London, 1992. ISBN 0 7137 2248 7

Fox, Nick: *Understanding the Bird of Prey* — Hancock House Publishers, Canada and the United States, 1995. ISBN 0 88839 317 2

Freethy, Ron: *Secrets of Bird Life* — Blandford, London, 1990. ISBN 0 7137 2154 5

Glasier, Phillip: *Falconry and Hawking* — B. T. Batsford Ltd, London, 1984. ISBN 0 7134 0232 6

Gooders, John: *Field Guide to the Birds of Britain and Europe* — Kingfisher Books, Grisewood & Dempsey Ltd, London, 1990. ISBN 0 86272 504 6

Grossman, Mary Louise and Hamlet, John: *Birds of Prey of the World* — Bonanza Books, Crown Publishers Inc, USA, MCMLXIV. Library of Congress Catalog Card Number 64-8391

Hosking, Eric and David: *Eric Hosking's Birds of Prey of the World* — Pelham Books, London, 1987. ISBN 0 7207 1756 6

King, A S and McLelland, J: *Birds – Their Structure and Function* — Baillière Tindall, London, 1984. ISBN 0 7020 0872 9

Lascelles, Gerald: *The Art of Falconry* — C. W. Daniel Company Ltd, Saffron Walden, England, 1985. ISBN 85435 031 4

Layton, David: *German Shorthaired Pointers Today* — Ringpress Books Ltd, Hertfordshire, England, 1994. ISBN 0 948955 78 3

Mavrogordato, Jack: *A Hawk for the Bush* — C. W. Daniel Company Ltd, Saffron Walden, England, 1985. ISBN 85435 082 9

McBride, Anne: *Rabbits & Hares* — Whittet Books, London, 1988. ISBN 0 905483 67 7

McKay, James: *The Ferret and Ferreting Handbook* — The Crowood Press Ltd, Wiltshire, England, 1994. ISBN 1 85223 772 4

Mackenzie, John P S: *Birds of the World – Birds of Prey* — Harrap Ltd, London, 1986. ISBN 0245 54475 5

Moxon, P R A: *Training the Roughshooter's Dog* — Swan Hill Press, Shrewsbury, England, 1994. ISBN 1 85310 501 5

Newton, Doctor Ian (Consulting Editor): *Birds of Prey – An Illustrated Encyclopedic Survey by International Experts* — Merehurst Press, London, 1990. ISBN 1 85391 131 3

Parry-Jones, Jemima: *Falconry – Care, Captive Breeding and Conservation* — David & Charles, Newton Abbot, England, 1989. ISBN 0 7153 8914 9

Roberts, M B V: *Biology – A Functional Approach* — Thomas Nelson and Sons Ltd, Walton-on-Thames, England, 1986. ISBN 0 17 448019 9

Upton, Roger: *Falconry – Principles & Practice* — A & C Black, London, 1991. ISBN 0 7136 3262 3

Wellstead, Graham: *The Ferret and Ferreting Guide* — David & Charles, Newton Abbot, England, 1981. ISBN 0 7153 8013 3

White, T H: *The Goshawk* — Pan Books, London, 1988. ISBN 0 330 30410 0

Woodford, M H: *A Manual of Falconry* — A & C Black, London, 1987. ISBN 0 7136 5614 X

Young, J Z: *The Life of Vertebrates* — Oxford University Press, Oxford, 1989. ISBN 0 19 857173 09

Useful Addresses

The Hawk Conservancy
Weyhill, Near Andover
Hants SP11 8DY
01264 773850
www.hawk-conservancy.org.uk

The National Birds of Prey Centre
Newent
Gloucestershire
GL18 1JJ
0870 990 1992
www.nbpc.co.uk

Welsh Hawking Centre
Wyecock Road
Barry
South Glamorgan
CF62 3AA
01446 734687
www.aboutbritain.com/WelshHawkingCentre.htm

British School of Falconry
Gleneagles Hotel
Auchterarder
Perthshire
Scotland PH3 1NF
01764 694347
www.highlandtrail.co.uk

Independent Bird Register
White House Business Centre
Hatton Green
Hatton
Warwick CV35 7LA
0870 6088500
www.ibr.org.uk

Index

Please Note: Page numbers in **bold** text refer to relevant illustrations